AQA

Theatre Studies

AS

QA

Su Fielder
Pat Friday

Nelson Thornes

Published in 2008 by:
Nelson Thornes Ltd
Delta Place
27 Bath Road
CHELTENHAM
GL53 7TH
United Kingdom

12 / 10 9 8 7 6 5 4

A catalogue record for this book is available from the British Library

ISBN 978 0 7487 8291 8

Cover photograph by Corbis
Illustrations by Carrie Southall and Pantek Arts Ltd, Maidstone
Page make-up by Pantek Arts Ltd, Maidstone

Printed in China by 1010 Printing International Ltd

The authors and publisher would like to thank the following for permission to reproduce photographs and other copyright material:

piv: Getty; pvi: Fig. 1, Tom Stewart/CORBIS; pviii: Fig. 2, Donald Cooper/Photostage; p3: Fig. 2.1, Sandro Vannini/CORBIS; p4: Fig. 2.2, John Heseltine/CORBIS; p5: Fig. 2.3, V & A Images, Victoria and Albert Museum; p6: Fig. 2.4, Bettmann/CORBIS; p7: Fig. 2.5, Lebrecht Music and Arts; p8: Fig. 2.6, Georgian Theatre Royal, Richmond; p9: Fig. 2.7, Jeremy Hoare/Alamy; p12: Fig. 3.1, E.O. Hoppé/CORBIS; p13: Fig. 3.2, Getty Images, p14: Fig. 3.3, Hulton-Deutsch Collection/CORBIS, p16: Fig. 4.1, Fig. 4.2, Stephen Moreton-Prichard; p19: Fig. 4.3, RSC Hire Wardrobe; p20: Fig. 4.4, Fig. 4.5, Bridge House Theatre in Warwick; p21: Fig. 4.6, Fig. 4.7, RSC Hire Wardrobe, p22: Fig 4.8, Strand Lighting; p25: Fig. 4.9, © Catherine Ashmore, Coram Boy, National Theatre; p26: Fig. 4.10, Robbie Jack/CORBIS, p27: Fig. 5.1, Michael Nicholson/CORBIS; p28: Fig 5.2, Rex Features, Fig. 5.3, Donald Cooper/Photostage; p29: Fig. 5.4, Nigel R. Barklie/Rex Features; p32: Fig. 6.1, Brian Rasic/Rex Features, p33: Fig 7.1, Bettmann/CORBIS; p51: Fig. 12.1, Donald Cooper/Photostage; p54: Fig 12.2, Hekimian Julien/CORBIS SYGMA; p56: Fig. 12.3, Getty Images; p58: Fig. 12.4, Nick West/ArenaPAL; p60: Fig. 12.5, photo by Alexander T Knapp reproduced by permission of the Tower Theatre Company, London; p69: Fig. 14.1, Bettmann/CORBIS; p70: Fig. 14.2, Drew Farrell/Lebrecht Music & Arts, p74: Fig. 14.3, Donald Cooper/Photostage; p77: Fig. 14.4, Donald Cooper/Photostage; p78: Fig. 14.5, photo by Malcolm McKee; p81: Fig. 15.1, Alastair Muir/Rex Features; p84: Fig. 15.2, Alastair Muir/Rex Features, p85: Fig. 15.3, Donald Cooper/Photostage, p86: Fig. 15.4, Donald Cooper/Photostage; p88: Fig. 15.5, 15.6, Alastair Muir/Rex Features; p89: Fig. 15.7, Alinari Archives/CORBIS; p90: Fig. 15.8, Donald Cooper/Photostage; p91: Fig. 15.9, Fig. 15.10, RSC Hire Wardrobe; p96: Fig. 16.1, Donald Cooper/Photostage; p98: Fig. 16.2, Bettmann/CORBIS; p99: Fig. 16.3, Bettmann/CORBIS; p104: Fig 16.4, Donald Cooper/Photostage; p106: Fig. 16.5, photo by Alexander T Knapp reproduced by permission of the Tower Theatre Company, London; p119: Fig. 18.2 Donald Cooper/Photostage; p123: Fig 19.1, Donald Cooper/Photostage; p127: Fig. 21.1, Roger Viollet/Getty Images, Fig. 21.2, Tristram Kenton/Lebrecht Music & Arts; p130: Fig. 21.3, DV8, *The Cost of Living*, UK production (2003), Alastair Muir; p131: Fig. 21.4, Richard Melloul/Sygma/CORBIS; p132: Fig. 21.5, *The Dawn*, devised by Nomand Theatre Company, designed by Carrie Southall; p133: Fig. 21.6, Ralph Koltai; p139: Fig. 23.1, Moscow Art Theatre Museum, p140: Fig 23.2, Moscow Art Theatre Museum; p141: Fig. 23.3, Tristram Kenton/Lebrecht Music & Arts; p143: Fig. 23.4, Galway Youth Theatre; p145: Fig. 23.5, Steve Tanner, p146: Fig. 23.6, Steve Tanner; p163: Fig. 25.2, Alastair Muir/Rex Features; p163: Fig. 25.3, mask created by Beckie Kravetz, The Mask Studio; p164: Fig. 25.4, Thinkstock/Corbis; p169: Fig. 27.1, student production of *Haroun and the Sea of Stories*, South Dartmoor Community College; p171: Fig. 27.2, Robbie Jack/CORBIS.

pp64-65: Viking Penguin, a division of Penguin Group (USA) Inc for extracts from Sophocles, Antigone from *Three Theban Plays* by Sophocles, trs. Robert Fagles (1982) pp67-8, 70, 75, 78-9. Copyright © 1982 by Robert Fagles; p68: Faber and Faber Ltd for extracts from Sean O'Casey, *The Shadow of a Gunman* from Plays 2 by Sean O'Casey (1921) Act 1, Scene 1; pp113-114: David Higham Associates on behalf of the translator for extracts from Henrik Ibsen, *A Doll's House*, trs. Michael Meyer, Methuen Drama (1994), Act 1, pp30-40, 38-9.

Contents

AQA introduction

Nelson Thornes and AQA

Nelson Thornes has worked in collaboration with AQA to ensure that this book offers you the best support for your AS or A Level course and helps you to prepare for your exams. The partnership means that you can be confident that the range of learning, teaching and assessment practice materials has been checked by the senior examining team at AQA before formal approval, and is closely matched to the requirements of your specification.

Blended learning

Printed and electronic resources are blended: this means that links between topics and activities between the book and the electronic resources help you to work in the way that best suits you, and enable extra support to be provided online. For example, you can test yourself online and feedback from the test will direct you back to the relevant parts of the book.

Electronic resources are available in a simple-to-use online platform called Nelson Thornes learning space. If your school or college has a licence to use the service, you will be given a password through which you can access the materials through any internet connection.

Icons in this book indicate where there is material online related to that topic. The following icons are used:

Learning activity

These resources include a variety of interactive and non-interactive activities to support your learning.

Progress tracking

These resources enable you to analyse and understand examination questions (On your marks...).

Research support

These resources include WebQuests, in which you are assigned a task and provided with a range of web links to use as source material for research.

Study skills

These resources support you as you develop a skill that is key for your course, for example planning essays.

Analysis tool

These resources help you to analyse key texts and images by providing questions and prompts to focus your response.

When you see an icon, go to Nelson Thornes learning space at www.nelsonthornes.com/aqagce, enter your access details and select your course. The materials are arranged in the same order as the topics in the book, so you can easily find the resources you need.

How to use this book

This book covers the specification for your course and is arranged in a sequence approved by AQA. The introduction contains information on what to expect in the drama and theatre studies course, as well as how you will be assessed. Unit 1 is split into two sections which relate to the two sections of your examination paper. Section A is designed to help you with section A of the examination, and is about your critical response to live theatre. The section includes background information about the theatre, directors, designers and performers, preparation for a theatre visit and follow up on your theatre visit. The section ends with advice for success in this section of the exam.

Section B of Unit 1 relates to section B of the examination, and is about the prescribed play, laying out a summary of each available set text and relating them to the interpretation of the director, designer and performer. The skills of analysis and interpretation that you will need to use in section B of the examination are described and practised using examples from the set texts. Again, the final chapter is advice for success in this section of the examination.

Unit 2 deals with your coursework task, introducing key practitioners that may be chosen for study and giving you detailed guidance and advice on how to choose a play, make best use of the skills of your group, rehearse, write supporting notes and evaluate your work.

Definitions of any words that appear in bold can be found in the glossary at the back of this book.

Learning objectives

At the beginning of each section you will find a list of learning objectives that contain targets linked to the requirements of the specification.

The features in this book include:

Key terms

Terms that you will need to be able to define and understand. These terms are coloured blue in the text book and their definition will also appear in the glossary at the back of this book.

Who's who

The names of key drama practitioners. The short biographies given are intended to enhance your understanding of the subject and encourage further research.

Think

A short reflective activity. Thinking about the issues brought up in this feature will help you develop an interesting range of ideas that you can write about in your exam and coursework.

Theatre trivia

Fun facts about the theatre to add variety to your study.

Links

Links to other areas in the text book which are relevant to what you are reading.

Background information

Interesting facts to extend and support your background knowledge.

Activity

Activities which develop skills, knowledge and understanding that will prepare you for assessment in your drama and theatre studies course.

Further reading

Suggestions for other texts that will help you in your study and preparation for assessment in Drama and Theatre Studies.

AQA Examiner's tip

Hints from AQA examiners to help you with your study and to prepare for your exam.

AQA Examination-style questions

Questions in the style that you can expect in your exam.

AQA examination questions are reproduced by permission of the Assessment and Qualifications Alliance.

Introduction to drama and theatre studies

What will I be doing on this course?

Whatever type of school or sixth form you are attending, embarking on your drama and theatre studies course means that you'll be joining like-minded people on an exciting course of learning in a subject that has fascinated A Level students for over 30 years and the general public for well over 2,000!

Fig. 1 *Students in rehearsal*

One of the main appeals of any drama and theatre studies course is that study is based on group activities, so learning takes place through the shared experience of watching **theatre** and of making **drama** as part of a group. In choosing drama and theatre studies, you have already 'signed up' to a partnership with your fellow students which will get stronger and more enjoyable as you progress through the course.

If you studied drama as one of your GSCE subjects you will already understand the importance of group work in a practical subject like this. If you are new to the subject, you might be surprised to discover how much you come to rely upon and trust the other group members, and also to discover just how much fun an AS Level subject can be!

Your teacher will introduce you to a range of different activities to help you to gain knowledge and understanding of the different elements of the drama and theatre studies course. Some activities will involve reading and interpreting plays, or finding out about playwrights and theatre practitioners. Others will be based on practical group exploration of plays in your drama room or studio. Some activities will involve you visiting the theatre, watching plays and/or talking to directors, actors and designers. This course book has been written to support you throughout each and every aspect of your studies.

■ What will I study on the drama and theatre studies course?

You will study how drama is produced, what plays mean and how theatre is created by a production team, to convey that meaning to an audience.

You will also learn to appreciate a range of practical theatre skills and you will study the work of one significant **theatre practitioner** whose ideas have influenced modern theatre.

■ What will drama and theatre studies lessons be like?

No two drama lessons are ever quite the same. In one lesson your teacher might be introducing you to the background to one of the set plays chosen for Unit One. For example, if you are studying *Oh! What a Lovely War*, you may be learning about the dreadful conditions endured by soldiers fighting on both sides in the trenches in the First World War. Your teacher might show you photographs of the battlefields; you might look at some war poetry; you might even watch a clip from the television comedy series *Blackadder Goes Forth* to give you a sense of the period of the play. Knowing about the background to the play will help you decide how to use theatre elements to interpret the First World War setting for your audience.

In the next lesson you might be working practically on the script, thinking up ideas for how you might design an appropriate stage setting for the 'trench' scene in the play, so that your audience will understand the context. You might be in the drama studio, working as a group of actors, exploring the meaning of the lines and discussing how to bring the scene to life on stage for an audience.

In another lesson you might be preparing for a theatre visit; looking at the text of the play that you are going to see, reading a couple of scenes from it, thinking about its staging needs and discussing what you might expect to see on stage. You will be preparing yourselves to be informed members of an audience.

Other lessons might involve rehearsing your own production for Unit Two, experimenting with performance and staging techniques to create meaning for your potential audience.

Although no two drama lessons are ever the same, there will be one feature common to all: you, your fellow students and your teacher will be working together to understand drama and to create theatre. You will learn that what the audience experiences is at the centre of every aspect of your studies.

■ How will my work be assessed and examined?

You will take one written paper, Unit One, at the end of the AS course, to assess your knowledge and understanding of your chosen set play and your appreciation of a live theatre production.

You will take one practical test, Unit Two, in the spring or summer term, where your knowledge and understanding of a further play, chosen by you and your group, will be assessed in performance.

■ Key terms

Theatre practitioner: an individual, or group of individuals, who work in the theatre in a practical way. In this course, the term 'theatre practitioner' refers to directors, performers, theatre companies and designers.

AQA Examiner's tip

Whatever play you are studying, research the period when the play is set as soon as you can. This will help you to visualise the characters and their world when you are reading the play. Also look for pictorial evidence that might trigger ideas for authentic settings and costumes.

■ Further reading

In the e-resources there is a link to the BBC history website, which is a great source of pictures and articles covering a wide range of historical periods.

The units at a glance

Unit 1: Live theatre productions and prescribed play (written exam)

Unit 1 is assessed by a written paper, divided into two sections, A and B. Section A contains questions based on your visits to live theatre productions. You will have seen a number of different productions during the course, including several different types of theatre. You will have made plenty of notes about each production and you are allowed to take *two sides* of notes (A4) *for each production* into the examination with you.

You should choose the most appropriate production that you have seen to answer one question from a choice of four. Questions will ask you to discuss the total effect of the chosen production or they will ask you to write about specific elements of that production. You need to be able to offer a personal assessment of the success of the production that you choose to write about.

Aspects of presentation to be considered should include:

- the theatrical style and genre of the production
- directorial interpretation
- the choice of venue
- the choice of staging form
- performance skills
- integration of movement and language in performance
- the stage setting and design
- use of space
- costume
- technical elements: lighting and sound
- creation of pace, mood, atmosphere and specific effects
- creation of specific effects for an audience
- the actor-audience relationship.

Section B contains questions based on your study of one of the set plays. There will be a choice of two questions on each of the set plays. You will have studied *one* of the following:

Antigone, by Sophocles

The Taming of the Shrew, by William Shakespeare

A Doll's House, by Henrick Ibsen

The Shadow of a Gunman, by Sean O'Casey

Oh! What a Lovely War, by Joan Littlewood and Theatre Workshop

Playhouse Creatures, by April de Angelis.

The exam questions will ask you to adopt the point of view of a director, an actor or a designer. You will be asked to write about either directing a specific section from the play, performing a specific role in one or two scenes from the play, or designing for a specific scene of the play. You will have your copy of the play with you in the examination.

You will need to be able to refer to some of the following aspects, depending on your choice of question:

Link

See Chapter 9 for further information about notes for the examination.

Link

See Chapter 8 for further information about aspects of presentation.

Think

In Shakespeare's *The Two Gentlemen of Verona*, one character is accompanied on stage by his dog. In *A Winter's Tale*, there is a stage direction 'Exit, pursued by a bear'. Modern directors tend to use a real dog for *Two Gentlemen ...* , but what might they use instead of a bear in *A Winter's Tale*?

Fig. 2 Two Gentlemen of Verona

- choice and use of staging form
- choice and use of performance space
- actor-audience relationship
- casting and appearance of characters
- physical qualities, for example, age, build, height and facial features
- movement, posture, gesture and facial expression
- vocal qualities, for example, volume, pitch, accent, pace, timing, intonation, phrasing and emotional range
- visual qualities, for example costume, make-up, mask, use of props
- character motivation and interaction
- development of pace and pitch/climax
- stage directions and practical demands of the text
- patterns of stage movement
- creation of mood and atmosphere
- design fundamentals, for example, scale, shape, colour, texture
- use of scenic devices, for example, revolves, trucks, projections
- use of lighting, for example, direction, colour, intensity, speed
- use of sound, for example, direction, amplification, music and/or sound effects, both live and recorded
- other technical elements, for example, pyrotechnics, smoke machines, flying
- visual elements
- use of space.

Unit 2: Presentation of a play extract (practical exam)

For this unit, you will be working in groups to present an extract from a play of your choice. Your group should contain between two and eight students offering acting as their chosen skill and may include, in addition, a director, a set designer, a costume designer and one or two technical designers. The extract, when performed, should last between 15 and 40 minutes depending upon the size of your group.

Your teacher will guide you in your choice of play. The play should be suitable for you to demonstrate your understanding of the influential theatre practitioner that has been selected to support your study for this unit.

▉ Theatre terminology

As with any subject that you wish to study in depth, you will need to understand and use specific **terminology**.

For this course, you will need to learn to recognise and to use a whole range of terms, phrases and words that have a special meaning in the world of the theatre. You may think of it as a code that you have to understand and adopt in order to communicate your own theatrical ideas clearly and accurately. All the words that appear in **bold** in this book are explained in the glossary at the end of the book.

If you studied drama at GCSE you already have a head start, but if you are new to the subject you may initially find some terms confusing. We have already tried to distinguish between the terms 'drama' and 'theatre',

▉ Link

The different aspects listed are fully explained in Chapters 14 to 17.

Examples of exam questions are in Chapter 19.

AQA Examiner's tip

One student might choose to offer both lighting and sound design, or one student might offer lighting and another offer sound design.

▉ Link

See Chapters 21 and 22 for further details about suitable practitioners and plays.

▉ Key terms

Terminology: specialised vocabulary used in any particular sphere of life. For example, doctors use medical terminology and lawyers use legal terminology. As students of drama and theatre, you need to acquire and use theatrical terminology.

Key terms

Play: a written script consisting mainly of dialogue, which may be read and enjoyed by a reader, but which does not fulfil the playwright's intentions until it is performed by actors in front of an audience.

Production: what the play (or ballet, opera or mime, etc.) is turned into once it has been interpreted by a director working with performers and with a production team consisting of designers, stage managers, technicians, scene builders and a wardrobe department.

Performance: the interpretation of a play, ballet or opera by actors, dancers or singers. Some performances rely entirely for their effects upon the performers' words or actions, although most performers are also supported in a production by design elements.

Performance elements: all aspects of the performers' work; the acting/performing within a production.

Production elements: all aspects of a production reflecting the work of a production team, which can be made up of some or all of the following personnel: a director, an assistant director, actors, stage manager(s), stage/set designer, lighting designer and technicians, sound designer and technicians, costume designer, make-up, artist, musical director, choreographer, fight director – even animal trainers, depending upon the production.

AQA Examiner's tip

Some students become confused about the spelling of playwright and they often put 'playwrite' by mistake. Rather than simply 'writing' a play, the word 'playwright' suggests that the author is someone who 'crafts' plays. Historically, wheelwrights and cartwrights were craftsmen working with wheels and carts.

Further reading

In the e-resources you will find website addresses that will enrich your understanding of theatrical concepts and devices.

but what about a 'play', a 'production', and a 'performance'? Is there any difference? Some people use these terms as if they are interchangeable.

For example:

> Sophie: *What did you do last night?*
>
> Rob: *I went to see a* **play** *– it was The Taming of the Shrew.*
>
> Ryan: *I went to see a* **production** *of The Taming of the Shrew.*
>
> Emily: *I went to see a* **performance** *of The Taming of the Shrew.*

In this context, all the answers to Sophie's question use theatre terminology in a perfectly acceptable way. Although Rob, Ryan and Emily use three different terms to describe what they saw at the theatre, each is used accurately.

However, all these words – 'play', 'production' and 'performance' – have slightly different meanings when we come across them in exam questions and wider reading in drama and theatre studies. Look carefully at their definitions in the key terms boxes.

When we talk about **performance elements** and **production elements** in this course book and when you come across the terms in your examinations, they will have the fixed meanings given in the adjacent key terms box.

Start your own glossary notebook or e-notebook, which you can add to throughout the course. It will not only help you to understand how theatre works but will equip you with the correct terms with which to express yourself in both written and practical situations.

1   Introduction to live theatre

In this section you will learn about:

In this section you will learn about:

- how to prepare for and get the most out of live theatre experience

- how different performance spaces affect the way plays are presented

- how performers, directors and designers work together to communicate meaning to an audience.

Key terms

Production team: all members of the theatre involved in preparing the production for the audience.

This section is intended to prepare you to make the most of your theatre visits, to enable you to watch theatre with an educated eye and to discuss your experience of theatre with confidence and perception, using appropriate specialist vocabulary.

In your written exam for this unit, you will be expected to write in a critical way about a live production that you have seen. Your visits to the theatre will give you the opportunity to watch how others have put into practice all the various techniques that go to make up a live theatre performance.

When you see live theatre you will be witnessing the result of very close cooperation between directors, designers and performers. Although the end result is one presentation, it is important to look at the individual contributions made by these people. This section considers the role that each of these members of the **production team** plays in presenting live theatre.

This section also gives more detail about the different types of theatre space that are used for live theatre, and how they affect the choice and presentation of performances. There is also advice on how to find information about the particular performance you are seeing, how to take notes and, finally, how to use that material to answer the exam question.

Remember, this part of the course is an important foundation for the rest of the AS Level. Understanding live theatre will enhance your appreciation of your set play and also give you a broad spectrum of ideas that you can draw from when you plan and present your own extract of a play in Unit 2.

2 Theatre buildings and spaces

Key terms

Auditorium: the space where people sit or stand when listening to or watching a performance.

Proscenium arch: The word 'proscenium' comes from Greek, and means literally the area in front of the stage. In modern theatre it refers to the archway shape through which one views the stage in most end-on theatres. It is sometimes referred to as 'picture-frame theatre'.

Black-box theatre: a relatively small studio space where the 'stage' area is defined by black drapes, or 'black legs' as they are called.

Theatre-in-the-round: theatre layout where the acting area is enclosed on all sides by seating. There are sometimes a number of entrances through the seating. Careful thought needs to be given to the positioning and size of furniture or scenery, as the audience's view can easily be blocked.

People have been watching drama and plays for over 2,500 years. During that time the size, shape and positioning of the stage have changed considerably in different countries and cultures. When going to theatre today you might have the expectation that you will find a platform at one end of an **auditorium,** with an archway framing the 'picture' created by the actors and the designers. However, this is only one of many different staging arrangements that exist today.

This chapter will explore the ways in which performance space affects the relationship between actors and their audiences and shapes both their experiences.

As a member of an audience nowadays, you might witness a performance in a Greek-style amphitheatre and be one of an audience of thousands of people, or you could be one of several hundred people in the theatre space, mentioned above, watching the action through the **proscenium arch.** Alternatively, you could be part of a relatively small audience in a **black-box** studio theatre or even watching a performance taking place in a space that is not an actual theatre building.

Theatre, at its most basic level probably originates in the hunting rituals of primitive people. People's instinct for story telling, ceremony and musical performance evolved into the basis of theatre worldwide. It is tempting to think of such 'theatre' taking place within tribal communities as an early example of **theatre-in-the-round** lit by the light of the sun or a primitive camp fire!

Debate continues as to whether the Egyptians had a theatre form, but dramatised story-telling seems to have been important in Africa from the 1st century AD and mask plays have a long history in South America.

In India, the Hindu temple ritual play of the 2nd century developed by the 17th century into the present day version of Kathakali, a highly stylised form of theatre.

The Noh theatre of Japan originated in the 12th century and reached its peak in the 17th. It was performed on a platform viewed from two sides and the masked actors were lit by people known as 'shadows' who carried a light on a pole. There was no scenery but the costumes were extremely elaborate. In the 17th century, Kabuki, a more popular form of theatre developed.

Although many of these forms originated as serious ritual, linked to religion and worship, the urge to entertain emerged in many different cultures. The fact that theatre has been practised all over the world since ancient times suggests that theatre-going serves a fundamental human need and is an important activity in its own right.

Think

As you read about the different developments in theatre spaces, think carefully about how each one affects the actor-audience relationship and the audience's.

Activity

In your groups, choose one of these theatre forms to find out about on the internet then share your discoveries. You might try out each style in a practical session.

Greek and Roman theatres

Fig. 2.1 *Epidarus theatre*

Think

What are your first impressions of the theatre at Epidaurus as an acting space? Some Ancient Greek and Roman theatres survive today and put on traditional performances. How might the audience experience differ from that in a modern theatre?

The theatre pictured above is at Epidaurus in Greece and is one of the best surviving examples of the type of theatre built by the Ancient Greeks. Greek theatre dates back to the 6th century BC, when theatre-going was regarded as a **civic duty** and plays were performed as part of a religious festival dedicated to Dionysus, the god of nature and of wine.

This theatre is huge – it seated 14,000 spectators! You might wonder how the spectators sitting in the back row could hear what was being said. In fact, the **acoustics** of the structure allow everyone to hear with great clarity. The Greeks used their skill in mathematics to calculate the optimum size and shape of the seating area for maximum acoustic effect. If someone stands in the centre of the circular acting area, and tears a piece of paper, it can be heard perfectly everywhere in the auditorium.

Because of the size of venue, the actors wore masks so that fixed facial expression could still be seen. The mouthpiece of the mask was constructed like a funnel, creating a megaphone effect. Platform shoes and coloured wigs made the actors look taller and more visible. All these elements helped the audience to follow the action.

In Roman times (approximately the 3rd century BC until after the fall of Rome in the 5th century AD) all theatres were similar in design.

Theatre trivia

According to legend, the Greek playwright, Aeschylus was killed when an eagle attempted to break the shell of a tortoise on his head; apparently the eagle mistook Aeschylus' bald head for a stone!

Key terms

Acoustics: the quality of the sound in a place, which is influenced by its size and shape.

Activity

In Ancient Greek theatre, the colour of the wigs and costumes had a particular significance. If you are studying *Antigone*, explore whether you could still use these codes to help a modern audience watch and judge the play.

Fig. 2.2 *Roman theatre at Orange*

Fig. 2.2 shows the semicircular acting area of the Roman theatre built in the South of France, about 500 years later than Epidaurus. Notice the marble-clad walls, typical of the period, which acted as the backdrop or scenery.

▓ Medieval theatres

Western theatre went into decline after the fall of the Roman Empire but two types of performance evolved in Medieval times and each influenced later theatre forms:

- ▓ religious plays, performed by the **guilds**
- ▓ travelling players, presenting juggling and acrobatics; minstrels and troubadours.

Religious plays

The medieval Church held elaborate processions and pageants to celebrate saints' days and festivals. These were performed and led by the **clergy** and became so popular that they eventually moved out of the church building and onto the broad church steps. The congregation would gather around to watch, becoming, in effect, an audience.

The plays that developed from these pageants became known as Miracle or Mystery plays, dating from 12th to the 15th century. Each major town had its own cycle of plays, which retold stories from the Bible to a largely uneducated audience. Some of the plays were humorous, while others, such as the one depicting the Crucifixion, were violent or moving.

These cycles of plays were performed on pageant carts, which moved through the town, stopping periodically to perform their individual play.

▓ Theatre trivia

The expression **'to out-herod Herod'** means to exceed, on stage, even the villainy of the worst of tyrants. The phrase originates from the medieval depictions of a ranting King Herod on the stage.

▓ Background information

One such mystery play was *The Second Shepherds' Play*, in which a sheep is stolen, wrapped as a baby and disguised in a crib. The robber is punished by tossing him in a blanket and then the shepherds go to see the baby Jesus in the stable.

Fig. 2.3 *Painting of a pageant cart from Brussels*

The picture in Fig. 2.3 dates from 1615 and suggests the general style of these pageant carts, which were temporary structures. It also gives an indication of the style of presentation of performances and the proximity of the audience.

One advantage for the medieval audience was that the plays were performed only metres away from them. Although the players were members of the medieval guilds and not professional actors, the competition to present the best play within the cycle was great.

Special effects were created to amaze the audiences, including smoke pouring out of a 'Hell's mouth'. Cut-out scenery and even trap doors could all be included. In some performances, members of the audience were also pushed into the hellish mouth in an early form of audience participation.

Activity

Religious plays from medieval times are still performed, for example in Wakefield, York, Chester and Coventry. Read or watch one or more of these plays and you should be able to work out the type of theatre and audience for which they were created.

Background information

In a few plays comedy characters were developed far beyond their biblical personas to amuse the audience; for example, Noah's wife was presented as a nagging wife, creating an early form of stereotyping of this kind of woman.

Travelling players

Bands of travelling players were entertaining their audiences with a much more light-hearted style of performance at about the same time as the Miracle plays were educating audiences. The travellers' juggling, acrobatics and fire-eating performances had more in common with our modern circus.

Key terms

Commedia dell'arte: a theatrical style that flourished in Italy from the 16th to the 18th century. Each actor played a stock character, for example, the old man, or the zanni (the comic servant). The companies were skilled in comedy techniques and, in particular, in improvisation.

Theatre trivia

A **'slapstick'** was a stick used by Harlequin to beat his opponents in many commedia dell'arte plays. The resulting 'thwack' sounds as if a really heavy blow has been struck, but the design ensures that no damage is done to the other actor! The term nowadays describes knockabout humour.

Further reading

The Seventh Seal (1957) is a classic black-and-white film, directed by Ingmar Bergman. It shows something of the life of groups of travelling players. It is of general interest, but is particularly relevant for students of film and media.

Italy saw the beginnings of the **commedia dell'arte** style. These troupes of actors relied on improvisation and based their devised plays on **stock characters** and situations.

They provided a form of street theatre that could take place in any open space with little preparation. The audience would be passers-by, including a cross-section of the community and they could come and go throughout the performance. The concept that theatre can happen anywhere (which is often mistakenly regarded as modern), was evolving.

Activity

Find out about the different stock characters of the commedia dell'arte from the internet and devise your own commedia scenarios in a practical session.

Elizabethan and Jacobean theatres

From the middle of the 16th century, what we now refer to as Elizabethan or 'Shakespearean' theatres began to develop.

Fig. 2.4 *Model of a reconstructed Elizabethan theatre*

Theatres were built to house permanent companies of actors; their design echoed the courtyard performances favoured by travelling players. The courtyards provided a defined flat area around which the audience could stand; because they were also surrounded by windows and galleries more people could watch the action from above.

In 1576, the first theatre was built in London. It was called The Theatre. This was soon followed by The Curtain, The Rose, The Swan and The Globe. (There were two theatres called The Globe because the first one burned down during – or soon after – a performance of Shakespeare's *Henry VIII*.)

The Globe is the most famous theatre because it was where the Chamberlain's Men performed, and they were the company to which Shakespeare belonged. The Globe was the venue for the first performances of many of his plays.

By the beginning of the 17th century, plays were being written in vast numbers and theatre-going had become a popular pastime for all levels of society.

An Elizabethan audience would talk of going to 'hear' a play, since they would need to listen carefully to the words that indicated details such as the time of day, the weather and the setting for the action. Scenery and stage effects in Elizabethan theatres were limited and the playwright himself had to provide all the necessary information. Audiences today go to 'see' a play, and although they should, of course, listen to the dialogue, the lighting and set designs provide them with much of the information they need to understand the play.

The late 16th and early 17th century was probably the most important period in British theatrical history and yet we know relatively little of the actual stage conditions. We know that part of the audience stood; these were called **groundlings** and they watched the performance from an open-air vantage point, liable to be rained on! People paid more to watch from the sheltered galleries. The performance took place on a raised platform, viewed from three sides.

The sketch in Fig. 2.5 is by Johannes de Witt, who was simply an early 'tourist' in London; it is the main source of our understanding of what the inside of a theatre of the period looked like.

Fig. 2.5 *Sketch by Johannes de Witt*

An Elizabethan audience's experience would have been different from ours. The plays did not have intervals, but snacks such as oranges, oysters and cobnuts were sold during the performances. Audience members would also shout out, at will, making for a lively, informal atmosphere.

There were some indoor theatres in Elizabethan times, such as Blackfriars. Admission prices were higher than those for outdoor theatres and there was no standing space. Although the indoor venues were not the most popular theatres during this period, their style did influence later developments. They were large halls with three galleries, benches instead of the groundling space, and a more elite audience. The stage was lit with candles and some scenery was used, paving the way for further developments.

Late 17th- to 20th-century theatres

By the late 17th century, theatre styles were changing and moving towards the fundamental features that are found in most conventional theatres today. Inigo Jones, the famous architect, is credited with introducing the proscenium arch theatre and this was to be the dominant style for the next three centuries. Many school halls are still designed on this pattern.

This style of theatre – placing the actors at one end of the area and seating the audience to view the action from one angle – dictated an acting style that made performers angle their bodies towards the audience in what appears as a slightly unnatural way. Such an arrangement does ensure that the audience share a similar view of the performance.

The theatre in Fig. 2.6 is the Georgian Theatre Royal, Richmond, and is one of the oldest working theatres in the UK. The seating capacity was originally about 400, which gave the theatre a very intimate atmosphere. Similar theatres can be found in Bristol and Bury St Edmunds.

Fig. 2.6 *Georgian Theatre Royal, Richmond*

Further reading

For more detail about Elizabethan theatre, read *The Shakespearean Stage, 1574–1642* by Andrew Gurr.

Look at the Globe Theatre website and if you have access to London, go to watch a performance in the reconstructed theatre. Backstage tours are also available.

In this picture you can see the old painted backdrops and the footlights that lit stages until the 20th century. The audience boxes at the side of the auditorium offer a lopsided view of the stage, but keep the audience close to the action and the performance is still viewed from only one side of the stage.

During the 18th and 19th centuries theatres became larger, and some had elaborate **stage machinery,** although the basic shape of the stage remained the same. New mechanisms were installed, which could fly scenery in and out, enabling the producers to create some complex and impressive scenery and illusions.

The picture of Drury Lane Theatre in London (Fig. 2.7) shows how ornate theatres became during this period. The prices of seats varied enormously. The 'upper circle' provided cheap seats for a fairly rowdy audience. The more sophisticated folk sat in the 'dress circle' and the stalls. The boxes such as the two Royal Boxes in Drury Lane separated wealthy audience members from the 'hoi polloi' and allowed their occupants to be seen as well as to see.

This theatre seats over 2,000 people reducing any sense of intimacy between the actors and audience, but the viewing angle is the same: the audience is on one side of the proscenium arch and the actors are on the other. The concept of the audience looking into a rectangular set with one 'wall' removed had been established.

Key terms

Stage machinery: machinery installed to enable the stage and scenery to be raised and lowered, sometimes with complete changes of scenery being hidden under the stage and then raised with the help of hydraulic lifts.

Background information

The famous director Stanislavski later elaborated on this idea of the audience watching from the other side of that invisible 'fourth wall'.

Fig. 2.7 *Drury Lane Theatre in London*

Further reading

For more information about changes to the theatre in the mid-17th century and the historical influences at the start of this period, read *The First English Actresses* by Elizabeth Howe.

Activity

Many theatres surviving from this period offer guided tours backstage. Try to arrange one for yourself or a group of classmates. These give you the opportunity to look in more detail at the whole structure of the theatre and its facilities.

Mid-20th century and 21st-century theatres

Although many present-day theatres were either built in an earlier period or follow the same proscenium arch style, in the second half of the 20th century there was a huge movement towards experimentation in theatre. The writing of radically different styles of plays throughout the mid and late 20th centuries inevitably challenged traditional ideas about the relationship between the performers and the audience. The experimental movement demanded a fresh view of what a theatre actually was, where the audience should be placed and how the venue could best contribute to the theatre experience.

Theatres today

In the 21st century, you may encounter any of the following shapes and configurations of performance space, as a member of a theatre audience:

End-on theatre

The conventional rectangular-shaped stage with the audience on one side.

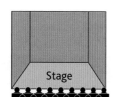

Fig. 2.8 *End-on theatre*

Apron stage

Where the platform used for the performance extends beyond the proscenium arch into the audience. Theatres such as Birmingham Rep have this shape, but many others will build a temporary apron for particular plays. The aim is usually to prevent the distancing effect that the proscenium arch can create.

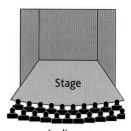

Fig. 2.9 *Apron stage*

Thrust stage

Where the stage platform juts out into the auditorium and the action is viewed from three sides. This is a version of the Elizabethan shape and can be seen is theatres such as the Swan Theatre in Stratford-upon-Avon. This is a useful way of reducing the space between the actor and the audience and is usually very popular with actors themselves.

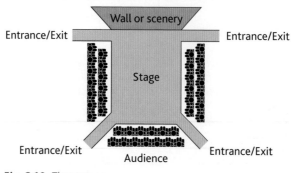

Fig. 2.10 *Thrust stage*

In-the-round

These theatre spaces evolved from classical models but on a smaller scale, where the audience sits on all four sides. Examples of this shape can be found at the Royal Exchange Theatre, Manchester, and at the Bolton Octagon. This style ensures that the audience are close to the action but causes both designers and actors to rethink their style of presentation. It is not possible to face the audience at all times and pieces of scenery have to be designed in such a way as to avoid obstructing some of the audience's view of the action.

Many studio theatres are built deliberately to provide alternative and adjustable spaces. The seats may be positioned to create any of the above but they may also create further options:

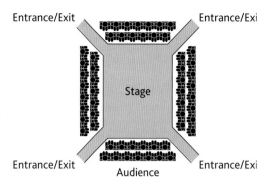

Fig. 2.11 *Theatre in the round*

- **Traverse**, where the audience sit on two sides facing each other and the action happens between them. The reactions of other spectators can be viewed very easily and can be an advantage or a distraction.
- A triangular or diamond-shaped acting area, which is viewed from two adjacent sides. This is yet another alternative for creating intimacy and allows the director to decide what angles will be most advantageous for the performers and the audience. (Recent productions in the Arcola Theatre in London, for example, have used these variations.)

Another variation is where seats are not used at all and the audience stand and walk around, following the action of the performance in different areas: this is known as **promenade theatre**. Though quite exciting for the audience, who feel almost part of the action, it is possibly the most difficult style to use as the audience will need guidance as to when and where to move.

Some productions take place outside theatre buildings. Venues include parks and gardens in the open air as well as, for example, factory spaces, disused tower blocks or warehouses, and even canal barges!

The size of the contemporary audience also varies enormously. The Theatre Royal, Drury Lane, has the capacity for 2,000 audience members, while a recent performance at the Roundhouse, London, shepherded audience members wearing headsets and guided by ropes one-at-a-time through a unique theatre experience.

When people today ask 'What is a theatre?' there is obviously no simple answer!

When you visit the theatre, look carefully at its structure and the way the acting area fits into the building. Consider which style or period has influenced this particular venue most. Try to see a variety of venues during your course and always think about the different impact that the stage layout and the configuration of the space has on the audience experience and the relationship between performers and audience.

▓ Think

How does modern promenade theatre link back to historical theatre? Try to identify when there was a similar relationship between audience and performers.

▓ Think

Consider Peter Brook's opening words of his book *The Empty Space*:

'I can take any empty space and call it a bare stage. A man walks across this empty space whilst someone else is watching, and this is all that is needed for an act of theatre to be engaged.'

▓ Activity

A practical exercise, to demonstrate the importance of the theatre and the positioning of the stage relative to the audience, is to take an extract from a play and perform in two different configurations, for example, end-on and in-the-round. You need only a relatively short extract and this can come from one of your set plays, a text you have seen performed or even from a text with which you are not familiar. (This final option is useful preparation for Unit 2 at AS and Unit 3 at A2.)

3 The work of the director

Theatre trivia

An angel is an American expression for a major financial backer of a play. Like the Ancient Greek *Choregoi*, the angel is a rich patron who puts up the money for a production.

Who's who

Thomas Betterton: those of you studying *Playhouse Creatures* will be familiar with the name of Thomas Betterton, as it is the actresses in his company that feature in the play.

Fig. 3.1 *Henry Irving in costume for a role*

In Unit 1 Section A of your AS course, you will be watching and evaluating a range of different theatre productions. You will be required to answer an exam question about *one* of these productions, assessing the effectiveness of its design or of the actors' performances or the success of the director's interpretation of its central issues. So, it is important that you have a thorough understanding of the role that these key people play in crafting a production and presenting it to an audience.

The director is the most influential person in the production of a play. Although he or she will not be seen by the audience, the decisions that the director makes will influence nearly every aspect of the play, including its interpretation, setting, design, technical presentation and the casting and performance of actors. The director will work with the whole production team, drawing on the expertise of individuals who specialise in different skills, but he or she will have overall authority.

The evolution of the director's role: pre-20th century

Although in contemporary theatre the director has the single biggest influence on a production, the role of the 'director' is a relatively modern one. Originally companies directed themselves, with the most important actor often dictating the moves and positioning of the rest of the cast.

In Greek and Roman theatre, as well as in the Elizabethan era, the playwrights themselves tended to take some responsibility for the staging of their plays.

In the 17th, 18th and early 19th centuries, theatre owners employed managers who took responsibility for the financial administration of the company as well as having the powers to engage and dismiss members of the company. Often, the 'big name' actors of their day eventually became managers and took on the role of training younger actors as well as 'directing' the company. Famous actors such as **Thomas Betterton** (1635–1710), David Garrick (1717–79) and Charles Kean (1811–68) were amongst this number.

In Victorian theatre the companies were often led by an **actor-manager**, who owned and ran the company and usually played all the leading roles. Some actor-managers concentrated on their own individual performance, rather than taking a broader view of the way the production as a whole would affect an audience.

However, not all actor-managers were self-obsessed. Henry Irving, the most famous English actor of the late 19th century, was highly respected by his company of actors and was famous for taking time to rehearse the crowds and not just the principals.

Theatre historians usually recognise the **Duke of Saxe-Meiningen** (1826–1914) as the first real theatre 'director'. The Duke was fanatical about the theatre and he not only directed but also designed costumes and scenery for all his productions. Meiningen revolutionised the way plays were presented, he aimed to make theatre look as realistic as possible. As a result of his European tour, (his ensemble style company visited 38 different European cities between 1874 and 1890) he changed the direction of modern theatre.

The director's role in the 21st century

Since the Duke of Saxe-Meiningen's influential tour of Europe there have been many theatrical innovations and a succession of significant 'movements' in the theatre. The 20th century saw an explosion of different theatre forms and styles and the emergence of a multitude of talented playwrights worldwide. The rapidly changing world prompted many playwrights to use the theatre to communicate their vision of truths about modern society.

The director's role is no longer simply about moving a crowd on stage or making sure that the principal actor is placed downstage centre. There is a great diversity of theatre available today from the all-singing, all-dancing West End musicals to the intimate **chamber theatre** style of experimental practitioners. There is also an awareness that some modern audiences expect to think as well as feel during a performance. Every type of contemporary theatre makes demands upon the director to capture the spirit of the production and to interpret it clearly for the audience.

Advances in technology and in theatre buildings have also brought new opportunities and challenges for theatre directors. Twenty-first century theatre audiences are constantly being surprised by the sensational technical effects that can be achieved on stage.

The role of the director in the theatre has become a highly specialised job. A modern director must coordinate a cast of actors, oversee complex design issues and, most importantly, interpret plays for an increasingly sophisticated audience.

Who's who

Duke of Saxe Meiningen (1826–1914): considered by many to be the first theatre 'director' in the modern sense. His theatre company, founded in 1874, was an inspiration to emerging writers and directors of the time. **Stanislavski**, who founded the Moscow Arts Theatre in Moscow, and **Antoine**, who founded the Theatre Libre in Paris, both saw the Meiningen company in the 1890s. They became exponents of the 'new' stage realism, undoubtedly influenced by the directorial style of the Duke.

Fig. 3.2 *Peter Hall takes a rehearsal*

■ Who's who

Edward Gordon Craig (1872–1966)
thought that a director's role
was one of complete control.
He experimented with lighting,
saw the actor as only a part of
the whole picture and designed
revolutionary sets, saying that
it made no sense to put a three-
dimensional actor in front of
a two-dimensional painted
backcloth.

Fig. 3.3 *Edward Gordon Craig*

Contemporary playwrights, often intent upon communicating a clear social or political message, make a conscious decision to write for the theatre rather than for any other form of media. They are usually acutely aware of the audience for whom they are writing as they shape their work.

The modern director has a duty to interpret both old and new plays to bring out meaning for a modern audience. This often means that a director works closely with a living playwright to ensure that the resulting production is faithful to the writer's artistic and/or political intentions. It also involves working closely with a dead playwright's work to ensure that the interpretation of it will be relevant to a contemporary audience and reveal something to them about 'life'. This is what we mean by communicating 'meaning' to an audience and it is the director's principal function in the theatre.

■ The director's role in interpreting a play

In modern theatre it is the director who has an overview of the whole production. He or she will start by studying the text of the play in detail to discover its meaning and uncover its relevance for a contemporary audience. This will lead on to decisions about how the characters will be interpreted and performed. The director will build up a general idea of the style of the set, costume, lighting and sound required to fit in with his or her interpretation of the play, although specialists will work on the details and technical demands.

The director heads the team of actors, designers and technicians who will all work to achieve what **Edward Gordon Craig** defined as 'a unified stage picture', in which all elements are working together to create the director's vision.

Different directors have different working methods and intentions. Some, such as Stephen Unwin, in his production of *Twelfth Night*, see their work on the playwright's text as all important while others, such as Julie Taymor, are equally concerned with visual spectacle as *The Lion King* shows. Some directors believe that production elements should be used sparingly in order to keep the focus firmly on the performance of the actors. Peter Brook, who has used far more complex directorial styles, adopted this approach in *The Grand Inquisitor*.

There are also occasions where a director begins a project without a script. Instead, the director guides the ensemble to devise an original piece of theatre based on a specific idea or issue; the plays of Mike Leigh, such as *Two Thousand Years*, are good examples of this style of working.

Sometimes a script-writer is shaping the work during the rehearsal process. **Max Stafford-Clark**, for example, has worked closely with Caryl Churchill, David Hare and Timberlake Wertenbaker to create scripted drama that has emerged from specific research and devising work with an ensemble cast. John Godber and Alan Ayckbourn are best known for directing the plays they have written themselves.

■ Who's who

Max Stafford-Clark is an example
of a director who works closely
with contemporary playwrights.
He could not break this habit when
directing *The Recruiting Officer*
(written by George Farquhar in
1706), so, as he worked on the
play, he wrote regular letters to
the dead playwright outlining his
directorial decisions!

■ The director's role in the production team

Although it is the director's vision that guides the whole performance, the director has to work closely with his production team in order to achieve this vision. He or she will appoint people whose skills can contribute to gaining the overall desired effect.

Many directors first appoint designers, in particular the set designer, because they need to know what the stage space will be like before the actors can make even basic plans for a performance. After initial discussions with the director, the set designer will sketch out some ideas for the set that will then be assessed and often elaborated on or modified by the director.

Another vital part of the director's initial work is the casting of the play. In plays with large casts the director may need to use the expertise of a **casting director** who will make a shortlist of actors whose skills, style and physical type make them suitable for a particular part. The director will then hold auditions, listen to the actors read and watch them move. The final selection of the cast is the responsibility of the director.

In some theatre companies the process becomes more complex if one group of actors is performing more than one play with the same or different directors. In these cases, the director needs to juggle the roles to find the 'best fit' for all concerned.

Other roles within the production team who help the director, are:

▮ The *costume designer* (sometimes the same person as the set designer but not always).

▮ The *lighting designer* (who is sometimes responsible for sound as well but in large productions this will be the responsibility of another specialist).

▮ The *stage manager* (whose responsibility is to run the show in performance, ensuring that every other aspect of the performance, from the entrances of the actors, the cueing of lights, the changing of set and the positioning of props is carried out with precision and perfect timing. In large productions the stage manager will have a team of people working for him or her).

▮ Specialists in a variety of other areas such as musicians, choreographers, fight directors and even magicians.

Whenever you visit the theatre, remember that your experience of the production has been consciously shaped by the director to ensure that you share his or her understanding of the original script. Your task for Section A of Unit One is to come away from each production with a clear understanding both of the director's interpretation and of how that interpretation has affected your experience.

AQA Examiner's tip

In Unit 2 of this course, you will need to make casting decisions within your group. You will need to consider how all the parts can best be performed by the people available. No play, whether a major professional production or a student examination piece, can survive with only one starring and suitably cast central figure.

4   The work of the designer

This chapter looks at the purpose of design in the theatre and the role that the setting, costume and technical design play within a production. The design of a play is an integral part of how an audience experiences a performance. You need to be able to comment on the following aspects of design when answering questions on live productions in the exam.

◾ Setting

The first impression that an audience gets of a play is usually the set design. In the past this was revealed when the main curtain rose, showing the stage and scenery behind. Nowadays the set is often on display while the audience enter the auditorium. This gives opportunity to observe the set and make initial judgements about the style of the production before the performance begins.

You need to be familiar with some of the different styles of design that a designer might choose to adopt.

Total realism

This is usually an indoor set which attempts to recreate the setting for the play as realistically as possible. If, for example, the action of the play is set in a living room or kitchen, the designer will create what appears to be a replica of that room in detail.

If the designer has done his or her job well, this type of set gives the audience a view of a room as if through a transparent **fourth wall.**

◾ Theatre trivia

In the play *Saturday, Sunday, Monday*, by Eduardo de Filippo, a complete meal has to be cooked and eaten on stage, so the appliances not only have to look convincing – they need to work!

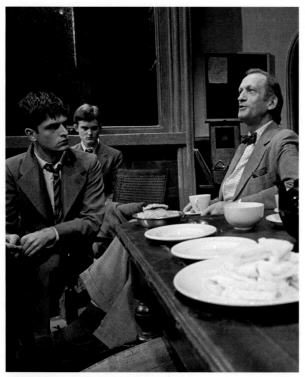

Fig. 4.1 *The set of* Another Country

Fig. 4.2 *The set of* Another Country

Figs 4.1 and 4.2 show the set of a production of *Another Country*, by Julian Mitchell. It shows a common room at a boys' public school. If you look carefully you will see how the **set dressing** is changed slightly between scenes to indicate the passage of time, adding to the realistic quality of the setting.

Partial realism

This type of set includes some realistic features but the designer has not attempted to replicate a real setting. An example might be a play set in Ancient Greece, which is suggested by a couple of Greek pillars. Such a design allows for a flexible use of the acting space while retaining a suggestion of the play's location. The action of the play may move from place to place, in different scenes, indicated by re-positioning or removing the pillars, as necessary, or simply by a change of lighting to suggest the passage of time.

This type of set gives the audience some visual information but the rest is left to the imagination.

Symbolism

In this type of set the designer reflects an important theme or concept which runs throughout the play in a non naturalistic way. For example, a 'symbolic design for **A Doll's House** might choose to symbolise **Nora's** 'doll-like' existence by setting the play behind a doll's house façade and using brightly painted dolls' house type furniture. Symbolic sets demand that the audience think carefully about the reasons why particular elements of the set have been included.

Fantasy

Plays that demand the creation of another world offer designers the opportunity to be particularly creative. Productions for plays such as *His Dark Materials* or *The Lord of the Rings* demand imaginative treatments.

Colourful, imaginative sets are needed so that the magic of the story, and the illusions it creates, transport the audience to a fantasy realm. A recent design for *Lord of the Rings*, for example, spread beyond the confines of the stage. The proscenium arch and the boxes at both sides of the auditorium were covered in a design resembling twigs and branches. The design stretched into the auditorium, drawing the audience into an alternative 'reality'.

Minimalist

A minimalist set or 'bare stage' setting contains no constructed set and is sometimes found in studio productions where the focus is entirely on the acting. The stage has little more than basic black drapes that mask the **wings**.

Practical considerations

We have considered some types of design and the effect they might be aiming to create. There are also practical questions that we need to ask when judging a set design.

Where are the entrances and exits?

These may be realistic doors or simply gaps between flats or drapes. There may be trapdoors in the stage floor, or the facility for harnessed actors to 'fly' on and off stage. Actors' entrances and exits are potentially

Theatre trivia

Antony and Cleopatra is set in 37 different locations. While most of them are in Rome, Egypt and Greece, there are many more separate settings mentioned, including scenes set in the midst of battle, one aboard a ship and several on the plains of Syria. Quite a design challenge?

Theatre trivia

A Vamp Trap or Vampire Trap is a piece of scenery designed to create the illusion of a ghost or spectral creature walking through a solid wall on stage. It consists of two spring flaps cut into a canvas flat.

very significant, so you need to be conscious of a designer's decision to highlight an entrance or to conceal it, to create surprise.

Has the designer left sufficient space for the action?

It is essential that there is enough space on the stage to accommodate all the play's action without forcing actors to appear bunched together or to sidle round items of furniture. Whatever the style of the set, it needs to enhance, rather than restrict, the action of the play.

What kind of scale and dimensions are used?

A designer might use an entirely realistic scale, mirroring the dimensions of an average house. Alternatively, the designer might exaggerate or diminish the scale of the set, perhaps to suggest a character's sense of isolation or confinement in a symbolically distorted environment.

What is the colour scheme?

Designers pay a great deal of attention to the **colour palette** of a production. They may choose to use strong, vibrant colours on the setting for a comedy or lively musical, while restricting the colours used to neutral or duller tones for more serious drama or tragedy.

Costume

The costume designer in the production team has to continue the illusion created by the set designer. Sometimes the same person will design both set and costume, giving one unified idea to the visual aspect of the production.

Although the style of costumes is almost limitless, it is worth considering some of the most common categories and look out for them when watching live theatre.

Whatever the production, whether modern or ancient, realistic or symbolic, the designer needs to address the following **design fundamentals**:

- the period and style of the costumes
- the use of colour, fabric and texture
- the fit and condition of the costumes
- hemlines, necklines, waistlines, lapel width, trouser shapes, jacket shapes
- wigs, masks, make-up, hairstyles, shoes, accessories, ornamentation.

Realistic modern dress

Designing costumes for a modern realistic production poses the following questions:

- In what decade is the production set?
- What is the situation of the characters in the play or scene?
- What are the characters like? How old are they? How fashionable are they likely to be?
- Are they at work or at home, dressed up or dressed down?
- Are they alone or in company?
- Are they at leisure or on display?
- Is this war or peace?

Theatre trivia

At the Royal Shakespeare Company ('RSC'), **costumes** are made and maintained by 28 members of the costume department. In the 2005 production of *A Midsummer Night's Dream*, Oberon's coat was made from over 320 individual pieces.

Realistic period costume

If a director wants an historically accurate production, the designer will need to research the period and location of the play. This might involve visiting costume museums, looking at paintings and sculptures from the era and looking at fashion prints.

The costume below (Fig. 4.3) is based on a realistic style for the 18th century but it is not simply a *copied* design. The designer has adapted it to the needs of a specific character – a high-class prostitute from *Jubilee*, by Peter Barnes. The gold beads and sequins will catch the light on stage, the elaborate cuffs will accentuate hand movements and the flimsy material around the waist and shoulders will float as the actress moves. The low-cut neckline and the tassels which raise the front part of the dress show that the character wants to flaunt herself!

Group costumes

In many plays, the designer will need to create groups of costumes. In a recent production of *The Producers*, by Mel Brooks, one scene involved a group of elderly ladies all dressed identically in lilac suits with curly white wigs. Later the same actresses played dancing girls in elaborately designed costumes with extravagant head-dresses representing Germany; one head-dress looked like a large pretzel, another was the shape of a frankfurter. Costumes can be designed to add humour to a scene.

Sometimes costumes can reinforce a relationship between characters. For example, members of the same family might be dressed in similar colours and styles to help the audience to identify them as a group. Warring parties may be given contrasting colours to distinguish them during fight scenes.

Fig. 4.3 *18th century purple dress*

The two photographs below show an aunt and her niece from the play *Warwickshire Testimony*, by April de Angelis. Their costumes highlight the relationship between them, as each wears a cardigan, a mid-calf-length skirt and sensible shoes. The costumes give out signals about the characters – the audience does not expect them to be cheerful and outgoing!

Fig. 4.4 *Aunt from* Warwickshire Testimony *by April de Angelis*

Fig. 4.5 *Niece from* Warwickshire Testimony *by April de Angelis*

Use of symbolism in costumes

In some productions, designers use costumes to reinforce a symbolic interpretation of a play. For example, in a production of *The Country Wife*, by William Wycherley, the designer dressed the promiscuous female characters solely in their undergarments, consisting of corsets and wire-framed underskirts. The production emphasised the loose morality of the late 17th century, echoed in the risqué costumes.

Fantasy costumes

Fantasy costumes pose a different challenge to the designer. Before designing for *A Midsummer Night's Dream*, for example, a decision has to be made about whether fairies are fragile, pretty creatures from a story book or more menacing and mischievous like hobgoblins. A designer for *Toad of Toad Hall* would have to decide whether to make the animal characters look human or as 'beastly' as possible. The designer of 'fantasy' costumes has endless options.

Practical considerations

Can the actor move easily in the costume?

The costume should allow for all necessary stage activity and should be safe for the actor to wear. Trailing hems or slippery shoes are to be avoided.

Is the costume durable; can it be cleaned effectively?

Costumes need regular cleaning and need to be able to withstand both wear and tear and laundering. A **distressed** costume needs to remain 'distressed' even after washing!

Can the audience see the important detail of the design?

The detail of stage costumes needs to be exaggerated, to ensure that it is visible to the whole audience. A few specks of dirt or blood, or a subtly shabby outfit, will not be noticed by the majority of the audience. Fig. 4.6 shows the costume used for the beggar Christopher Sly in *The Taming of the Shrew*. It was torn, patched, dyed and attacked with a cheese grater, to make it sufficiently shabby.

Fig. 4.7 shows the costume used for the body of Julius Caesar, after he has been stabbed. A special solution has been used around the neckline to make the blood look wet under the stage lights. The amount of 'blood' is exaggerated to make an impact on the audience.

Fig. **4.6** *Christopher Sly,* Taming of the Shrew

Fig. **4.7** *Costume for stabbed Julius Caesar*

 Theatre trivia

At the RSC, for example, **stage blood** is created by mixing glucose, sugar and fruit colourings. Black treacle is used to darken the blood.

Activity

Take turns to select and wear three items of randomly chosen clothing. Ask the group to tell you what type of person you appear to be. Then change one item to try and alter the whole impact of the 'design'.

Further reading

Costume and Fashion – A Concise History, by James Laver (Thames & Hudson, 1988)

Technical design

Increasingly, in contemporary theatre, directors have come to rely on technical elements to help them to bring out meaning for their audiences. Technical design includes lighting, sound and special effects, which, used separately or together, can make a huge contribution to the experience of the audience.

Lighting

Lighting is a vital part of any theatrical production and yet it is often overlooked by students both when they visit the theatre and when they prepare their own work.

In order to recognise its importance, let's consider why stage lighting is used. At the simplest level, it enables an audience to see what is happening, but it can achieve much more than that.

Think about the opening moments of a production: the convention is that the **house lights** are dimmed. The audience are in the dark, which is the signal for the action to begin. The stage will then be lit, and from then on the audience's attention is manipulated by the lighting designer.

Here are just some of the ways in which lighting affects the audience's focus and perception:

- A bright area of light over the whole or part of the stage will draw the audience's attention to it.
- If only one part of the stage is lit, this suggests that important action will take place there.
- The level of light and use of colour may suggest the time of day and year.
- A particular colour of **gel** will suggest a mood appropriate to the scene as a whole or to the main character.
- **Gobos** can create the impression of a place or define the style of the room; they may give the light pattern associated with prison bars, or of sunshine through leaves, or of an ornate doorway or window.
- The angle of light and the number of lanterns used will usually eliminate shadows; however, by lighting a character from below, a sinister shadow may be created, while lighting from behind presents an anonymous figure whose facial features are in darkness.

In order to assess and discuss lighting used in a production, you need to be aware of what effects the lighting is achieving and how they are created. So, ask yourself some of the following questions:

- How many lanterns are being used? This can vary from one single spot to banks of lights.
- What angle are they coming from? An angle of 45 per cent is the usual, because this eliminates distracting shadows, but a **birdie** can be used from ground level or a spotlight may be shone directly downwards.
- What area of the stage is being lit? Even when the whole stage appears to be lit, you might find that the upstage corners are far less bright or that the designer has suggested a natural light source beyond the 'room' by means of a brighter light by a doorway.
- Is there a spotlight on a particular character? This is used a great deal in musicals for the soloist but sometimes the main character is quite subtly picked out from a crowd by extra lighting.

Theatre trivia

The theatre's **shortest play** is Samuel Beckett's *Breath* (1969). It lasts about 30 seconds and has no dialogue, nor any actors. Using recorded sound and light, the play attempts to depict life from the cradle to the grave. It begins with the sound of a newborn baby's cry and ends with the dying gasp of an old man.

Fig. 4.8 *Lantern*

- What colour is being used? Pastel shades are the norm for realistic plays, conveying a degree of warmth, according to the mood of the play. Deep colours, such as green or red, can add strange, even surreal qualities.

- What level are the lights at? This goes from 0 to 10, with 10 being the brightest and, without gels or frosting, the most clinical. The very lowest numbers hardly register.

Once you have identified the style of lighting used in a production, and the intended effect, try to judge how successfully it has been achieved.

▥ Activity

Using a powerful torch and differently coloured gels, experiment with the effects you can create. Remember that the mixing of colours using lighting produces different colours from those produced by mixing paint (for example, red and green lights mix to make yellow, not brown).

▥ Further reading

The Stage Lighting Handbook, by Francis Reid (A&C Black: Sixth Edition, 2001)

Sound

The use of sound in a theatre production can be as effective and important as lighting. Sound effects create a world outside the confines of the stage, allowing the audience to imagine an extended reality beyond the play's setting.

Sound is used in a variety of ways in a theatre production:

- to produce sound effects demanded by the plot of a play
- to create realism in a setting
- to enhance the mood of a scene (usually abstract sound)
- to produce music with songs and instruments.

AQA Examiner's tip

Sometimes a question may focus on the use of sound in a production referring to both 'live' and 'recorded' sound. Read the question carefully to ensure you understand exactly what you are being asked to focus on. You may be expected to include something on actors' vocal skills.

Sound effects demanded by the plot of a play

In several of the set plays there are examples of sound effects that are crucial to the plot of the play.

In *A Doll's House* the sound of the door slam at the end creates a powerful climax and makes a statement about the determination behind the exit.

In *The Shadow of a Gunman* there are several important sound effects described in this text. In Act Two 'a rapidly moving motor', which suddenly stops, then, 'a violent and continuous knocking, followed by the crash of glass and the beating of the door'. The sound effects represent the army, their activities and the threat they pose.

Sounds to create realism in a setting

Some sounds are used to enhance the impression of realism, for example:

- bird song and the drone of insects can suggest an open-air feel to a scene
- waves crashing on a beach can evoke the impression of a sea shore
- traffic noises can suggest an urban setting
- the sound of a single car may herald the arrival of a character.

Abstract sound to enhance the mood of a scene

In some productions abstract sounds are introduced to build up atmosphere, in particular tension and suspense. The source of these sounds can be deliberately obscure or ambivalent. For example, in *The Woman in Black*, adapted by Stephen Mallatratt from the book by Susan Hill, the sound of the rocking-chair is heard before its source is obvious to the audience. Many people take it to be a heartbeat because of the rhythm.

Music through songs and instruments

Many plays include a variety of songs and music. The song may be part of the text and sung on stage, such as **Mr Grigson's** singing in **The Shadow of a Gunman**, or the numerous songs in *Oh! What a Lovely War*. In *A Doll's House* the sound of the party at which **Nora** dances the tarantella is the prelude to the climax of the play.

Musicians on and off stage are used to enormous effect to add atmosphere to performances.

Sound equipment

Sound equipment can vary from the simplicity of a wind chime to the complexity of a sophisticated, computerised sound desk.

Certain sounds effects have been used in theatres for centuries. For example:

- a wind machine – a wooden wheel covered with canvas and turned by a handle; as the wheel turns the wood rubbing against the canvas creates an impression of wind
- a rain machine – a circular drum with small stones inside which makes the appropriate sound as the drum is rotated
- a thunder sheet – a large sheet of metal, suspended and with handles at the bottom, which booms like thunder when shaken.

Nowadays CDs, minidisks and downloaded sounds can be programmed into a computerised system. The quality of the sound can be manipulated and is usually convincingly realistic.

However, even with modern equipment, some sounds are tricky to create and sound designers rely on manual methods. For example:

- An Elizabethan beheading can be effectively evoked by the sound of a white cabbage being chopped in two.
- The sound of birds' wings flapping can be obtained by opening and shutting an umbrella.
- Horses' hooves are recreated by banging two coconut shells together with the appropriate rhythm. (Yoghurt pots can be used as a substitute.)

Most sounds are more effective if played into a microphone and relayed through speakers. Microphones (or 'mikes') themselves are a vital part of the sound equipment. Hand-held mikes are not usually appropriate in stage plays, but spot mikes will pick up just one person. Ambient mikes will cover a more general area and radio mikes are sometimes worn by individual actors, particularly in musicals, where it is essential to ensure that the singer's voice can be heard above the level of the accompanying orchestra.

The balancing of sound in the theatre is an essential skill. The volume is controlled in the same way that the intensity of lighting is controlled.

Try to become *consciously* aware of the sound accompanying a play and its method of production. Then analyse how it affects your responses.

■ **Activity**

Explore the quality of various sounds and decide how they might fit into a piece of theatre. Devise a story which you tell the group while they have their eyes shut. See how powerfully you can evoke the experience. Remember that many sound effects are not recordings of the real event.

■ Further reading

Theatre Sound, by John A Leonard (A&C Black, London 2001)

See reference to radio mikes in e-resources: interview with Gandalf, 'Lord of the Rings'.

Special effects

In addition to lighting and sound there are other special effects that designers can employ to add impact to a production. Special effects are used to create the impression of natural elements such as smoke, fog, rain, snow, water and fire, as well as the consequences of violence.

Smoke and fog

A smoke machine can create fog and mist. It can be used in a variety of ways, for example, to create heavy billows for a witches' scene or a light mist for an urban street. Some smoke machines are portable and can be activated by actors on stage, ensuring the smoke emerges at just the right time and in the right place. A cold fog machine will, with the help of ice cubes, create a fog that clings to the ground and flows like water. The fog settles as a blanket on the ground and can hide the actors' feet or the wheels of **trucks**, for example.

Water, rain and snow

There are many ways to achieve the effect of water, using lighting or fabric, together with mime. Some productions use real water to create scenes, for example in a channel to suggest a river.

Rain can also be created effectively on stage, although if real water is used the drainage has to be efficient to avoid actors slipping on stage.

Snow is usually either created by snow machines, which produce snow with a very low water content, so it evaporates almost instantly, leaving the stage dry, or with tiny bits of white paper or plastic which are blown by hidden fans.

Fire and pyrotechnics

Fire can create great impact on stage. In Shakespearean plays, flaming torches can cast powerful moving shadows and look very authentic in scenes such as when Banquo is murdered in *Macbeth*. Rings and jets of fire (gas fuelled) can be created on stage, adding to the dramatic impact.

Pyrotechnics can also create impressive moments. A device is usually concealed on stage and set off by an electrical charge. Spouts of flame, explosions, puffs of smoke, even curtains of fire, can evoke scenes of celebration, or of war, or 'magical' transformations.

Flying, drowning and hanging

Special effects in the theatre are not new. Actors representing gods were flown in Elizabethan theatres, using a crane-type device; in a modern production the actor may be flown using expensive winches, which can raise an actor in a *Spider-Man*-type movement at two metres a second and can be programmed to stop to an accuracy of one millimetre. The flying of actors in *Peter Pan* has provided many children with their first experience of the magic of theatre.

In the National Theatre's production of *Coram Boy*, three characters are flown in order to create an image of drowning in water. With the addition of a transparent curtain, appropriate lighting and, of course, the skill of the actors, the effect was disturbingly convincing and powerful.

Fig. 4.9 Coram Boy

The Scottish play refers to Shakespeare's *Macbeth*. Theatrical superstitions abound about this play; early performers of it claimed to have seen ghosts on stage and there have also been sightings of additional cast members materialising in the murder scenes!

Theatre trivia

Unlike a 'magic carpet', the Tragic Carpet, which was used in 17th-century English theatre, was simply a green baize cloth that was spread over the stage boards to protect the actors' clothes during the performance of a tragedy where their characters collapsed and died on stage!

Cleverly constructed harnesses can give the impression of a person being hanged. Concealed wire supports the body, rather than the rope which is around the neck.

Bloodshed and mutilation

Even a limited knowledge of Elizabethan plays will make you aware of the use of the severed head, for example Macbeth's at the end of the play, but in other plays from that period there are severed hands, tongues, a heart freshly cut out and many more.

The Elizabethans used sacks of animal blood, worn by the actors who burst them by hitting them at the appropriate moment.

Nowadays sacks of fake blood in cling film are simple but effective. Blood capsules held in the mouth are bitten at the appropriate moment and there are even exploding squibs that give an effective impression of a gunshot wound. Liquid can be pumped from beneath the floor to leave a body lying in what appears to be an enormous and ever-growing pool of blood.

There are many more, but whether it's a handful of poppy petals to symbolise the loss of life in the First World War or a car that flies above the heads of the audience, special effects add some of the most memorable moments to any theatrical production.

Fig. 4.10 *A gory prop from a production of* Macbeth, *1989*

5   The work of the performer

Further reading

The Art of the Actor, by Jean Benedetti (Methuen, London 2005)

This chapter looks at the role of the performer. What actors do on stage is the principal way that meaning is communicated to an audience. It affects the audience experience of a production more than any other single element.

The actor through the ages

Throughout history, the actor's role has evolved considerably. The Greeks and Romans saw acting as an extension of the art of public speaking and actors as voices of persuasion. Nowadays, modern audiences appreciate the performer's ability to combine vocal with physical skills to communicate the whole spectrum of human experience.

Styles of acting have changed significantly over the centuries. What might have been considered good acting in the 18th century would certainly be condemned today as unnatural or affected. The exaggerated pose by David Garrick in the picture below is a fairly unrealistic example of theatrical shock.

Fig. 5.1 *David Garrick as Richard III*

▓ Who's who

Dame Judi Dench: (1934–) popular and award-winning actress of stage and screen (big and small); classically trained at Central School of Speech and Drama in the 1950s and famous for theatre roles both traditional and modern, as well as having screen credits including 'M' in the James Bond films.

Sir Ian McKellen: (1939–) classical actor who graduated from Cambridge in 1961 and went directly into professional theatre. Amongst a string of famous roles played both at the RSC and the National, his performance as Macbeth is considered one of his finest. (See page 32 for another picture of McKellen.)

Steven Berkoff: (1937–) British actor, dramatist and director, best known for his starkly expressionistic visions of modern life and his adaptations of classical works such as *Agamemnon* and *Coriolanus* as well as Kafka's *Metamorphosis* and *The Trial*.

While theatre goers of the past would be accustomed to the particular style of delivery that reflected the taste of the times, contemporary acting styles are many and varied. Compare the minute naturalistic acting of performers such as **Ian McKellen** or **Judi Dench** with the exaggerated, expressionistic style of **Steven Berkoff**.

In today's theatre, there are actors who speak and move naturally on stage, simulating different emotions, delivering their lines in prose or verse and manipulating the intellectual and emotional responses of their audience.

There are other actors whose performances are closer to dance or athletics. The pieces are physical and frenetically paced and the effects on the audience can be exciting, disturbing or mesmerising.

Fig. 5.2 *McKellen and Dench in* Macbeth, *1976*

Fig. 5.3 *Steven Berkoff in* Messiah – Scenes from a Crucifixion, *2003*

Nevertheless, what all actors have in common, from Sophocles to **Frantic Assembly** is the impulse to communicate meaning to an audience.

▓ Key terms

Rehearsal: a session or series of sessions where performers practise for a public performance; the rehearsal is usually led by the director or assistant director.

To act: to play the part of a character in a dramatic performance, using a combination of vocal, physical and facial expression.

To improvise: to make something up on the spot; to act or compose something, especially a sketch, play or piece of music without any preparation or set text to follow.

▓ What actors/performers do

What performers do, both in **rehearsal** and on stage, varies enormously depending upon the style of the theatre piece that they are performing, as well as the working methods of the director of the show.

Whatever the style, what most performers 'do' is **act**, taking one part or several parts within a piece of theatre, adding to the total effect of the show. Before they get to act, almost all performers also have to rehearse their work. The exception to this is where actors **improvise** work before an audience.

Some rehearsal periods can be as short as three weeks, while others last several months or, exceptionally, even years. Where the rehearsal period is very short it is most usual for the performers to learn their lines and their moves, take direction about how to deliver their speeches, and effectively 'do as they're told'.

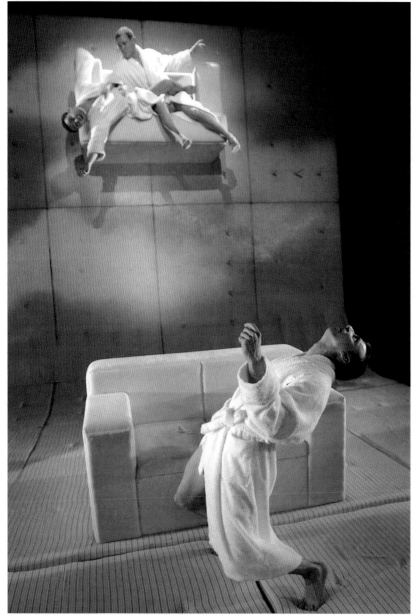

Who's who

Frantic Assembly: Formed in 1994 and in collaboration with a wide variety of artists, Frantic Assembly's artistic directors – Scott Graham and Steven Hoggett – create new work that places equal emphasis on performers' movement, design, music and text.

Fig. 5.4 *Frantic Assembly on stage in* Heavenly, *2002*

Longer rehearsal periods allow both the director and the performers time to explore a text in detail; sometimes performers are involved throughout a lengthy period of research, practical exploration and experiment before the opening of the play. In these situations, the work of the performer can include the making of meaning, not merely the communication of it.

The performers' relationship with the director and fellow actors

In the early part of the 20th century, performers were accustomed to working with 'autocratic' directors who ran their rehearsals like military campaigns. They arrived at the first **read-through** of the play with the actors' moves already '**blocked**' and the meaning of the play unalterably fixed in their minds. Such directors took a dim view of any actor who challenged his or her decisions.

■ Link

See Chapter 16 for more detail about the performer's analysis and interpretation.

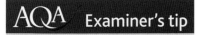

There are not many directors working in contemporary theatre who adopt such a rigid approach. However, there are still directors, especially those working with a tight rehearsal schedule, whose aim is to impose their vision of the play on the performers at all costs.

Most plays have main parts and most theatre companies have traditionally had leading actors who would play those parts, with supporting actors taking the lesser roles. Nowadays, there are also companies of performers whose work is far more democratic in nature. In these companies, an actor might be playing a king in one production and a spear-carrier in the next, although the director will still be exercising the powers of direction over king and subject alike.

Other contemporary companies such as **Complicite** and **Shared Experience** work as a creative **ensemble**, where the performers take as much responsibility for creating meaning, during the rehearsal period, as the director.

The performers' relationship with the text and with the audience

All performers have work to do on their role, whatever kind of director they are working for and whatever kind of role they are playing. Of course, every performer must learn his or her part (if it is text based) and this is usually the first task to be accomplished before beginning the real process of exploration.

Most actors will study and analyse their parts and relationships with other characters before beginning to build the role vocally and physically.

Performers also have to think about their relationship with the audience, although this will be dictated by the style of the play to be performed. Even when performing in a naturalistic play, which demands total concentration on the stage action and does not break '**the fourth wall**' in any way, performers have to communicate with their audiences.

Preparing for a theatre visit: style

Link

Look back at Chapter 2 for further detail about theatre buildings and spaces.

This chapter describes some of the styles of theatre you may encounter and suggests ways in which you can maximise the value of each theatre visit. Preparation before a visit will help you to assess what you see.

The venue

Theatres vary enormously in shape and design and each venue will produce a different audience experience.

You will be better equipped to assess the effectiveness of a production if you know about the size and lay-out of the **auditorium** in advance.

Theatres sometimes have separate auditoria and most studio theatres can vary the acting and seating areas between productions, so check out the precise configuration before your visit. If you are unfamiliar with the venue, look on the theatre's website. This may provide photos or even a virtual tour.

Find out if the play is designed specifically for one performance space or if it is a touring production, visiting many theatres. A touring set has to adapt to stages of varying dimensions and has to be easily transported.

The style of the production

Prepare for your theatre visit by identifying the *style* of the production in advance. Some styles are detailed below.

The classical play

These are plays from earlier periods, such as Greek, Elizabethan or Restoration, that have been performed regularly over the centuries. They may be serious or comical, but they usually rely a great deal on language for their effect. Such plays may be staged and costumed to preserve their original style or brought up to date in a contemporary treatment.

The naturalistic play

In the **naturalistic** play, the plot, characterisation and design elements are largely realistic. This category includes serious plays exploring important themes and issues as well as comedies presenting relationships, and 'whodunit?'-style plays, based on detective stories.

The pantomime

Traditionally these are Christmas entertainments, primarily aimed at children. They often have sketchy plots, loosely based on fairy tales, and include music and song, slapstick sketches and topical references. A woman in tights usually plays the principal boy, while the comic dame figure is taken by a male actor. Today's pantomimes are often spectacular and feature leading TV stars and/or pop groups among the cast.

The musical

Musicals are plays in which the dialogue is mainly sung. Storylines vary enormously and include a wide range of settings from the Biblical

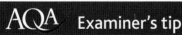

background of *Joseph and his Amazing Technicolor Dream Coat*, to the more contemporary setting and themes of *Blood Brothers*. Musicals generally combine a mixture of big chorus numbers with solos from the leading characters and they invariably include spectacular staging effects.

Physical theatre

Physical theatre is a relatively recent theatrical style, drawing on the skills of both mime and dance. The extent of physicality employed varies greatly. In some productions, physical movement is used to support the text, in others it is the dominant form of expression. Popular physical theatre groups include DV8, Complicité and Kneehigh.

Specialist theatre: puppetry, mask work and circus skills

A number of theatre groups integrate puppetry and/or masks into their productions and some groups are dedicated exclusively to puppet or mask-based drama. This style of theatre is not necessarily aimed at children. **Trestle Theatre** once specialised exclusively in mask work while groups such as **Faulty Optic** present powerful and moving themes, using puppetry to convey disturbing, cartoon-style productions.

There are also several touring circus groups, such as **Cirque du Soleil** who blend the skills needed for circus and drama to create spell-binding theatre of the extreme.

Preparation before the performance

Being prepared for each theatre visit will allow you to concentrate on what's happening on stage. It will enhance your enjoyment of the show as well as boost your ability to discuss and write about the production afterwards.

- Visit the theatre company's website to find information about the group's aims and ethos, as well as particular details about the type of play you are about to see.
- Read publicity material about the show.
- Use all forms of media to gather information about a piece. Actors are often interviewed on television, radio, in newspapers or magazines when a play is opening.
- Read reviews of the performance in your local or a national newspaper.
- If the text of the play is available, read at least part of it before you go. Alternatively, read a synopsis of the plot in order to leave you free to concentrate on *how* it is being performed.
- If you are seeing a play based on a novel or a film, try to read or watch the original source material.

7 Preparing for a theatre visit: audience

Activity

Draw up a list of rules for members of an audience. First on your list should be: turn off your mobile phone!

Previous chapters in this section have considered the work of many people in the theatre. This chapter looks at the role of another important group of people – the audience. The word 'group' is significant here since theatre going is a group activity with codes of behaviour that should be observed by all.

When you go to the theatre, it is important to remember that both the actors and the audience are an essential part of the theatre experience. The actor-audience relationship works two ways and the actors are very much aware of the responses of an audience. They can sense if the audience is enthralled or bored, amused or amazed.

A good audience is attentive from the moment the house lights go down, the curtains open or the performers start to perform, depending on the style of the show.

The normal expectation of an audience is that they should be silent and alert for the duration of the play, though they may laugh at appropriate moments and applaud at the end of the performance.

There are occasions when silence is inappropriate. In many shows, a degree of audience participation is invited. Actors in pantomimes, for example, make it clear that the audience is expected to 'boo!' the villain, or to join in with some singing. Actors are skilled at indicating to an audience what is expected, so a good audience takes its cue from them.

The length of productions varies, but two-and-a-half to three hours is average. Concentrating for every second of that time is impossible, which is why most shows have an interval to allow the audience to reflect on what has taken place as well as to refresh themselves. Most people find that if they concentrate hard at the beginning of a play they soon become absorbed in the action and lose track of time.

At the end of most performances the tradition is to applaud. If the emotional impact of the play is very strong, this applause may not start the instant that the play finishes. A pause may ensue, as the audience digest the emotion of the piece.

At the end of musicals, on the other hand, there are often several curtains calls, during which the audience are encouraged to sing along, or to applaud rhythmically.

At the end of an outstanding performance an audience may react by giving a **standing ovation**. This standing up and clapping is a way for people to express their strong appreciation of the actors and production team.

Fig. 7.1 *A detail from* The Laughing Audience *by William Hogarth*

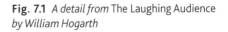

8   Preparing for a theatre visit: content

In this chapter you will learn about:

- the difference between the content and the style of a production
- the features of a production that you need to identify and evaluate.

Activity

Use the internet to research the history of the Cinderella story and its many versions through the ages.

This chapter looks at three different potential productions of the Cinderella story and explains how each one is made distinctive by the choices made by the production team. It will help you to *identify* and *evaluate* the specific qualities of a particular production, relating to its direction, to the acting and to the design. These are the necessary skills for tackling exam questions in this section of Unit 1.

Cinderella – three virtual productions

The story of Cinderella is centuries old and it has been retold in various theatrical forms as well as in countless films, cartoons and storybooks. The story is often performed as a pantomime, although there are also more serious modern performances that focus on the neglect of the Cinderella figure, living in a household with a hostile stepmother and two sisters whose ugliness is more than skin deep.

The playlet *Ashputel* in *Grimm Tales* (1996) by Carol Ann Duffy, as well as the play *The Ash Girl* (2000) by Timberlake Wertenbaker, both explore the more sinister elements of the story. Both these versions include the episode from the original fairytale where the two 'ugly' sisters cut off parts of their own feet in order to trim them to a size that will make the magical slipper fit and guarantee them the Prince!

This chapter will look at details from three *entirely imaginary dramatised versions* of the story:

- *Cinderella* – a pantomime
- *Ella and the Ashes* – a piece of physical theatre
- *Cinders* – a naturalistic retelling of the story, with a social message.

The productions described below are **fictitious** but analysing them should help you to recognise and categorise the features of *any* production of *any* play that you go to see. Note that the headings (from 'Style and genre' to 'The actor-audience relationship') are the same as those listed in the syllabus specification, so do use them to arrange your own observations of performances that you see. See the introduction on page viii for more detail.

Imagine that you are seeing each of the three performances listed above and that in preparation for your visits you have learned about the intended style of each. The examples below will then help you to differentiate between the contrasting theatrical approaches to the same 'content'.

Style and genre

Cinderella – a pantomime

The publicity material for this production has described it as a 'traditional pantomime with magical effects, suitable for all the family'. The term 'traditional pantomime' suggests the performance will be colourful and the staging quite elaborate; the mention of 'magical effects' suggests that the **transformation scenes** will be creative and exciting, and the tag 'suitable for all the family' suggests a wide target audience; this production aims to please everyone.

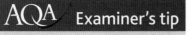

Examiner's tip

Knowing the *style* of the production that you are about to see will be valuable preparation for the visit.

Ella and the Ashes – a piece of physical theatre

This production is described as an 'innovative physical presentation' and 'visually stimulating'. The movement skills of the actors will be physically taxing and impressive, and they will be aiming to tell the story visually rather than through the delivery of lines. This production may rely on the audience already knowing the story.

Cinders – a naturalistic re-telling of the story

Described as 'a re-examination of the traditional story', this version looks at the social implications of Cinders' situation in a naturalistic way. There will be no magic; instead the company will be concentrating on the reality of the social and emotional problems of the characters. Unprepared audience members may not recognise this as *Cinderella* at all!

The directorial interpretation

Cinderella

The director of *Cinderella* has a reputation for creating exciting and beautiful pantomimes, and people book tickets annually for a family Christmas treat. This means that they arrive with high expectations, remembering the flying sequence from a previous year's *Peter Pan*. The transformation scene, where Cinderella's coach and dress appear, will be the most theatrical moment of the show, using spectacular effects and 'no expense spared'. Gasps of amazement from young and old alike will be the desired response. The role of Cinderella in this production will be played as the conventional heroine of slim build, long fair hair, graceful movements and a fairly high-pitched voice. Her animal friends will be cute.

Ella and the Ashes

The director of *Ella and the Ashes* has worked in modern dance and physical theatre, and has built up a company who explore their plays through extreme physicality. In preparation for your visit to this production you might have visited the website of the physical theatre company DV8; you might even have watched their DVD.

In this version the actor playing Cinderella has enormous physical dexterity and flexibility and her animal friends are represented by very human-looking performers, who present the physicality of mice and frogs in stylised ways. When Cinderella is transformed before the ball, the animals form a pyramid and she is lifted three metres above the stage as her new dress descends onto her.

Cinders

The director of *Cinders* usually works on plays such as Ibsen's **A Doll's House** and Chekhov's *The Seagull*. She wants to explore the suffering of a girl in a dysfunctional family who, in desperation, elopes with a man she has known for only a few hours. In this version the director wants to create sympathy for the other characters – the stepmother and the sisters. The body language and proximity of the members of the family indicate that they are not merely 'wicked' and the casting, costuming and make-up of the sisters in no way suggests ugliness, either in appearance or in personality.

Choice of venue and staging form

Cinderella

Cinderella is being performed in a theatre with a proscenium arch stage and seating for an audience of 1,000. The size of the audience helps to pay for the elaborate production. Setting the piece on a stage that is slightly

AQA Examiner's tip

The director's interpretation emerges in performance; take careful note of what you believe the director is intending to communicate to the audience.

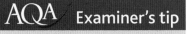
AQA Examiner's tip

The staging form makes a huge difference to the audience's experience.

removed from the audience allows special effects to be created using the trapdoors, the flies and **pyrotechnics**. The tiered seats and **raked** (slanting) stage help the smaller members of the audience to see reasonably well. The size of the stage itself allows for a spectacular ballroom scene, which can be clearly seen in particular from the circle and the upper circle.

Ella and the Ashes

Ella and the Ashes is performed on a thrust stage with an audience of about 400, seated on three sides and in raked seating, but with a flat stage since the complexity of the movement, and especially the **lifts,** make a rake difficult to work on. This touring company have a good reputation and should easily fill all seats for the six performances before it moves to a similar venue 200 miles away. The audience are relatively close to the stage and can see the grace, strength and concentration of each performer.

Cinders

Cinders is in-the-round in a 120-seat studio theatre with seating arranged in three rows. The stage area itself is small and intimate. The audience is close enough to the actors to see the smallest change in facial expression as they discuss the seriousness of their respective problems. There are only six actors in this version, and the budget for the production is small.

Performance skills

Cinderella

The performers in *Cinderella* are expected to be able to sing and dance as well as act. A girl plays the **principal boy**, the dashing Prince Charming, while the ugly sisters are played by men, in true pantomime tradition, to create comedy for the audience. The actors in the chorus are playing the animals in the transformation scene as well as the guests at the ball, so their movement skills need to be adaptable. Some of the actors speak directly to the audience.

Ella and the Ashes

The performers in *Ella and the Ashes* specialise in physical theatre so their movement skills are outstanding. They slightly exaggerate the physicality of each moment to create vivid pictorial images of the emotions being expressed; in the ballroom scene, the dances are unconventional, with many extreme **lifts** and jumps; they also climb up the framework of the set, creating a three-dimensional picture.

Cinders

The performers in *Cinders* place emphasis on communicating their emotions in a subtle way through their truthful facial expressions and the naturalistic delivery of dialogue. The confrontation between Cinders and her mother when she announces she is eloping is performed with great emotional intensity. As Cinders leaves, her sisters stand silently watching her go while her mother, on the verge of tears, sinks into a chair.

Integration of movement and language in performance

Cinderella

Movement and language are exaggerated in style, which helps to tell the story to young children. To entertain both young and old, the language of *Cinderella* is peppered with silly jokes and also slightly risqué innuendo, directed straight to the audience. There is a slapstick sequence where the ugly sisters end up throwing make-up all over each other, as they prepare

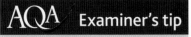

AQA Examiner's tip

When evaluating performance skills, consider the vocal, physical and facial expression of the performers, as well as the delivery of their lines.

Theatre trivia

Madame Vestris (1797–1856) was not only the first woman to manage a theatre; she was also the first ever **principal boy** in the English Pantomime, *Puss in Boots*.

AQA Examiner's tip

While watching a live production, think about how much meaning is communicated through language alone, how much through movement alone and how these two combine to reinforce meaning for the audience.

for the ball, where no words are spoken. Chorus songs are delivered energetically, while the duet between Cinderella and Prince Charming is romantic and tuneful.

Ella and the Ashes

Physical movement conveys both the plot and the emotions very powerfully in this production, although not in a realistic form. The use of dialogue is relatively restricted, but when words *are* used they are even more noticeable; at times they are delivered in chorus to give extra weight and they are synchronised with the movements.

Cinders

From the first entrance of the actor playing Cinders it is clear this is not a pantomime-type approach. Her work in the kitchen is realistic, chopping real vegetables and actually mending the sisters' clothes with needle and thread, while explaining to her family, in a totally credible tone, why she feels she is being treated unfairly. Her voice is quiet but the sisters have quite harsh tones and a clipped, yet still naturalistic delivery. Movement is entirely naturalistic throughout.

Stage setting and design

Cinderella

Most of the scenery is very bright, using mainly primary colours. The set for the kitchen scenes has a two-dimensional painted backcloth showing a kitchen range with pots and pans. This conceals an opening through which the fairy godmother appears. The ballroom has a magnificent gold and silver double curved staircase, creating an elaborate semicircle around the dancers, and offering a high platform for Cinderella's entry in her stunning ball gown.

Ella and the Ashes

The set comprises a large, non-naturalistic framework at the back of the thrust stage. The scaffolding-type structure is constructed of silver poles, providing the performers with a visually pleasing variety of levels on which to stand or from which to suspend themselves and to jump. The magic coach is created using the bodies of the ensemble cast, in a feat of great agility, suggesting precisely the shape of the coach and using umbrellas to suggest the wheels.

Cinders

Cinders has no constructed scenery and comprises one permanent set. There is minimal furniture, but what there is, including the props and set dressing, is all realistic and establishes the period for the play as present day. The largest item is the kitchen table which is placed centre stage so that the in-the-round audience can see the whole action.

Use of space

Cinderella

The huge stage space enables the spectacular magic coach to rise on hydraulic lifts from beneath the stage. A chase scene involving Buttons and his nephew, Zipper, is especially comic as they disappear into the wings and then reappear instantly, from the other side of the stage, using look alikes. The chase extends into the auditorium with Zipper climbing over the seats in the stalls and then trying to hide under one man's coat, while Buttons shouts at him from the circle.

AQA Examiner's tip

The set design is an important means of signifying location and/or the style of production to the audience. Think carefully about how the actors use the set, in performance, to contribute to the communication of the meaning of the piece.

AQA Examiner's tip

Notice how the abstract notion of space has a specific effect on the audience's experience of a production and it can thrill, engage sympathy or suggest 'reality' through the way it is used.

Ella and the Ashes

The cast make the best use possible of the floor space, at one point lying down and rolling from one side to the other, to suggest Ella's emotional turmoil. Entrances are made from the aisles between the seats in the auditorium; the sudden and scurrying entry of six 'mice' in this way startles many of the audience.

Cinders

The performers are surrounded by the audience but are careful not to make eye contact with them as this would ruin the realism of the piece, which is maintained by using the 'kitchen' space entirely naturalistically.

Costume

Cinderella

Cinderella's ball-gown is white with a sequinned bodice and an enormous hooped skirt. The other dresses in the ball scene are of a similar design but hers stands out because it catches the light and the skirt is covered in frills. The over-elaborate bright pink and fluorescent greens of the ugly sisters' dresses also stand out! The fairy godmother's dress is a particular favourite with some of the little girls in the audience because it is silver and pink and incorporates flappable wings.

Ella and the Ashes

The costumes for all the cast are eminently practical, allowing freedom of movement. They are designed in shades of creams and browns. Ella's 'rags' contain a mixture of these colours attached to a costume that enables her to physicalise her part. Her ball gown and Prince Charming's costume are made from a light chiffon material threaded with silver which floats and reflects the light as the pair dance ever faster around the stage.

Cinders

The costumes are contemporary; the characters wear clothes that could have come from a high street store. Cinders herself wears grey throughout and the sisters wear tight-fitting black tops and trousers. All the cast look as though the colour had been drained from their lives. The only splash of colour is Charles' blue shirt, worn with grey trousers, suggesting he is different from the others but somehow linked to Cinders.

Technical elements

Cinderella

Cinderella uses an enormous array of technical effects. The lighting is bright but varied. **Gobos** are used to change the pattern of light on the floor and gels change the colour. A **glitterball** in the ballroom scene shines on the audience as well as the cast. When the clock strikes midnight, the noise is deafening, and adds to Cinderella's panic. Pyrotechnics help to disguise the arrival and departure of the fairy godmother.

Ella and the Ashes

The lighting is the outstanding technical element because it is used to alter mood. The coloured gels reflect off the silver poles of the set and create a sombre ice-cold scene with pale blue gels when Ella is left alone. Dry ice flows down the set and creates a white lake on the floor. There is also a complex **soundscape** throughout the performance, which involves some music but also more abstract noise appropriate to the atmosphere of each moment.

AQA Examiner's tip

Notice the detail of each costume design; the colours, fabrics and cut, as well as accessories used, such as shoes, jewellery and head-gear.

AQA Examiner's tip

Remember that, while some lighting and sound effects are easy to see and hear on your theatre visit, more subtle uses of light and sound are designed to create an ambience rather than a direct effect. You need to recognise and evaluate each of these approaches.

Cinders

Technical elements are not needed in this production beyond very subtle lighting to create a realistic effect. There is a conventional bulb and shade suspended over the central table which appears to be the light source in most scenes. The stage is actually lit by approximately 40 **lanterns**, but they are positioned to make facial expressions clear and to eliminate shadows, not to create noticeable effects.

The creation of pace, mood and atmosphere

Cinderella

The pace varies from the slow and lyrical love duet to the frenetic chase sequence; the lighting enhances the mood in every scene, and encourages the audience to join in the songs creating a light-hearted atmosphere throughout the performance.

Ella and the Ashes

The energy of the performers is exhausting to watch but the gentler, slower and more reflective moments, when Ella is alone, serve to change both the pace and the mood. The atmosphere is tense for most of the performance because the emotions are very powerful; the audience may well forget that the story traditionally ends happily.

Cinders

This carefully directed piece contains a variation of pace, matching the rhythms of real life. The preparations for the night out are much faster, while the pace of the first meeting between Cinders and Charles is very slow because of their initial shyness. The mood and atmosphere is generally serious and tense.

The actor-audience relationship

Cinderella

As in all pantomimes, the cast take every opportunity to look at, or speak to, or invite reactions from the audience. The audience enjoy booing the ugly sisters as they plot against their stepsister and singing along with the chorus numbers. Children in the stalls are showered with sweets from time to time and one little girl gets to dance with the Prince. The actor-audience relationship is an essential part of the fun of the performance, confirmed by the excited 'buzz' as the audience leave their seats.

Ella and the Ashes

The company involves the audience through their use of the auditorium, but their skilful performance leaves the audience gasping at their dexterity and ingenuity. There is no interaction between actor and audience during the production.

Cinders

Although the actors perform very close to the audience, the actors perform as though they are entirely oblivious to their presence. The company expect (and achieve) the total focus and concentration of an audience attentive to a very new slant on a very old story.

AQA Examiner's tip

Be sensitive to the general pace, mood and atmosphere of the production, as well as noting the variations in these elements throughout the piece.

AQA Examiner's tip

Always consider the actor-audience relationship when discussing a production that you have seen. In particular, you should refer to the way it affected *your* experience of the performance.

Activity

Take any well-known fairytale and perform the same basic plot in two different styles. You may not be able to use all the theatrical elements mentioned in this chapter but consider what they might be and how they would help to define the style and affect the audience.

9   After a theatre visit

In this chapter we are going to focus on how best to record your experience of each theatre visit, so as to retain your impressions of it long after the **curtain call.**

Going to the theatre and watching the performance is only the beginning of the work that will equip you to answer your exam question in Unit 1. What you do afterwards is crucial.

Most performances include a huge amount of visual and aural detail. The design and each nuance of performance, as we have seen, have been carefully chosen to contribute to the meaning of the play.

From a two-to-three hour performance we will remember only a fraction of these details as time passes unless we make a conscious effort to document what we have seen.

When you sit your AS exam you are allowed to take some notes in with you, so that:

- you spend your time productively, rather than struggling to remember details of the show

- you can illustrate your answer with precise references.

There are three steps to follow to ensure your notes are as helpful as possible:

- making notes immediately after the visit
- discussing the visit
- rewriting your notes.

AQA Examiner's tip

Remember that you might be seeing the performance several months before the examination, so it is vital that you make clear, concise notes to prompt your memory.

Making notes immediately after the visit

Do this as soon as possible and begin by being totally unselective. Write down absolutely everything you can remember of the production; make a sketch of the set design(s), write about the style and the colour of the costumes. List the lighting and sound effects that you noticed. These first impressions should be committed to paper or computer within 24 hours of the visit; you should edit and organise them later.

Activity

Keep a list of positive and negative words, which can be used to define each performance seen.

Discussing the visit

Discuss the strengths and weaknesses of the production with your group as well as with your teacher. You should try to focus on:

- Style. (Look back at Chapters 7 and 8.) Ask yourself what the style was. How was it revealed?

- Audience response. Ask yourself what the audience response was. Were you moved to tears or laughter, or made to think?

- Performance details. Ask yourself which were the outstanding elements. (Refer back to the headings in Chapter 8.) Which details that you remember fit which category?

- Themes and issues. Ask yourself what were the main themes, issues, messages, aims. How were these made clear for an audience?

- Total effects. Ask yourself which were the most effective moments and which were less effective; how did these affect the total theatre experience?

Some of the details you remember will be the same as everyone else's. However, good theatre creates a variety of responses. Express and share *your* opinions.

During discussion, try to develop appropriate vocabulary with which to express your experience. 'Boring' or 'great' are not helpful terms; 'slow moving', 'energetic', 'exciting', 'surprising' are more specific. Try to find the appropriate word or words to define your response to each and every element of the show.

▮ Rewriting your notes

Before the exam, you should review, refine and rewrite your notes.

The notes you take into the exam *must* be:

▮ in note form rather than sentences
▮ no more than two sides of A4 on each play,

and *may* be:

▮ handwritten or word-processed
▮ sketches, to help you answer on design topics.

These notes must be your personal notes and should not include any printed material such as reviews or programmes. Take care to make them clear, easy to follow, detailed and accurate.

As a 'rule of thumb', each point you record should contain enough detail to be developed into a decent-length paragraph of about 70 words. To write a fully developed exam answer you will need to write between 12 and 15 of these paragraphs, so make sure that you have the material for at least that amount.

Be selective when you write your final notes. During the course you should have seen at least four different productions. If your notes about, say, *The Woman in Black*, include hardly any details about costumes, you will be ill-equipped to choose a costume question based on that play, so concentrate on other aspects in your rewritten notes. If the acting in *Macbeth* was the outstanding feature of the production, then include as much detail as you can about the performances of two or three actors.

It is always worthwhile allowing yourself about half a page per production to write simply *everything* you can recall about one or two particular moments from the play. Exam questions often demand reference to 'particular moments' and you don't want to find yourself remembering the show as one great blur!

▮ Think

Record your own impressions and don't be tempted to write about exactly the same moments or aspects as everyone else in your class. A personal response is what's needed!

▮ Think

The answer you give in your AS exam for Section A will count for 30 per cent of your AS marks, so do make sure you prepare for it carefully!

AQA Examiner's tip

To help you formulate and develop your critical responses and vocabulary, read newspaper reviews and listen to any media discussions of the production *after* your visit; think carefully about whether you agree or disagree with them and why.

10 How to be successful in the examination

▤ Choosing a question

In the exam, you will be faced with a choice of four questions; you need only answer one of them. You need to select the question that gives you the most opportunity to write, in detail, about *one* of the productions that you have seen.

Here are examples of the type of exam question you will find in the Unit 1 paper, Section A.

1 Outline the set design(s) in *one* live production that you have seen where the designer adopted a non-naturalistic approach, and evaluate the success of the designs in creating a suitable setting for the action, at particular moments of the play.

2 Outline the use of period styling, colour, condition and accessories within the costume design of *one* live production that you have seen and assess its success in communicating character to the audience. You should consider the costumes worn by at least two characters at particular moments in the play.

3 Explain how *one or more* performers used vocal, physical and facial expression to engage the audience, at particular moments within *one* live production that you have seen, and assess the effectiveness of their performances.

4 Explain how the performers used both their props and the setting within *one* live production that you have seen and assess their contribution to the creation of a sense of realism at particular moments within the production.

In the exam, after you have read all four questions, you need to select the one that you can answer best.

Assume you have seen the three imaginary productions, based on *Cinderella*, that featured in Chapter 8. Which question would give you the best opportunity to write a good answer on *one* of these 'productions'?

Question 1 would be a good choice for either *Cinderella* the pantomime or *Ella and the Ashes*, the physical theatre. However, it would be totally inappropriate for *Cinders*, the naturalistic version.

Cinderella, with its painted backdrop and 'fairy-tale' ballroom would be a good example of a non-naturalistic set, which is two dimensional, initially, and also has a fantasy quality. You could write well about this, remembering to:

▨ outline the kitchen and ballroom sets, using a sketch

▨ discuss the bright colours used

▨ define the non-naturalistic qualities of the set, such as the painted kitchen range

▨ discuss the bright colours used throughout and the spectacular gold and silver staircase in the ballroom

▨ describe precisely how the sets were used at particular moments and evaluate how suitable they were for the action; remember the concealed entrance for the fairy godmother's sudden appearance, for example, and the emergence of the coach from below the stage.

The set of *Ella and the Ashes* is also a good example of a totally non-naturalistic setting, where you could write about:

- the complex scaffolding structure used to climb up and hang from
- the silvered poles shimmering in different coloured lights
- the use of the set at particular moments, for example, when the mice appear, or when the actors physicalise their emotions, forming complex patterns within the three-dimensional structure.

Cinders had virtually no set and the limited furnishings used were entirely naturalistic. It would be very difficult to answer this particular question based on this production.

Writing your answer

When writing your answer you need to communicate your personal opinions in an appropriate way. Read the two examples of students' statements below. Decide which would gain more marks in the exam and why.

> 'This play was rubbish and the actors were useless.'

> 'This play was slow moving. The actors' voices became monotonous as they rarely changed the pitch or pace of their delivery, even during the sequence involving the trying-on of the slipper.'

Remember that, unlike your teacher and other group members, the person marking your answer has probably *not* seen the performance. Your answer should enable the examiner to:

- visualise the performance
- understand your response to it
- appreciate the assessment you offer.

Make your answer achieve these aims by using the following sequence of questions to structure the points that you make: *What? When? Why? Was it effective?* For example:

What? Cinderella let out a short, sharp, ear-piercing scream.

When? When her fairy godmother suddenly appeared in a puff of purple smoke

Why? To show Cinderella's amazement, to startle the audience and to make them laugh.

Was it effective? Yes, it was effective because although the audience were initially startled by the loud scream, they soon laughed at Cinderella's fear of the completely non-threatening, white-haired, elderly fairy godmother.

How to write a successful answer

If you follow all the advice offered, you will be well on the way to writing a successful answer in the exam. All you need now is to see some varied and exciting theatre. Remember:

You gain marks for:

- writing appropriately about a production which is suitable for your selected question
- including detail in your account of your experience as an audience member

Activity

Look at the other three questions and, by relating them to the imaginary Cinderella productions, decide which would give you the most opportunity to write a detailed response to questions 2, 3 and 4.

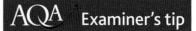

AQA Examiner's tip

Check that you are addressing *all* the parts of the question. For example, if you are answering question 3, you don't need to give *equal* weight to 'vocal', 'physical' and 'facial expression' but you must give some consideration to each.

Think

Look at the descriptive detail used in this short sequence to bring this 'particular moment' to life. Make a list of the different adjectives/adverbs that have been used to describe the moment in a vivid way.

■ offering personal assessment, in response to the precise focus of the question

■ referring to particular moments from the production to support your opinions.

The following weaknesses will prevent you from gaining good marks:

■ ignoring the focus and writing in a generalised way

■ choosing a question that does not match your experience of live theatre

■ reproducing your notes, unselectively

■ failing to take appropriate notes into the exam.

Enjoy your theatre visits, make helpful notes and good luck in the exam!

■ Summary of this section

In these chapters you have learned about:

■ different theatre spaces and how each affects the audience experience of a production

■ theatre buildings through the ages

■ what directors do and who they work with to realise their vision of a play for the audience

■ how set designers create specific effects for an audience

■ how costume designers interpret period and character on stage

■ how technical designers create their effects

■ what performers do and how they relate to the other members of the production team

■ preparing for a theatre visit

■ different styles of theatre

■ what is expected of an audience

■ how different theatre styles affect an audience differently – even when communicating the same 'story'

■ how to analyse the experience of each theatre visit and to make useful notes

■ how to prepare for and revise for the exam

■ how to choose a question in the exam

■ how to answer the precise demands of the chosen question

■ where to find information about historical as well as contemporary theatres and theatre companies, directors, designers and performers.

Don't forget that these chapters are not intended to be read just once. You should revisit these chapters throughout your course. For example, before you complete a homework task based on a theatre visit, read the relevant chapters again. You should read the whole section again before school or college exams, as well as before your actual AS exam.

Remember that the e-resources, and the weblinks contained within them, should also be revisited repeatedly. They are there to extend your knowledge and stimulate your interest in drama and theatre as well as to provide you with tools to support your studies.

11 Introduction to the set plays

In this section you will learn about:

- how your set play relates to its historical, social and cultural context

- how style, form, period, mood, action and characterisation can be interpreted in performance to create specific effects for an audience

- specialist terminology, so that you can use it accurately and with confidence

- how to respond to your set play imaginatively.

Activity

With a partner, take any play off the shelf in your drama library. Each of you read the opening two pages, note down your first thoughts about the setting, casting and stage action, then share your 'directorial' ideas. No two interpretations will ever be exactly the same.

Exploring a play

In this section we will be looking at different ways to explore your chosen play. Sometimes you will be studying your set play in the classroom or at home in your own space; sometimes at your computer and sometimes you will be in a drama studio. Wherever you are and whatever your set task might be, you need to think of yourself as an interpreter of the text.

You need to think about *what* the playwright is trying to communicate to the audience and about *how* a director, the actors, the designers, or a whole production team working together might bring the playwright's intentions to life.

Interpreting a play

Whenever you pick up a new play to read, you become, in effect, a new interpreter of that play. As you read, you begin to imagine what the play would look like on stage; moving the characters around an imaginary space, in your head; visualising the characters' faces and expressions; imagining their movements and 'hearing' their voices speaking the lines that you are reading. In fact, you are already looking at the play with the eyes of a director.

As you read on, you mentally 'cast' the characters of the play to fit in with the information supplied by the playwright, either in stage directions or in the way that the characters behave and interact with each other, imagining them as youthful or elderly, powerful or weak, beautiful or ugly. Reading a play is always more like being a director than like being a member of an audience, because the audience is always presented with a play that has been read and interpreted for them; all the casting and staging decisions have already been made. When reading, *you* are firmly in the director's chair.

As you gain more experience of the theatre, both by reading more plays and watching live productions, you will develop your ability to form clear mental pictures of the characters and action. You will even begin to fill your imaginary stage with suitable furnishings that create a location for the action in your mind; you will begin to envisage the costumes, lighting and sound effects.

Which play?

Your teacher will choose a play from the following list of possible set texts:

- *Antigone* by Sophocles
- *The Taming of the Shrew* by William Shakespeare
- *A Doll's House* by Henrik Ibsen
- *The Shadow of a Gunman* by Sean O'Casey

Further reading

There is further guidance about the choice of text for Unit 2 in Chapter 24.

Think

Read some of the set plays as well as the one you are studying. This will enhance your knowledge of drama and theatre as well as deepening your understanding of the process of interpretation. You might also discover a type of play that you might like to explore for Unit 2.

■ *Oh! What a Lovely War* by Joan Littlewood and Theatre Workshop
■ *Playhouse Creatures* by April De Angelis

The selection will be made according to which is most suitable and enjoyable for your group. You will be answering a question on your set play in the exam at the end of Unit 1, so your teacher will also be considering which play you are most likely to write about well. He or she will also bear in mind which practitioner you may be working on for your practical presentation in Unit 2 because the plays that you study in Units 1 and 2 must be different in period and genre.

Although each of the set plays in Unit 1 is very distinct, in terms of its style and original context, the demands that are placed on you as you work through the play are very much the same, whether you are studying *Antigone*, the 'oldest' play and a tragedy, or *Playhouse Creatures*, the most modern of the set plays and a comedy.

Rather than devote separate parts of this section to each of the set plays, after an initial introduction to the context, period and genre of each play, we are going to discuss approaches to interpretation that are common to all plays, using specific examples from each of the set texts to illustrate those approaches along the way.

Each play is highlighted in a different colour, to help you find references to your chosen text more easily. However, please remember that *all* the points made will be relevant to you, whichever text you are studying. The examples from the plays that you are not studying are presented so as to be meaningful to all readers of this book.

■ In the exam

Since the exam questions that relate to this unit invite you to give answers from the perspective of a director, an actor or a designer, it makes sense to give equal attention to issues of staging, performance and design. Chapters 14–17 are therefore divided up according to these three broad headings.

However, do remember that you need to understand how directors, designers and actors work *together* to achieve a complete theatrical realisation of a play for an audience. It is the result of this combined effort that the audience experiences when watching a production unfold in the theatre; only in the exam paper in Unit 1 do we separate out these individual theatrical elements.

12 Context, period and genre

In this chapter you will learn about:

- the context, period and genre of your set play
- researching the background to your set play.

The terms 'context', 'period' and 'genre' often appear together in this book and in the drama and theatre studies specification, but they have separate meanings and it is essential that you understand them fully. When you begin to study your set play, the first questions that you should be asking yourself are:

- What is the *context* of the play?
- What *period* was it written in?
- What *genre* is it?

'Context' refers to the circumstances or events surrounding the writing or the setting of the play. These might include, for example a political context, such as the political instability in Ireland in the 1920s that formed the background both to the writing and the setting of **The Shadow of a Gunman**.

It is also important to consider the theatrical context of your set play. Some of the plays on the set text list are chosen because they are representative of a particular type of play, as they were written in the style that was most common in the theatrical context of their day. Others have been chosen because they signal a radical departure from the theatrical context of their day. *Oh! What a Lovely War*, for example, was considered ground-breaking compared to the plays that made up its theatrical context.

'Period' refers not simply to the precise date when the play was written but rather to the 'interval of time' within which that date falls. For example, *The Taming of the Shrew*, written in the 1590s, is referred to as a product of the Elizabethan period, because it was written during the reign of Elizabeth I. Some of Shakespeare's later plays were written during the early part of the reign of James I. *The Tempest*, for example, is Jacobean in period.

'Genre' refers to the dramatic category that the play fits into, which may be determined by the style or form of the play. *Antigone*, for example, belongs to the genre of tragedy, a form of play that deals mainly with nobility; the action of the play entails the ruin of a previously 'great' character, usually due to personal weakness or pride; tragedies end unhappily. *The Taming of the Shrew* belongs to the genre of comedy, a form of play that usually involves a broader social class and which ends happily, often with a marriage.

What follows is a brief guide to the context, period and genre of each of the set plays. Do not be tempted to skip the plays that you are not studying; there is material that you will find useful in all of the sections below.

Antigone – 441 BC

Period and production context

Antigone was written around 441 BC by the foremost tragedian of his day, Sophocles.

Sophocles is believed to have written over a hundred plays, although only seven of his tragedies survive. Sophocles lived to be 90 years old and during his lifetime he won at least 18 victories in the **City Dionysia**.

Further reading

You can research more about your play's context, period and genre from a variety of resources including the introductions to your set plays, standard encyclopedias, general reference books and the internet.

This was the annual spring state festival of drama organised by city officials in celebration of Dionysus, the Greek god of fertility, wine and ecstasy.

Competition to present drama at the festival was fierce and state organisers had to select from many applications from aspiring playwrights when they were arranging the programme. Athens was the most important city state for drama. All the Ancient Greek tragedies that have come down to us through the ages were written for the Athenian festival by Athenian playwrights, Aeschylus, Sophocles and Euripides.

The City Dionysia was held in Athens in late March and early April and lasted between five and six days. Several playwrights presented a **tetralogy** consisting of three tragedies and a **satyr play**, which was like a comic 'after-piece' to the main event, the tragedies.

i It was every citizen's duty to attend the festival which had evolved from earlier religious ceremonies and rituals and, since attendance was mandatory for all citizens, free seats were provided for those who could not afford the modest price of admission. While the state paid for the actors and the **chorus**, all other expenses involved in the production were paid for by wealthy citizens called the **choregus**, who acted as sponsors for the playwrights.

Context to the play's action

Sophocles based his 'Theban' trilogy upon the saga of the house of Laius. The trilogy consists of *Oedipus the King*, *Oedipus at Colonus* and *Antigone* and it follows the cursed family of Oedipus, a man doomed by fate to kill his father and to marry his mother.

Antigone is the third play in the sequence, although it was probably written first. In order to understand the background to **Antigone's** own actions and character it is useful to be aware of her family history. Legend has it that Laius and Jocasta, the king and queen of Thebes, consulted the **oracle** of Apollo at Delphi, who gave them the prophecy that any son that they had would, in time, murder his father. So, when Jocasta gave birth to Oedipus, the baby was handed to a shepherd, to be abandoned on the hillside with his little feet pierced through with metal pins.

The shepherd took pity on the baby. Instead of carrying out his orders, he gave the boy to a fellow shepherd, who then took him to Corinth and gave him to the childless king and queen, Polybus and Merope, to bring up as their own son. In due course, Oedipus visited the oracle at Delphi for himself and was horrified to be told that he would murder his father and marry his mother. In the belief that Polybus and Merope were his birth parents, Oedipus immediately left the city of Corinth and set out for Thebes.

On his journey, Oedipus encountered an old man and his servants in a carriage at a narrow place in the road. There was a dispute about the right of way and, in an ancient fit of road rage, Oedipus killed the old man and his entourage. He continued his journey to Thebes, ignorant of the fact that he had just killed the king of the Thebans, his birth father.

When he arrived in Thebes, Oedipus found a state terrorised by a monster, the Sphinx (a winged lion with a woman's face). The Sphinx threatened to blight Thebes until someone answered her riddle. Oedipus answered the riddle correctly and the Sphinx threw herself to her death. Oedipus was rewarded for saving the city by being married to the widowed queen, Jocasta – who was, unbeknown to him, his birth mother.

■ **Think**

Have you heard of the 'Oedipus complex'? It is a term coined by the Austrian psychiatrist Sigmund Freud (1856–1939), to describe a mental state whereby a young man has obsessive feelings either for his mother or for older women in general.

■ **Think**

The Sphinx's riddle was: 'What goes on four feet, three feet and two feet and is most vulnerable when on four feet?' The answer is humans, who crawl on four feet as a baby, use two feet in adulthood and three feet (two, plus walking stick!) when old.

For many years, Oedipus was a successful and popular king. He and Jocasta had four children: two sons, Eteocles and **Polynices**; and two daughters, **Antigone** and Ismene.

When Thebes was struck by plague, however, the oracle at Delphi predicted that the city could only be saved when the killer of old King Laius had been discovered. Oedipus took every step to discover the murderer and eventually he unearthed the truth about his own origins and the horrific fact that he had committed both **patricide** by killing his father and **incest** with his own mother. He had unwittingly fulfilled the prophecy that he had tried so hard to escape.

In an act of self-loathing, Jocasta hanged herself and Oedipus put out his own eyes with the pins from her robes. Jocasta's brother, **Creon** assumed power in Thebes, ruling alongside Eteocles and **Polynices**, the sons of Oedipus. Offended by his sons, Oedipus pronounced a curse upon them that they would die by one another's hands and he left Thebes, with **Antigone** as his guide, to become a wandering beggar along the highways of Greece.

Oedipus's curse on his sons was fulfilled when, having failed to gain the Theban throne for himself, **Polynices** raised an army against Thebes at Argos. He engaged in battle against his homeland and his brother, Eteocles who fought in defence of Thebes. The play *Antigone* opens after Thebes's victory has been secured, the brothers have killed one another and the state is finally in **Creon's** sole control.

Genre

Classical Greek tragedy is a form that was first documented and described by the Greek philosopher and critic, Aristotle (384–322 BC). His definition of tragedy appeared in a volume called, simply, *Poetics*, written nearly 100 years after Sophocles wrote *Antigone*. Aristotle defines tragedy as a play devoted to the downfall of a great man, through the combination of his own *hubris* (pride) and the will of the gods – sometimes described as fate. The fall from happiness to misery is so complete that the audience, watching the fate of the **protagonist** unfold, experiences both pity and fear in an emotional release which is called **catharsis**.

Antigone is a good example of Classical Greek tragedy, as defined by Aristotle. **Creon** is the tragic figure in this play, whose fall is brought about by **Antigone's** challenge to his authority and to the laws that he represents. By ignoring the laws of the gods to give **Polynices** a proper burial, **Creon** exhibits the fatal flaw of *hubris* and, deaf to the pleas of his own son, to the advice of the prophet **Tiresias** and to the consistent questions of the chorus, he condemns Antigone to death and offends the gods. Their **retribution** upon him is swift and devastating.

Further research

You will find a comprehensive section on Greek theatre in general, and Sophocles in particular, in the *Oxford Illustrated History of the Theatre* (OUP, 2001).

Other standard reference books on drama and theatre history include:

- *The Oxford Companion to the Theatre*, edited by Phyllis Hartnoll (OUP, 1983)
- *History of the Theatre*, by Glynne Wickham (Phaidon Press, 1992)
- *Theatre History Explained*, by Neil Fraser (The Crowood Press, 2004).

Theatre trivia

Deus ex machina, meaning literally 'god out of a machine' describes the moment, in Greek theatre, where a stage machine lowers an actor playing one of the gods descending from mount Olympus to resolve human difficulties on earth. It now refers to any improbable resolution to a play.

Activity

Try to see a live production of your set play. You might stage at least a section of your play using full production elements.

Books devoted to classical Greek theatre include:

- *Images of the Greek Theatre: Classical Bookshelf*, by Richard Green *et al.* (British Museum Press, 1995)
- *Public and Performance in the Greek Theatre*, by Peter D. Arnott (Routledge, 1991)
- *Guide to Greek Theatre and Drama*, by Kenneth McLeish (Methuen Drama, 2003)
- *Greek Theatre Performance: An Introduction*, by David Wiles (CUP, 2000).

If you are using Robert Fagles' translation of *Antigone* within the volume of *The Three Theban Plays* (Penguin Classics, 1984) you will find ample background material to the play in Fagles' excellent introductory chapter.

The Taming of the Shrew – early 1590s

Period and production context

Shakespeare (1564–1616) requires only a brief introduction, since you will have encountered at least some of his plays in your school study of English or drama.

Very little biographical detail is known about Shakespeare although commentators have suggested that he began his career in the theatre as a writer of history plays before turning his hand to both comedy and tragedy.

Shakespeare wrote at least 36 plays, although the authorship of some of these plays has been disputed. Whether or not future research reveals that there was more than one author of what we currently consider to be Shakespeare's plays, few people would dispute that they form a collection of entertaining, absorbing and often enthralling dramatic works.

Theatre companies in Elizabethan England were sponsored by wealthy courtiers. Some commentators suggests that Shakespeare's earliest theatrical experiences were gained as some kind of apprentice within the Earl of Leicester's company, which was based at Kenilworth Castle in Warwickshire. What we do know for sure is that, by the mid-1590s, Shakespeare had become an **actor-sharer** in the Chamberlain's Men, the company for whom he wrote the majority of his plays. The Chamberlain's Men performed their repertoire at the Globe theatre in London until it burned down in 1613 during, or shortly after, a performance of Shakespeare's play *Henry VIII*.

The company also performed at the Blackfriars Theatre, which was one of the first indoor theatres to be built in London. Lit by candlelight, the Blackfriars theatre allowed for night-time performances as well as performances in the winter. The Chamberlain's Men were great favourites with Queen Elizabeth I. After she died in 1603, James I came to the throne. The Chamberlain's men were renamed The King's Men and gained the direct patronage from the king himself.

Shakespeare's plays were written specifically for the company with which he was associated; many of the roles were tailored to match the strengths of a cast that he knew well, just as he knew exactly where each play would be performed. Shakespeare could also predict his potential audience, which could range from the Monarch and courtiers (in performances at court), gentlemen and gentlewomen, who would occupy seats of varying degrees of comfort and proximity to the action, all the way down to the **groundlings** who stood in the **pit** of the public theatres.

Groundlings paid a penny for the privilege of standing throughout the play, while seats in the public playhouses cost anything between sixpence and a shilling. The private playhouses had an audience capacity of 300–400 people, as opposed to the 2,000 who could be crammed into the public playhouse. Prices in the private playhouses would be about five times as great as those in the public playhouses.

Context to the play's action

The Taming of the Shrew was written in the early 1590s, during the reign of Elizabeth I. It is thought to be an adaptation of an earlier play with a similar name, but that play is no longer in existence.

The context of the action is contemporary to when Shakespeare wrote the play; set, for the most part, in 16th-century Padua, it tells the story of an Italian gentleman's attempts to get both his daughters married to suitable husbands.

In Elizabethan times, gentlewomen were financially dependent upon their families until they married. They did not work but prepared themselves for becoming wives and mothers by gaining accomplishments in music and needlework. Some enlightened parents also arranged for their daughters to receive education in the arts in order to prepare them for the society of their husbands and guests, once they were married.

So, marriage during the Elizabethan period was more likely to be a financial transaction rather than based on romance. Shakespeare's comedy presents the wooing of Bianca by Lucentio as romantic, but **Petruchio's** courtship of **Katherina** is more pragmatic. The generous dowry is Petruchio's main incentive to take on the 'cursed shrew'.

The action of the play follows the attempts of **Lucentio** to win 'fair **Bianca**' and the attempts of **Petruchio** to tame **Katherina** out of her shrewishness once he has married her for her hefty dowry. Both actions are linked to commercial considerations with **Petruchio** coming out of the bargain considerably richer than when he began, both in financial and romantic terms! He wins a lucrative wager as well as the love and respect of a woman whom he has come to love.

Fig. 12.1 *Petruchio and Katherina arriving at Petruchio's home*, The Taming of the Shrew

Genre

Elizabethan comedy spans a variety of styles, including the satires of John Marston, George Chapman and Ben Jonson, which are often peopled with cynical rogues and villains, as well as the more romantic comedies of Shakespeare.

Shakespeare's comedies themselves include a variety of plays but unlike the **city comedies** or **comedy of humours** of the earlier part of Elizabeth's reign, Shakespeare's comedies are more light-hearted in tone. They tend to end happily, often with a wedding or a scene of revelation or reconciliation. Shakespeare often focuses on cases of mistaken identity or disguise. Two of his comedies involve the exploits of identical twins. (*The Comedy of Errors* contains *two* sets of identical twins!) Shakespearean comedies also often feature witty, strong-minded women. In *As You Like It*, *Twelfth Night* and *The Merchant of Venice*, much of the comedy comes from the fact that the main female character disguises herself as a man.

Shakespeare's comedies include comic characters as well as situational comedy and all use wit and banter to create humour. Sometimes the comedy is less immediate to a modern reader, because Shakespearean language can be difficult to master. However, what seems unintelligible in the classroom can become hilarious when you see the plays in production.

Further research

- *Elizabethan–Jacobean Drama: The Theatre in Its Time*, by G.Blakemore Evans *et al*. (New Amsterdam Books, 1998)
- *The Taming of the Shrew – Shakespeare in Production*, by William Shakespeare *et al*. (Cambridge University Press, 2003)
- *The Taming of the Shrew: Shakespeare Handbooks*, by Margaret Jane Kidnie (Macmillan, 2006)
- *An Actor Working on the Elizabethan Stage: The Working Life*, by Stephen Currie (Lucent Books, 2003)
- *The Queen's Men and Their Plays*, by Scott McMillin *et al*. (CUP, 2006).

For further information online, see the e-resources.

Other versions of the play available on DVD include the famous Richard Burton and Elizabeth Taylor film production made in 1967, directed by Franco Zeffirelli (distributor Tristar).

There is also a 1983 version directed by John Allinson, starring Franklin Sealy and Karen Austin (distributor Quantum Leap).

A Doll's House – 1879

Period and production context

Henrik Ibsen (1828–1906) was a prolific Norwegian playwright who wrote in a variety of dramatic styles throughout his life. He is most famous for the series of **naturalistic/realistic** plays that he wrote in the 1870s, of which *A Doll's House* is a perfect example.

When Ibsen began writing his plays, theatre in Norway was in the very early stages of development. Despite becoming the artistic director of the Norske Theatre, Christiana, Ibsen was often frustrated by the lack of invention and experiment in the work of his fellow Norwegian dramatists, as well as by the conservatism of Norwegian audiences. He left Norway for Italy in 1864, having achieved modest success as

Further reading

There is a BBC film and DVD of *The Taming of the Shrew* starring John Cleese as Petruchio. If you can manage to see this very funny production you'll soon see why the play is so popular on the stage!

Think

In Elizabethan times the theatre companies were all-male and the roles of female characters were played by young men.

Theatre trivia

Although Shakespeare's plays are generally considered to be the works of a genius, he has not been universally admired. Charles Darwin, of evolutionary fame, recorded in his autobiography that, 'I have tried lately to read Shakespeare, and found it so intolerably dull that it nauseated me.'

Activity

Try to see a live production of your set play. You might stage at least a section of your play using full production elements.

Key terms

Realism: the faithful representation of life in literature and theatre.

Naturalism: a type of drama which began in the late 19th century as an offshoot of realism and which presented human character as being formed by heredity (inherited traits) and their environment.

a playwright, and travelled extensively in Europe. The exposure to developing European drama, especially in Germany and Denmark, made a great impression on him.

Ibsen's early plays were romantic, historical dramas written in verse. His middle period of composition included the poetic drama, *Brand* (1865) and the verse fantasy *Peer Gynt* (1867), both of which were intended to be read rather than performed. But it was with his social dramas, written when he was in his late forties and fifties, that Ibsen established his reputation. A collection of his plays was translated into scores of languages and performed in all the major European and American cities. When Ibsen returned to Norway, after an absence of 27 years, he was regarded as the undisputed 'father' of modern theatre, with an unrivalled reputation as a dramatist of international renown.

The plays that created such a sensation in the 1870s and 80s were those in which Ibsen exposed the hypocrisies of contemporary society, beginning with the ironically titled *Pillars of Society* in 1877, *A Doll's House* in 1879 and *Ghosts* in 1881. Performances of *Ghosts*, a play that deals with illegitimacy and madness inherited from a syphilitic father, caused outrage in several European cities when it was first performed. It received a particularly hostile reception, initially, in London and New York.

Nowadays, more than 130 years since the first performance of *A Doll's House*, it is difficult to imagine the shockwave that swept over audiences who first heard that slam of the door at the end of the play, signalling **Nora's** departure from her 'doll's house', her husband and her children.

Context to the play's action

Ibsen's play deals with the society of his time and he clearly intended to explore and expose the inequalities that existed between men and women in the mid-19th century. The play criticises the **paternalism** that is evident in **Torvald's** attitude towards **Nora**, an attitude that would have been a common characteristic of husbands towards their wives at the time. In the 19th century women did not have equal rights with men and the daughters of aristocratic or middle-class families were not expected to work; they were expected to marry.

In the society that Ibsen depicts in *A Doll's House* married women were seen as the property of their husbands and they could not enter into any legal or financial contracts without the consent of their husbands. In return, they received the protection of their husbands upon whom they were financially dependent, just they were on their fathers before they married.

The action of the play begins long after **Nora** has committed the fraud that allows **Krogstad** to blackmail her, but that act, which is discussed by **Nora** and **Mrs Linde** in Act One, underpins the whole play. By forging her father's signature in order to obtain a loan, **Nora**, unknowingly committed a criminal act. In her mind, because she borrowed money to fund the Italian trip that saved **Torvald's** life, the act of fraud was irrelevant; what mattered was saving her husband.

We learn from comments made by **Nora** to **Mrs Linde**, as well as by things that **Torvald** says, that **Nora** is a resourceful woman. She found herself a money-lender, when both her husband and her father were dangerously ill, and even though she was expecting her baby, she arranged the trip to Italy, recommended by the doctor as the only cure for **Torvald's** illness. In order to keep up with the repayments on the loan, **Nora** took on copying work to earn extra money and she economises on her own clothes.

Background information

There is some controversy about whether Ibsen's style is best described as realistic or naturalistic, as in recent years there has been a blurring of the distinction in discussion of the two forms. You will find that some commentators describe Ibsen as the 'father of realism' (despite the fact that his plays took many different forms) but for the purposes of this book and this course, we are describing *A Doll's House* as a naturalistic drama.

Theatre trivia

A Doll's House has a 'sequel' written by an Austrian feminist Nobel prize-winning author, Elfriede Jelinek in 1980 entitled *What Happened After Nora Left Her Husband*. This play presents Nora in a challenging world of industry, corruption and ill-fated love affairs, struggling to define her identity.

Think

Can you imagine life without photocopiers and printers? In the 19th century, all legal or financial documents had to be copied by hand.

Despite her resourcefulness, **Nora** plays up to the stereotype of being a sweet little feather-brain in order to please and flatter **Torvald**, who is conditioned by society to expect his wife to be attractive, amenable and docile. It is the arrival of **Mrs Linde** that acts as the catalyst to **Nora's** developing self-awareness and to her decision to leave **Torvald** at the end of the play.

Ironically, at the end of the play, independent, hard-working **Mrs Linde** finds happiness in the prospect of marriage, while pampered, innocent **Nora** abandons her marriage and her family to educate and 'find' herself.

Genre – modern tragedy/naturalism

In his notes to *A Doll's House*, Ibsen describes the play as 'a modern tragedy' although it is difficult, from the perspective of the 21st century, to see its action in quite those terms. A woman, apparently happy in a cosy but stifling marriage, has her illusions about the real nature of her husband utterly dashed. Feeling completely let down by him, she reassesses her life and decides to leave her husband and small children to embark upon a journey of self-discovery.

Told in this way, the plot hardly seems the stuff of tragedy to the contemporary eye.

However, looked at in context, **Nora** is taking a perilous step. In the 19th century once a woman willingly left her home, she became, in effect, a non-person. The husband had no further legal or financial responsibility for her. **Nora** is qualified for nothing and even as wife and mother she has had little to do with running the home or rearing the children, since the family have a full staff of servants.

Christine Linde, widowed and penniless, has had to work to provide for her bedridden mother and dependent brothers. Ibsen implies that, like Christine, **Nora** will find the real world outside her 'doll's house'

Fig. 12.2 *Torvald and Nora in A Doll's House*

a challenging place. To those of us living in a society where divorce is common and women are often earning the most money in a family, **Nora's** plight doesn't seem that bad. But then, perhaps the tragedy that Ibsen was contemplating was not **Nora's** but **Torvald's**.

According to the classical model of tragedy as outlined by Aristotle, we might say that **Torvald** is the tragic figure in this play. His *hubris* – a mixture of pride in his own unassailable position at the bank and arrogance in his dealings with both **Krogstad** and his own wife – leads to his downfall.

Although the play contains few allusions to fate or to God, **Torvald** is conventionally religious and in some ways the approval or disapproval of society fulfils the function of the gods in this play. **Torvald** will not retain his respectability in society once it becomes known that his wife has left him and he is left to bring up his children alone.

⁊ What is less contentious in terms of genre, however, is its naturalism. The action of the play takes place in a meticulously detailed reproduction of a comfortable and tastefully decorated room. The audience watch the play through the imaginary fourth wall and all the dialogue and action is realistic and believable. Ibsen explores some typical concerns of the naturalistic writer, for example, the effects of heredity and environment on individuals' actions and the possibilities of individuals exercising their free will within the restrictions of society.

All these features are indicators of the naturalistic genre of the play. However, as mentioned earlier, Ibsen's plays were quite diverse in style and even within apparently naturalistic plays like *A Doll's House* and *Hedda Gabler*, Ibsen introduces striking touches of **symbolism,** which are unusual in a naturalistic play.

Further research

There have been a number of film versions of *A Doll's House*, as well as several television productions. There is a good DVD version available starring Anthony Hopkins as **Torvald** and Claire Bloom as **Nora**. This is a 1973 production. The DVD was released in 2003.

Books that may be helpful in your study of the play include:

■ *Ibsen: A Doll's House*, by Egil Tornqvist (CUP, 1995)
■ *Ibsen's Lively Art: A Performance Study of the Major Plays*, by Frederick Marker and Lise-Lone Marker (CUP, 2005).

▧ *The Shadow of a Gunman* – 1923

Period and production context

Sean O'Casey (1880–1964) was an Irish playwright whose most popular plays present life among the slum-dwellers of Dublin, between 1915 and 1922, at the time of the Irish 'Troubles'. The Irish Troubles are too complex to explain in detail here but the term describes the eruption of violence during the 20th-century 'Home Rule' movement, which fought to establish Ireland as a separate country from Britain. ***The Shadow of a Gunman*** presents the events of one day in the life of a group of Dubliners in 1920 at the height of the Troubles, when Dublin was the power base of English rule in Ireland.

The play was written for **The Abbey Theatre** in Dublin, which opened in 1904. It had a reputation for promoting modern theatre and, in particular, supporting a form of cultural nationalism, so that most of

▧ Further reading

See p47 for ideas about classical tragedy in *Antigone*.

▧ Key terms

Symbolism: a movement in which concrete symbols represent aspects of characters' 'inner life'. For example, the Christmas tree in *A Doll's House*, which Nora decorates with baubles in the first act, represents Nora's optimism. In Act Two it is 'stripped of decoration and dishevelled', to symbolise Nora's loss of hope.

▧ Activity

How many examples of symbolism can you find in *A Doll's House*?

▧ Activity

Try to see a live production of your set play. You might stage at least a section of your play using full production elements.

its repertoire depicted Irish life in one form or another. When the play opened in 1923, the Abbey Theatre was under armed guard because of a threatened terrorist attack by the IRA, following the Abbey Theatre's public acceptance of an Anglo-Irish Treaty. The audience was warned before the play started that Act Two contained sound effects of a raid and of gunfire. The management were concerned that it might trigger a panic if people believed the attack was genuine.

Context to the play's action

The Shadow of a Gunman is set in a tenement room in Dublin, shared by two unlikely tenants, **Seumas Shields**, a self-educated peddler, and **Donal Davoren**, an aspiring poet, who people mistakenly believe to be an IRA gunman on the run. **Davoren**'s reluctance to disabuse his admirers of their mistake leads to a rumour about the whereabouts of an IRA gunman. This rumour reaches the ears of a notorious branch of the police force known as the 'Black and Tans' who raid the tenement. The police discover the bombs that **Minnie Powell** has taken to her room, in an attempt to protect **Davoren. Minnie** is arrested and bundled into a lorry, but when the Black and Tans themselves fall prey to an ambush by the IRA, **Minnie** jumps from the vehicle and is shot in the breast.

Characteristically for O'Casey, the play presents the relative cowardice of the blustering men in the play, **Davoren** and **Shields**, **Tommy Owens** and **Adolphus Grigson**, in contrast to the fortitude and moral courage of the women, especially **Minnie Powell**.

Genre – tragi-comedy

The Shadow of a Gunman is categorised as a **tragi-comedy**. The genre can take various forms; some tragi-comedies deal with serious issues but include comic insights or individually comic characters, while others are quite light-hearted in tone but generally end sadly. Shakespeare's plays, *Measure for Measure* and *Troilus and Cressida* and *Cymbeline* fall into the former category of tragi-comedy, while both O' Casey and Chekhov tend to write plays that fall into the latter.

Fig. 12.3 *A 1957 production of* **The Shadow of a Gunman**

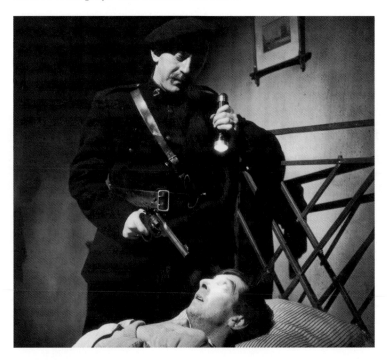

Some commentators might also make a case for **The Shadow of a Gunman** as belonging to the genre of naturalism, but whereas Ibsen and other 19th-century naturalistic playwrights focused on the lives of the aristocracy or middle classes, O Casey's plays are firmly rooted in the context of working-class Dublin. Some might argue that O'Casey's characterisation, for example of **Mrs Henderson**, is too much of a **caricature** to be truly naturalistic.

Further research

There is a DVD available of a Broadway production of the play featuring Richard Dreyfuss, amongst others.

Books that may be helpful in your study of the play include:

- *Faber Critical Guides: Sean O'Casey*, by Christopher Murray (Faber, 2000)
- *A Guide to O'Casey's Plays*, by John O' Riordan (Macmillan, 1984).

Oh! What a Lovely War – 1963

Period and production context

Oh! What a Lovely War (1963) is the product of a collaborative enterprise by the British ensemble, Theatre Workshop, which was originally established in 1945 by a group of actors who wanted to change radically the mainstream theatre of the day.

From 1953 the company established itself in the Theatre Royal in London's Stratford East and attracted like-minded actors. The company was headed by Joan Littlewood, as artistic director, with the writer Ewan McColl and with Gerald Raffles as general manager.

The Workshop was dedicated to invigorating contemporary theatre, which they saw as stale and very much the preserve of the middle classes. It encouraged writers to produce new plays about working-class issues as well as presenting innovative productions of the classics. Some of the playwrights associated with Theatre Workshop's repertoire include Brendan Behan and Shelagh Delaney. Shelagh Delaney's *A Taste of Honey* (1958) later transferred to the **West End** and was eventually made into a film.

Commercial success was also achieved by *Oh! What a Lovely War*, which transferred first to the West End, then to Paris and New York as well as both East and West Germany. It was made into a film in 1969.

Although the 1960s are often referred to as the 'Swinging Sixties', when hippies and 'love-ins' were part of the emerging culture, the decade also saw the height of what historians describe as The Cold War between the East (principally USSR) and the West (principally America). During this period both sides were building up their nuclear armaments to act as a deterrent to an attack. World annihilation was a real possibility. It is against this backdrop of growing unease about the outcome of the Cold War that the Theatre Workshop's critique of the First World War, as an emblem of *all* wars, should be seen.

Context to the play's action

The action of *Oh! What a Lovely War* depicts documented scenes from the First World War as well as anecdotes. It presents some key historical figures of the period, for example, **Emmeline Pankhurst**, **Sir John French**, **Sir Douglas Haig**, and shows their contrasting attitudes towards the war.

> **Activity**
>
> Try to see a live production of your set play. You might stage at least a section of your play using full production elements.

> **Further reading**
>
> The origins of *Oh! What a Lovely War* are recorded in an excellent introduction to your prescribed text, the Methuen edition of the play, published in 2006.

It also depicts soldiers in training for combat, soldiers in combat and in the trenches as well as civilians waiting at home for news of their loved ones.

Fig. 12.4 *Emmeline Pankhurst in* Oh! What a Lovely War *at the Roundhouse, National Theatre production, 1998*

There is no plot as such, since the play is constructed around a series of music-hall style songs and sentimental chorus numbers. The songs underscore the presentation both of individual scenes about the 'progress' of the war, as performed by the ensemble in their Pierrot costumes and authentic documentary slides from the front line, revealing the truly horrific conditions of war that were endured by ordinary soldiers on both sides of the conflict.

Genre – ensemble/devised, musical entertainment

You will see from this heading that *Oh! What a Lovely War* does not fit neatly into any specific genre. Different writers describe the play in different ways. For example, the *Cassell Companion to the Theatre* describes it as 'a musical lampoon' and a 'documentary collage', while Steve Lewis, in your set text, considers a range of possible categories from simple 'musical theatre' and 'documentary theatre' to 'total theatre'.

To conclude, this play is so unusual in terms of its content and form that it defies generic definition. The exam specification refers to it as an 'ensemble play with songs', but this has only been applied to help candidates avoid choosing a similar style in their choice of play to present for Unit 2.

Further reading

David Attenborough's film of *Oh! What a Lovely War* featured a cast of 'big names' of the period, including Laurence Olivier, John Gielgud, Ralph Richardson, Maggie Smith and Vanessa Redgrave. It is available on video and DVD, but remember that the film is very different from the original theatre production.

Further research

There is a detailed section about the context of the First World War in the introduction to your set text. You can access a great deal of background to the First World War on history websites.

One book that might be helpful in your study of the play is *Joan's Book: An Autobiography of Joan Littlewood*, by Joan Littlewood (Methuen, 2003).

Playhouse Creatures – 1993

Period and production context

April de Angelis wrote *Playhouse Creatures* for The Sphinx Women's National Touring Theatre in 1993. Its production context is specifically feminist theatre in the late 20th century, since the play was commissioned and performed by a group dedicated to raising awareness of feminist issues.

Although feminism as a political movement started in the 1960s, (as opposed to the 'Right to Vote' campaign orchestrated by the Suffragettes in the early 20th century), most feminists, even in the 21st century, do not believe that they have achieved all that they set out to. The late 1980s and 1990s were a period where women continued to challenge the limitations that were placed on them in many areas of modern life.

The history of British theatre up until the 1950s boasts few female playwrights. Since men have always dominated public life, both political and commercial, as well as dominating the world of literature and culture, it is not surprising that the majority of plays feature more men than women.

De Angelis has worked within a recognised form of political theatre by applying **historicisation**, a form of drama whereby the story is set in the past but the themes and issues are relevant to contemporary society. So, although De Angelis sets her play in the Restoration period of 'around 1670', the play's frank treatment of sexual exploitation of actresses offers a clear challenge to the presentation (in some areas of contemporary society) of women as sex objects.

Similarly, the comic treatment of the issue of the actresses acquiring shares in the theatre, in the way that their fellow actors did (delivered in the play as a one-sided conversation between Mrs Betterton and her husband) strikes a blow for equal pay and opportunities for women in both 1670 and 1993.

Context to the play's action

The action of *Playhouse Creatures* is set around 1670, shortly after the restoration of the monarchy following Oliver Cromwell's death in 1660. During the **Puritan Interregnum** all theatres had been closed. The Parliamentary Act cited religious and moral grounds for the closure but, in all likelihood, the Puritans closed the theatres because they were meeting places for pro-royalist groups and Parliament wanted to prevent civil unrest.

On Charles II's ascension to the throne, many of the measures taken by the Puritans were reversed. Charles was a great fan of the theatre. He granted licences for the first performances on the stage in England for over 20 years, and also licences for women to perform on the stage.

Theatre trivia

At the theatre oranges and other refreshments were sold. One of the most famous orange sellers was Mary Meggs, nicknamed 'Orange Moll'. Samuel Pepys mentions her in his diary which gives many fascinating insights into life (including the theatre) of his time.

At first there were only two theatre companies permitted to stage plays, The King's Men, who performed at Drury Lane, and the Duke's Men at Lincoln's Inns Fields Theatre. Even the *Cassell Companion to the Theatre* records that the most famous performers tended to be women 'because of their novelty value' and does not suggest that their reputations might have been based on their talent! Among the favourites cited are **Nell Gwynn** and Mary Saunderson, who was the wife of the **actor-manager** Thomas Betterton, and who appears as **Mrs Betterton** in de Angelis' play.

Playhouse Creatures follows the rise of **Nell Gwynn** from a common oyster seller in the London streets, to an orange seller in the Drury Lane Theatre, to an actress on the London stage and, as mistress to the king, to the height of her profession as a leading lady. De Angelis includes a scene in which **Nell** reveals that **Aphra Behn**, the only woman playwright of the era, has written a part especially for her in her latest play.

Genre – historical drama

While *Playhouse Creatures* is based on some real characters from the Restoration era and some historical facts, it remains an imaginative treatment of events from the past. So the term 'historical' to describe its genre takes account of the fact that much 'historical' drama and/or fiction is largely invented. The play contains a great deal of comedy, especially in its presentation of **Doll Common** and of **Nell Gwynn**, two outspoken women whose forthright views and practical approaches to life the audience are invited to admire.

Fig. 12.5 Playhouse Creatures

However, the play is also a serious examination of the inequalities that existed in Restoration times between men and women, especially in relation to the double standards that existed about male and female promiscuity. While showing a 'happy ending', of sorts for **Nell Gwynn**, the play reveals the dangers that women faced when entering into relationships with powerful men. What happens to **Mrs Marshall** in relation to the **Earl of Oxford** and what happens to **Mrs Farley** when she is rejected by the King, even though she may be carrying his illegitimate child, acts as a counterpoint to **Nell's** 'good fortune' in becoming **King Charles's** mistress.

The play is, of course, commenting on modern contemporary society in its examination of the past. It poses the questions: Have things really changed so much? Are women still the sex objects that they were in the Restoration era? Is there any such thing as equality of the sexes, even in the 20th or 21st century?

Activity

Try to see a live production of your set play. You might stage at least a section of your play using full production elements.

Further reading

There is more information on the Restoration period in your e-resources.

See the interview with April de Angelis about her career and the writing of *Playhouse Creatures*.

13   The director's interpretation – meaning

It is very important to have a well-developed theatrical imagination in this course, as you are asked in the examination to write 'as a director' or 'as a performer' or 'as a designer'. The purpose of this chapter is to help you to think and write as a director, whose job it is to interpret the play and, in collaboration with a production team and actors, to convey that interpretation to the audience.

A director needs strong, clear ideas about the play he or she is about to direct, because there are a huge number of choices to be made. Some of the decisions may be fairly straightforward and once they have been made they are rarely changed. For example, the following questions may be easily answered:

■ What performance space best suits this play?

■ Who should be cast in the main roles?

■ What style of production will this be?

■ Should this be a 'classic' treatment of the play, or a radical, new interpretation?

Other decisions are less straightforward, and they involve the director in teasing out meaning from the play; experimenting with the play in rehearsal and defining, refining and redefining their ideas about what the play means, over a course of several weeks or months. These decisions might relate to, for example:

■ When and where is the play set in terms of period and location?

■ What are the play's main themes and issues?

■ What is the mood or atmosphere of the play and how should it be created?

■ Which characters should the audience sympathise with?

■ What should the actor-audience relationship be?

■ Should some actors multi-role the characters or should there be one actor for each role?

■ How should the design features be used in performance?

■ How should the actors be directed, line by line and move by move?

On this course, you will have several months to become familiar with your set play. You will work through it methodically, both in the classroom and the studio, and come up with your own interpretation of it, based on the knowledge and understanding that you will acquire in your studies and in your practical exploration. You will need to find answers to all the questions listed above!

This chapter will take you through some, but not all, of the choices that directors face, and will consider how they might deal with them. Some of the set plays will be used as examples to illustrate certain points.

Activity

If you have already read through all of your set text, try to answer some or all of the listed questions.

■ Research

To begin, the focus will be on *Antigone*. However, the principles are the same, whichever set play you are studying.

Chapter 13 examined the context, period and genre of *Antigone* and, as a director of this play, you could not begin your work without this basic information. A director needs to undertake more extensive research than this, however, as simply knowing about the historical origins of the play is not enough to interpret the play for a contemporary audience.

You will also need to understand the issues at the heart of the play which were of burning significance to the original audience but which may appear to have little relevance to a modern audience. For example, *Antigone* deals with the conflict between two opposing viewpoints: the view of **Antigone**, who puts her loyalty to her brother and to the gods of the underworld above her loyalty to the city; and the view of **Creon**, for whom the city and its laws are more important than family ties.

Although a modern audience is familiar with the idea of divided loyalties, they might be surprised by the lengths that the characters are prepared to go to for the sake of their beliefs. **Antigone** is prepared to die rather than leave her brother's corpse unburied (which was considered a sacrilege against the gods of the underworld). **Creon** is prepared to impose a horrible death sentence on **Antigone** (who is not only his niece but also his son's fiancée) for defying his decree that the body should remain unburied. These apparently extreme attitudes would have been understandable to the original audience for whom ideas about a citizen's duty to the city, the rights and privileges of the gods, and the demands of family relationships were part and parcel of daily life.

A modern director would undertake a considerable amount of research into the customs and beliefs of the Greeks in the 5th century BC before embarking on a production of *Antigone* and would probably encourage his or her cast to do the same. This research is sometimes referred to as the 'invisible' work of an actor.

If this is your set play, you should explore the Greeks' views on the citizens' duties to the state, their religious beliefs and views about the afterlife and the underworld, as well as attitudes towards the inferiority of women in society.

Watching the production, the audience might not be aware of the research that has gone into its preparation. However, the fact that the actors playing **Creon** and **Antigone** fully understand their characters' attitudes towards Zeus and Hades and towards the concept of the city and the importance of the family will have an effect on their performance. It will make their acting more convincing and their motives clearer for the audience to understand.

The director's job is to make the modern audience feel something for the characters, even though they do not necessarily share their beliefs and concerns. This applies to any play.

💡 Key decisions about characters

Once armed with knowledge and understanding of the play's central debate, as a director you are in a position to interpret this aspect of the play for the audience. It will help you to decide who you want the audience to sympathise with and this will, in turn, affect the way you cast and direct your actors.

You can decide whether to depict **Creon** as a tyrant or merely as a misguided ruler and whether to emphasise **Antigone's** stubborn qualities or her religious fervour and genuine love for her brother. Supposing that, having explored the issues, you wish to interpret **Creon** as a fair-minded,

AQA **Examiner's tip**

Whenever you write about your set play in production, whether your interpretation is conventional or radically new, you should always think about presenting the play to a 21st-century audience.

Think

Many serious plays revolve around a central conflict or clash of ideas between two strong individuals – a **protagonist** and an **antagonist** – or between opposing groups. How many plays can you think of that follow this model?

Further reading

For more information about the beliefs of the Ancient Greeks, see Robert Fagles' introduction in the Penguin Classics edition of the play.

but misguided, ruler who believes very strongly in his duty to the state; you might direct the whole of his first speech to the Theban Elders to be delivered in a measured and reasonable way – as befits a statesman, newly in charge of the city. You may want to emphasise his sense of responsibility to Thebes and his fitness for the role as head of state.

On the other hand, you may wish to hint to your audience that **Creon** is not the wise ruler that Thebes deserves after the disruption of civil war. You may want to indicate something a little more unstable about him – even a touch of madness! If this is your interpretation, you will want his first speech to reveal something erratic about him.

Look at Interpretation One below. It shows the possibilities for emphasising **Creon's** statesmanlike persona through his calm tone of voice, his expansive gestures and reassuring nods to the **chorus** of Elders. As director, you may choose to emphasise **Creon's** relationship with the chorus: you might have him walking amongst them, clapping one of the counsellors on the shoulders, smiling, engaging in eye contact throughout. Remember, he is speaking about securing the future stability of the city. If you want to emphasise his duty to the gods you may have him speak the name of Zeus with reverence.

In the second version (Interpretation Two) the lines where **Creon** might show that he is less than reliable or stable are highlighted; as director you may wish to emphasise his authoritarian nature, you may place him above the chorus on stage, on a podium or throne. His gestures might be directed to be very emphatic, occasionally smashing his fist into the palm of his other hand or striking a table. You may direct him to speak at a varied pace, speeding up when he is angry. He may mention Zeus as if the word is a casual oath to reinforce his determination.

💡 Interpretation One – *Creon the statesman and dignified leader*

Creon strides into the midst of the chorus and puts his arms around the shoulders of two of the Elders, smiling as he speaks. He pauses before continuing, releasing his hold on the two men and looking around the whole chorus group.

Speaks enthusiastically, showing his high regards for the Elders.

Creon:

My countrymen,

the ship of state is safe. The gods who rocked her,

after a long, merciless pounding in the storm,

have righted her once more. ●

Out of the whole city

I have called you here alone. Well I know,

first, your undeviating respect

for the throne and royal power of King Laius. ●

Next, while Oedipus steered the land of Thebes,

and even after he died, your loyalty was unshakable,

you still stood by their children. Now then,

since the two sons are dead – two blows of fate

in the same day, cut down by each other's hands,

both killers, both brothers stained with blood –

Speaks gratefully and indicates the stability of the 'ship' with his hands.

Speaks fondly of the dead king.

Speaks with gratitude at the loyalty of the Elders.

as I am next of kin to the dead, ●————————

He shakes his head sadly, looking at the Elders and pausing before his next lines.

● I now possess the throne and all its powers.

Spoken with a sense of resignation.

Of course you cannot know a man completely,

his character, his principles, sense of judgement, ●————

Somewhat hesitant about his own powers.

not till he's shown his colours, ruling the people,

making laws. Experience, there's the test.

As I see it, whoever assumes the task,

the awesome task of setting the city's course, ●————

Speaks as if aware of the enormity of the challenge but growing in confidence.

and refuses to adopt the soundest policies

but fearing someone, keeps his lips locked tight,

he's utterly worthless. So I rate him now,

I always have. And whoever places a friend

above the good of his own country, he is nothing:

I have no use for him. Zeus is my witness,

Zeus who sees all things, always –

Interpretation Two – *Creon the power-hungry tyrant*

Creon:

                          My countrymen,

Spoken bitterly, pounding his fist into his hand to emphasise the suffering of the city.

the ship of state is safe. The gods who rocked her, ●————

Creon stands at a lectern, looking down on the assembled chorus.

● after a long, merciless pounding in the storm,

have righted her once more.

                          Out of the whole city

I have called you here alone. Well I know,

first, your undeviating respect

for the throne and royal power of King Laius. ●————

He sweeps his hand, complacently, to indicate that he knows they will continue to support him.

Next, while Oedipus steered the land of Thebes,

and even after he died, your loyalty was unshakable,

you still stood by their children. Now then,

since the two sons are dead – two blows of fate

in the same day, cut down by each other's hands, ●————

Delivery speeding up, showing anger at the unnatural deaths.

both killers, both brothers stained with blood –

A hint of megalomania as he points to himself proudly.

as I am next of kin to the dead,

● I now possess the throne and all its powers.

Of course you cannot know a man completely,

his character, his principles, sense of judgement,

He emphasises his power over the citizens – thumps the table.

not till he's shown his colours, ruling the people,
making laws. Experience, there's the test.
As I see it, whoever assumes the task,

Shakes his head, as if despairing at the responsibility.

the awesome task of setting the city's course,
and refuses to adopt the soundest policies
but fearing someone, keeps his lips locked tight,

Spoken with complete contempt.

he's utterly worthless. So I rate him now,
I always have. And whoever places a friend
above the good of his own country, he is nothing:
I have no use for him. Zeus is my witness,
Zeus who sees all things, always –

Pauses before 'friend' and spits the word out.

Raises his voice, looks intimidatingly at the chorus.

Bangs on the lectern. A throw-away oath.

Spoken threateningly, glowering at the chorus.

Activity

If you are studying *Antigone* as your set text, try a similar exercise on the second half of **Creon's** first speech, where he goes on to denounce **Polynices**.

If you are studying a different play, there are more suggested activities in the e-resources.

Of course, these are only two out of many possible interpretations of the role of **Creon**. Even if you decide that you agree with the interpretation of **Creon** as dignified statesman or **Creon** as tyrant, there are many ways that, as director, you could bring out that interpretation on stage, all quite different from the ones suggested above.

An interesting exercise to complete now would be to jot down some casting decisions for an actor chosen to play **Creon** as the 'dignified statesman' and some quite different ideas for the physical appearance and vocal qualities of the actor you might choose to perform as the slightly manic 'tyrant'. Remember that professional actors are very adaptable creatures and that the same actor could play the part either way.

Key decisions about issues

Whichever play you are studying for this Unit, you will find that each one has central issues. You will need to consider these issues carefully before you can offer a directorial interpretation of the play that helps an audience to understand it better and to engage with its characters.

For example, in both *The Taming of the Shrew* and *A Doll's House* you will need to understand the position of women in society at the time of the play's first production. The first is a lively comedy, which takes quite a light-hearted view of relationships between men and women in the 16th century, while the other offers a serious investigation into inequalities between men and women in the 19th century. Neither of these plays can be fully realised for an audience without you, as director, doing some background research.

Both *The Taming of the Shrew* and *A Doll's House* present women as possessions of both their fathers and their husbands – to be disposed of and dealt with as the fathers and husbands think fit. You will need to find out about dowries in the 16th century, about the role of women in the household and in society and about the obligations of fathers, daughters, husbands and wives, in order to be able to interpret *The Taming of the*

Shrew meaningfully. Similarly, when approaching *A Doll's House*, you will have to find out about the legal constraints upon married women in the 19th century and their exclusion from, amongst other things, the world of finance.

Playhouse Creatures also deals with the position of women, this time in the 17th century, but this play has a very specific focus. De Angelis writes about the experiences of the first actresses to appear on the English stage and the inequalities and exploitation that they suffered in their profession. To make sense of this play for an audience you will need to find out about the history of the theatre in this period, especially about the actresses of the time.

If you are studying **The Shadow of a Gunman** or *Oh! What a Lovely War* you will have to undertake research into the historical background of your set play. Remember, however, that **The Shadow of a Gunman** contains many more issues than those related to the war of independence in Ireland in the early 20th century. Some commentators have described the play as an examination of the nature of illusions; perhaps less fancifully, the play might be described as an exploration of the differences between bravado, cowardice and true courage.

Similarly, *Oh! What a Lovely War* examines the relationship between war and profit and it presents, through its **juxtaposition** of sentimental songs with slides of harrowing war-time photographs and horrifying statistics, a fairly cynical attack on the **establishment** during the First World War. The use of the Pierrot show as a setting and the design of the costumes which made all the cast appear to be Pierrots serves to underline the **universality** of the issues being presented.

■ Preparation for the examination

In the examination of this section, questions often ask you to interpret a character or scene, as a director. You can prepare yourself for this type of question by taking any character or scene from your set play and framing the question:

1 How would you direct The Sentry or Gremio or Mrs Linde or Mr Gallogher or Sir John French or Mrs Betterton in his or her first appearance of the play, in order to bring out your interpretation of the role for your audience?

Then carry out an exercise like the one above on **Creon**, to prepare your ideas, before writing a sample response.

■ **Further reading**

You can research more about the 'rights of women' through the ages in any encyclopaedia, or check it out at Wikipedia.

There is useful material on *The Taming of the Shrew* in *Shakespeare's Division of Experience*, by Marilyn French (Abacus, 1983).

A good source of further information is in Elizabeth Howe's book, *The First English Actresses*.

You can also find information about Restoration Theatre on the internet – key 'Nell Gwynne' or 'Drury Lane' into a search engine.

■ **Activity**

Who are the characters in *The Shadow of a Gunman* that best fit the three qualities of 'bravado, cowardice and true courage'? Try putting a different character under each heading. You may find that more than one character appears under some of them.

■ **Activity**

If you are studying *Oh! What a Lovely War*, suggest contemporary issues that appear equally ripe for attack; imagine that you are about to devise your own political musical piece. What slides and what soundtracks would you put together?

The director's interpretation – staging decisions

Key terms

Staging form: the arrangement of the acting and audience space. In a proscenium arch theatre, for example, the actors perform on a raised stage which is enclosed behind a large arch, separating the action from an audience, who view the performance 'end on'.

Stage directions: the playwright's descriptions of characters, costumes and settings as well as indications of entrances and exits and suggestions for the delivery of lines or of reactions to the unfolding events on stage.

Activity

Look back at Chapter 2. Which type of venue do you think best suits your set play?

List the pros and cons of each staging form for your set play.

What do we mean by 'staging'?

When we refer to staging in this book and in the course we are referring to all the theatrical aspects that a director might include in translating a text from page to stage.

These aspects include the choice of **venue** and **staging form** selected, as well as the **design concept** that he or she is working within and the direction of the performers.

Choice and use of performance space

A director's choice of performance space is fundamental to his or her approach to a play. Many directors are employed by particular theatres and are therefore more likely to choose a play that suits the space, rather than choose a space to match the requirements of their chosen play.

On this course, however, you are in the position of having to make decisions about a play already chosen for you by your teacher. You need to give careful thought to your choice and use of a performance space that meets the requirements of your play and of your intended treatment of it.

Responding to stage directions and the practical demands of the text

To begin, the focus will be on O'Casey's play *The Shadow of a Gunman*. This is a good example to illustrate how a director might respond to the very detailed **stage directions** that playwrights sometimes offer.

On the first page of O'Casey's text there is more than a page of stage directions, before the characters begin their dialogue. It starts:

> A Return Room in a tenement house in Hilljoy Square. At the back two large windows looking out into the yard; they occupy practically the whole of the back wall space. Between the windows is a cupboard, on the top of which is a pile of books. The doors are open, and on these are hanging a number of collars and ties. Running parallel with the windows is a stretcher bed; another runs at right angles along the wall at right. At the head of this bed is a door leading to the rest of the house. The wall on the left runs diagonally, so that the fireplace – which is in the centre – is plainly visible. On the mantelshelf to the right is a statue of the Virgin, to the left a statue of the Sacred Heart, and in the centre a crucifix. Around the fireplace are a few common cooking utensils. In the centre of the room is a table, on which are a typewriter, a candle and candlestick, a bunch of wild flowers in a vase, writing materials and a number of books. There are two chairs, one near the fireplace and one at the table. The aspect of the place is one of absolute untidiness, engendered on the one hand by the congenital slovenliness of Seumas Shields, and on the other by the temperament of Donal Davoren, making it appear impossible to effect an improvement in such a place.

Interpreting the stage directions in naturalistic plays

When you try to visualise or sketch the set that O'Casey has described, you will find that the directions are a mix of factual details (for example, 'in the centre of the room is a table') and more abstract ideas (for example, the suggestion that the room's 'untidiness', which is a result of the personalities of the inhabitants of the room, might communicate to an audience that it is 'impossible to effect an improvement in such a place'). Now, how does a director convey this to the audience as the play begins in such a setting?

Despite the difficulties of realising all of O'Casey's intentions in simple staging terms, it is clear that these stage directions offer much help in guiding the director's interpretation of the type of environment in which **Seumas** and **Davoren** live. The director may choose to ignore the exact positioning of the beds and is free to present the play is an entirely different setting if he or she wants, but the playwright's intention to surround **Seumas** and **Davoren** with a heap of untidiness is clearly central to interpreting this opening scene.

One crucial detail that helps to make sense of the scene for the audience is the religious **icons**. They indicate to the audience that the room is occupied by Catholics, which, given the context of the piece during the Irish 'Troubles', is a vital piece of information for the audience.

■ Activity

Whether or not you are studying *The Shadow of a Gunman*, try sketching this set now, paying close attention to O'Casey's directions.

■ Key terms

Icon: a symbol or emblem. The religious icons referred to in O'Casey's directions – the crucifix, the statue of the Virgin and the statue of the Sacred Heart – are all emblems of Christian and, specifically, Catholic beliefs.

Fig. 14.1 The Shadow of a Gunman. *How closely has the director followed O'Casey's stage directions in this production?*

There are several other items of staging that are indispensable. **Seumas** needs to be in bed at the start of the play, **Davoren** must have a typewriter at which to practise his poetry writing, and the vase full of wild flowers is referred to by **Minnie** in the text of the play.

If you are studying *The Shadow of a Gunman*, go through all the stage directions to see if there are any items mentioned that are not referred to specifically in the text or action of the play.

The Shadow of a Gunman is a **naturalistic** play, in terms of its setting, and all the action takes place in one room. The precise references in the text to events that occurred in Ireland in May 1920 mean that it would be very difficult for a director or designer to strip the play of its original context and still communicate O'Casey's intention to an audience. A director undertaking the staging of this play must be aware of this.

🔍 *A Doll's House* is also a naturalistic play and, like O'Casey, Ibsen outlines his suggestions for the Helmers' 'tastefully, but not expensively furnished room' in great detail at the beginning of Act One. Ibsen describes the layout of the set/room with its various doors as well as describing the items of furniture that the set/room must contain. These indicators of middle-class comfort and style are helpful in guiding the director to make decisions about staging. However, there are no specific references in the text as to *when* exactly the play is set, other than that it is Christmas time. Because the play deals with the timeless issue of the relationship between husbands and wives it means that a director of *A Doll's House* is free to interpret the play afresh for a contemporary audience.

In staging terms it is easier for the director of *A Doll's House* to **transpose** the play from its original setting in 19th-century Norway than it is for the director of *The Shadow of a Gunman* to make changes to its location in time and place.

▥ **Key terms**

Transpose a play: change a play from its original setting or period to an alternative one. The decision to transpose a play needs to be based on a valid reason, for example to highlight a link or parallel between the original and the alternative setting.

Fig. 14.2 *A non-naturalistic production of* A Doll's House, *2007*

▥ **Activity**

If you are studying *A Doll's House* try to think of alternative settings that might help you to realise Ibsen's intentions in examining the relationship between husbands and wives at any time over the past 150 years.

Interpreting the stage directions in non-naturalistic plays

It isn't only naturalistic plays that contain detailed stage directions from the playwright. Theatre Workshop's *Oh! What a Lovely War* is very far from offering a naturalistic approach to the period of the First World War, and yet the stage directions at the opening of the play and throughout the text are just as precise as O'Casey's or Ibsen's.

Take a look at the following directions from *Oh! What a Lovely War*.

Act One

Overture

'Long, Long Trail'

'Land Of Hope And Glory'

'Oh, It's A Lovely War'

'Mademoiselle From Armentières'

'Goodbye-ee'

Line of 'Land Of Hope And Glory'

'Long, Long Trail'

'Pack Up Your Troubles'

Line of 'National Anthem'

'I Do Like To Be Beside The Seaside'

Newspanel: SUMMER 1914. SCORCHING BANK HOLIDAY FORECAST … GUNBOAT SMITH fouls CARPENTIER in sixth round … OPERA BLOSSOMS UNDER THOMAS BEECHAM.

The company stroll on, in their own time, towards the end of the overture. They smile, wave at someone in the audience or just take their place, sit quietly and chat among themselves. The M.C. enters, wearing a mortar board. He ad libs with the audience. When ready, he announces the opening number, 'Johnny Jones'.

Band: Row, Row, Row

The mime to the song represents a day on the river. Two Pierrots hold a light blue drape across the stage about six inches high. On the intro, one of them runs across with one end. Another Pierrot takes a pole and punts across the stage. A fourth 'swims', balancing himself on a minute platform on wheels. The rest mime while they sing on the imaginary bank upstage:

Song: Row, Row, Row

If you aren't studying this play, these directions look a bit bewildering. Unlike the description of the Return Room in **The Shadow of a Gunman** and the 'tastefully furnished' living room in **A Doll's House**, the stage directions for *Oh! What a Lovely War* tell us nothing about the way the stage looks to the audience.

The first section of directions lists the songs that are played as part of the 'Overture' to the piece. The next set of directions describes what is written on the projections that flash up on the 'Newspanel'. The next set of directions explains what the actors do, in their **mime**, to create an impression of 'a day on the river'.

These directions seem to be both less precise in terms of setting and more precise in terms of acting than what we have seen in the directions of the other two plays. In an edition of the play published in 1965, when *Oh! What a Lovely War* was first performed, there were some more specific suggestions for the staging:

> *The stage is set as for a Pierrot show of fifty years ago with red, white and blue fairy lights, twin balconies left and right and coloured circus 'tubs' , which are used as seats, etc., throughout the play. Above the stage there is a Newspanel across which messages are flashed during the action. There is also a screen behind the acting area, on to which slides are projected.*

As a director, which of these two sets of stage directions do you find most useful? The one where you are told how to set out the stage or the one that leaves it up to you? Do you think that the suggestions for creating 'a day on the river' should be followed slavishly? Are there other ways to present 'a day on the river' on stage?

Patterns of stage movement, groupings, levels

Not all plays contain stage directions written by the original playwright. Apart from indications of entrances and exits you will find almost no stage directions at all in *Antigone* or *The Taming of the Shrew*. If you do have some in your copy of either of these plays, they have probably been inserted by a modern editor.

However, irrespective of whether there are stage directions in a play or not, the director must take responsibility for all staging decisions that involve the actors. He or she must consider their movements, their groupings and their use of stage space, as well as their use of the set or personal props, in order to communicate a coherent interpretation of the play to the audience.

If the play is naturalistic in style, like *A Doll's House* or **The Shadow of a Gunman**, or if the director wants to give a naturalistic treatment to a play such as *Antigone* or *The Taming of the Shrew* or *Playhouse Creatures*, then the directions relating to movement and groupings will be dictated by realistic motivations.

For example, in **The Shadow of a Gunman** Donal Davoren is sitting at his typewriter attempting to compose poetry when he is disturbed by **Minnie Powell**. She pretends to be looking for **Seumas Shields**, whom she has probably seen just go out, whereas her purpose in dropping in is undoubtedly that she wants a chance to talk to **Donal** alone.

When **Donal** tells her that **Seumas** has just gone out she is clearly unconcerned.

Remind yourself of O'Casey's stage directions that explain the layout of the room and then look at the following dialogue and think about how you might direct your actors to move in this section.

[There is a gentle knock at the door.]

Davoren: Another Fury come to plague me now!

[Another knock, a little louder]

Davoren: You can knock till you're tired.

[The door opens and Minnie Powell enters … She is a girl of 23 … Her hair is brown … Her well-shaped figure … is charmingly dressed in a brown tailor-made costume, her stockings and shoes are a darker brown tint than the costume, and all are crowned by a silk tam-o'shanter of a rich blue tint.]

Minnie: Are you in, Mr Shields?

Davoren: *(rapidly)* No, he's not, Minnie; he's just gone out – if you run out quickly you're sure to catch him.

Minnie: Oh, it's all right, Mr Davoren, you'll do just as well; I just come in for a drop o' milk for a cup o' tea; I shouldn't be troubling you this way, but I'm sure you don't mind.

Davoren: *(dubiously)* No trouble in the world; delighted I'm sure. *(Giving her the milk)* There, will you have enough?

Minnie: Plenty, lashins, thanks. Do you be all alone all the day, Mr Davoren?

Davoren. No, indeed; I wish to God I was.

■ **Background information**

A tam-o'shannter is a hat, similar to a beret.

■ Activity

Imagine that you are directing this play. Make some notes about how you would direct your actors to move and to use the stage and the props in this extract. Draw a sketch or make this a practical activity, directing two actors.

Assuming you have, as a director, decided to keep to O'Casey's ideas more or less, you would start the section with **Donal** sitting centre stage at the typewriter, writing his poetry. **Minnie** must enter through the single door that leads to the rest of the house. However, as a director you need to decide on a great many things in order to bring this scene to life.

Below is a series of questions that you should ask yourself before directing even this brief section:

▨ What are my intentions for the audience in directing the section?
  – Do I want the audience to respond positively to **Minnie**, or to recognise her artfulness?
  – Do I want the audience to sympathise with **Davoren** having his work interrupted yet again, or to feel that he is too rude to young **Minnie**?

▨ Where will I place **Davoren**? Should he be directly facing the audience as he sits at his desk, so that they can see his facial expressions? Should his table be angled slightly towards the door, so that we can see the exchanges between **Davoren** and **Minnie** more clearly?

▨ When **Minnie** knocks how does **Davoren** react, physically and/or facially?

▨ When **Minnie** enters, how far into the room does she come?

▨ Has **Minnie** brought her own little milk container with her? Does she indicate it to **Davoren**, as she asks for the milk? How is she holding the milk jug? It is a key prop; it is the pretext for her visit, after all.

▨ At what point, in the text, does **Davoren** stand up to fetch the milk?

▨ Where is the milk kept in this squalid room? How far away from **Minnie** does **Davoren** have to go to fetch the milk? Does he turn his back to her? Can the audience still see his facial expressions? If so, what are they?

- If **Davoren** has his back to **Minnie**, what facial expression might she assume?
- Does **Minnie** stay by the door? Does she come further into the room while **Davoren** fetches the milk? Does she follow him to wherever the milk is kept? Does she wait for him by his desk?
- How long a pause, if any, is there between the lines 'delighted I'm sure' and 'There, will you have enough?' Is there any movement at this point?
- On the stage direction '(*Giving her the milk*)', how close is **Davoren** to **Minnie**? Does he keep the table between **Minnie** and himself, to act as a barrier between them? Does he attempt to get rid of her by striding to the door and holding out the milk container for her there? Or does he engage in a moment of eye contact as he hands her the jug at quite close range?
- At what point, precisely, does **Minnie** take the milk? Has **Davoren** given her enough milk for her tea? Is 'Plenty, lashins, thanks' spoken sincerely or not? Does **Minnie** even look to see how much milk there is? How long a pause before she asks, 'Do you be alone all the day, Mr **Davoren**?'
- **Minnie** wants to stay in the room with **Davoren**; how will you direct her to reveal this? Does she clutch the milk jug to her chest or put it down on the table to indicate that she has no intention of going just yet?
- Where are the two actors standing for the final exchange of this section? Are they by the door? Is **Davoren** standing with the door open just hoping she will go through it? Has **Davoren** already gone back to his desk? Is **Minnie** hovering behind him? Does he have his head in his hands?

So, there are many possibilities to consider here! Not all of them are confined to stage movement, groupings, levels and spatial relationships, but they will all contribute to decisions made about those aspects. Directors do not consider 'stage movement, groupings, levels and spatial relationships' as an end in themselves but merely as a means of communicating meaning to the audience.

Activity

Repeat the previous exercise based on different answers to the questions above. How many quite different, yet appropriate, interpretations of this section do you think there are?

Now try selecting a short section from your set play and take a director's approach to any single page of text. Ask yourself a similar series of questions about what motivates the characters to move, stand, sit, enter or exit. Photocopy your single page and make up your own 'prompt book' page for that short section. (See Chapter 25, Unit 2 for more detail.)

Fig. 14.3 *Minnie* and *Davoren* in **The Shadow of a Gunman**

◎ Staging decisions – creating mood and atmosphere

The next aspect of directing that we are going to look at is the way in which **mood** and **atmosphere** can be created on stage.

Scenes can be described as having either moods or atmospheres. However, when we talk about the arrival or departure of a character on stage as altering the emotional tone of the scene, we would invariably use the term 'mood'. The mood is changed from one of happiness to anxiety in *A Doll's House*, for example, when **Krogstad** interrupts **Nora's** game with her children, by appearing suddenly in the doorway, looking rather sinister. It would be up to the director of the play to decide how abrupt a change he or she wants to create here. The more boisterous and laughter-filled the game of 'hide and seek' is and the more sudden **Krogstad's** somewhat threatening appearance is made to look, the more acute the change of mood will be.

When we are discussing levels of tension in a scene, we are more likely to refer to the 'atmosphere' of the scene. *The Shadow of a Gunman* becomes increasingly tense, for example, once **Davoren** has discovered the bombs in Maguire's bag. Again, the director must decide how tense he or she wants the scene to become and decide upon the rate of the increase of tension as events spiral towards the shooting of poor **Minnie Powell**. However there is a only a very small distinction between the precise meaning of these two terms and it is one that you need not worry about too much.

In order to alter the mood or atmosphere of a scene the director has the following means at her or his disposal:

▉ The direction of the cast, including:
 – movement, interaction, pace and stillness
 – delivery of dialogue, pitch, pace and pause
 – use of space and groupings.
▉ The use of sound, including:
 – sound effects and silence
 – ambient noise.
▉ The use of lighting including:
 – naturalistic or symbolic lighting
 – strobe light
 – specials.

Let's keep the focus on *The Shadow of a Gunman*. As the play is described as a 'tragi-comedy' you might expect it to have more potential than most plays for varied moods; and, indeed, it does. Following on from the unrelieved, mild humour underlying the situation presented in the dialogue and action of Act One and the beginning of Act Two, the second half of Act Two is, by contrast, extremely tense.

▉ Link

See p162 in Chapter 25, Unit 2 for more detail on prompt books.

▉ Activity

Find the number of actors that you need for your selected extract and direct them using your prompt book.

▉ Key terms

We use the terms **mood** and **atmosphere** almost interchangeably, or often together, to refer to the emotional tone of a scene or section from a play. You will be familiar with terms such as 'a sombre mood' or 'a tense atmosphere'.

The scene is still set in the squalid tenement room shared by **Seumas** and **Davoren**. This time, however, the scene is set at night. There's a raid imminent and, having discovered that the bag left earlier in the day by Maguire is full of bombs, both **Davoren** and **Seumas** are scared.

Look at what O'Casey gives a director to build tension with:

1   a night-time setting; the room is quite dark but visible as it is lit alternately by moonlight and candle light; **Seumas** and **Davoren** are in bed, though not asleep

2   the sound of a volley of gunshots

3   the uninvited presence of **Mrs Grigson** and her drunken (potentially violent) husband, **Adolphus**, staggering around the darkened room; his drunken song

4   the sound of an approaching motor and of the vehicle stopping close to the house

5   sudden silence in the room; **Davoren** lights the candle again and begins hunting frantically for **Mr Gallogher's** letter, addressed to the IRA

6   more gunshots from outside, followed by loud shouts of 'Halt, halt, halt!'

7   the **Grigsons'** abrupt departure

8   the continuing panicky search for the letter

9   the finding of the letter, which **Davoren** burns – brief moment of relaxed tension

10   the discovery of the bombs

11   **Minnie Powell's** rushed entry, only partly dressed and in a state of 'intense excitement' because of the imminent raid

12   the sound of violent knocking at the street door, 'followed by the crash of glass and the beating of the door with rifle-butts'

13   **Minnie's** exclamation, 'There they are, there they are, there they are!' – she seizes the bag of bombs and leaves hurriedly

14   the sound of the street door being broken open and 'heavy steps' heard in the hall, shouts of 'put 'em up'

15   the Auxiliary enters the room brandishing a revolver and torch

16   the Auxiliary's aggressive interrogation of **Seumas** and **Donal**; his reckless handling of the revolver; his search of the room

17   **Mrs Grigson's** re-entry and her anxiety for 'Dolphie'

18   the Auxiliary's rapid exit when hear that there's whisky to be drunk in the **Grigsons'** room

19   the increasingly loud and varied commotion created by the raid in progress, shouting, the sound of 'ransacking' and moving of furniture

20   the sound of **Minnie** being manhandled into the lorry; angry male voices shouting 'Get in the lorry'; **Minnie's** hysterical shout of 'Up the Republic'

21   Mrs **Grigson's** frantic exit and return, screaming about **Minnie's** room having been full of bombs

22   a brief interval of comparative quiet when Dolphie returns and lies about his bravery

23   the deafening sound of the ambush: two exploding bombs, fierce gunfire, clamour of voices, a rifle-shot, then the cries that reveal that **Minnie Powell** has been shot – 'they say she's dead'

24   the horrified reactions of **Mrs Grigson**, **Seumas** and **Davoren**.

You might think that, with all this going on, the director has little to do to create tension, but you would be wrong. The tension is created by the actors' **reactions** to the sound effects and terrifying events, as well as by the noises themselves.

Remember that in rehearsal the director is working with her or his cast without the support of the technical elements. He or she will need to direct the cast to assume the appropriate facial expressions, gestures and movements to convey the escalating tension in the scene. In a scene like this it is vital to vary the tempo and pace of the action.

Not all of the plays available on the course have sections of such extreme tension. However, all plays need to be directed to bring out the prevalent mood or atmosphere of individual scenes for the audience.

If you are studying one of the other set plays, look at the following sections and identify the key features for mood and atmosphere.

Antigone

Look at the final sequence of the play, from **Eurydice's** entrance to the end of the play:

1 **Eurydice** enters the play for the first time; she has heard a voice filled with sorrow at some terrible news
2 the **Messenger** must confirm to this loving mother that her only surviving son, **Haemon**, is dead and that he took his own life because of her husband's stubbornness
3 she turns away without speaking and returns abruptly to the palace
4 the **Chorus** express their alarm and the **Messenger** follows her, hoping to prevent her from doing something rash
5 **Creon** enters, now a broken man; his attendants carry the dead body of his son
6 **Creon** blames himself for **Haemon's** death, in a painful lament
7 the **Messenger** re-enters to break the news to **Creon** that **Eurydice** has killed herself out of grief for her son; he tells **Creon** that, just before she died, having stabbed herself, she cursed **Creon** for bringing about the death of her two sons
8 **Creon's** misery is boundless; faced with the bodies of his dead wife and son, he becomes a 'wailing wreck of a man' and is led away into the palace
9 the **Chorus** deliver, to the audience, a brief condemnation of **Creon**, whose pride has invited the 'mighty blows of fate'.

Admittedly, this section does not have the excitement of gunfire or an ambush, but it is still powerful drama.

Activity

Try directing this section using the rest of your group to take the parts. If you are studying a different play, you might still like to experiment with directing a group of actors' reactions to the listed sound effects.

Fig. 14.4 *Antigone is led to her death*

Like the death of **Minnie Powell**, the deaths of **Haemon** and **Eurydice**, (and **Antigone** herself, of course) take place *off*stage. The director's job is to convey the shock and the horror that these deaths cause *on*stage, using movement and facial expression as well as directing the delivery of the speeches.

If *Antigone* is your set play, try working through this section as a director, paying close attention to the emotional temperature of the scene.

Since *The Taming of the Shrew* is a comedy, we would not expect there to be the same type of terror or horror affecting the scenes, but there is still tension between the characters, and the audience keenly anticipates seeing **Petruchio** 'tame' his 'shrew'. Look at Act Four, Scene Three, where **Katherina**, half-starved and utterly exhausted, is tantalised both by **Grumio's** descriptions of the food he has no intention of bringing her and by **Petruchio's** presentation of new, fashionable clothes that he has no intention of letting her wear.

The final part of *A Doll's House* also offers the director the opportunity to use staging elements and the direction of the actors to create a tense mood. Near the end of Act Three, **Nora** is almost out of her mind with worry about **Krogstad's** letter, which will expose her fraudulent act of forging her father's signature and, she believes, cause **Torvald** to ruin his own reputation in protecting hers. She has done everything she can think of to keep **Torvald** from opening his post.

Look at the section from **Torvald's** exit into his study to read his post up to the end of the play. How would you ensure the ebb and flow of tension here? What mood do you think Ibsen wants you to create for your audience through the final exchanges of **Torvald** and **Nora**?

Fig. 14.5 *Rifle Drill scene from Oh! What a Lovely War*

If you are studying *Oh! What a Lovely War*, look at the Christmas Day scene towards the end of Act One. Here, as director you need to vary the mood of the scene to match the swift changes in the soldiers' experiences. The soldiers' initial state of bored resignation to their conditions in the trenches, in the first winter of the war, is punctuated, first by the sound of the 'distant bombardment', then by the German voice singing 'Silent Night/Heilige Nacht'. The reactions of the soldiers are critical here in emphasising the unfamiliarity of such lyricism amid the hellish scenes of war.

After the **First Soldier** answers the carol with his own coarse rendering of 'Christmas Day in the Cookhouse' the mood lifts as the soldiers from both nations meet in No Man's Land for their famous exchange of gifts.

As director, once again, you have plenty of 'ingredients' to work with to create different moods with your cast.

Finally, if you are studying *Playhouse Creatures*, look at Act Two, Scene Two. This scene begins with **Mrs Betterton's** conversation with her husband, and gathers momentum as **Mrs Farley's** pregnancy is discovered and she first attempts, and then halts, the procedure to abort her baby. The scene ends sombrely with **Mrs Farley** leaving the company but threatening, darkly to **Mrs Marshall**, 'Maybe you should have a care. Maybe your luck will run out.'

The moods and atmosphere in this scene are very different from the others we have looked at, but the director needs just as much skill in every case, first to decide upon the effects he or she wishes to create, and then to achieve those effects using the staging methods available.

15   The designer's interpretation

Think

You could take a more expressionistic or abstract approach to either of these plays, but you must ensure that your ideas are carefully thought out and justified.

This chapter looks at the way in which designers contribute to the audience's experience of a production. It also focuses on how to approach a chosen text from a designer's perspective.

All the plays in this Unit offer excellent opportunities for the designer. Some of them, such as *The Shadow of a Gunman* and *A Doll's House*, invite a **naturalistic** approach to setting, costume and technical design. This means that a designer needs to undertake meticulous research into the period in which they were set. For example, *A Doll's House* is set in a **bourgeois** home, so the fashions and furnishings on the set should reflect the sort of clothes and décor that a middle-class family would have had at the time. In contrast, the costume and set for *The Shadow of a Gunman* need to reflect life in a run-down **tenement** building in Dublin in the 1920s.

While **Minnie** presents herself 'charmingly', and **Adolphus Grigson** also takes care of his appearance, the general poverty of the characters in the cast should be reflected in the overall designs.

Some of the other plays are more flexible in their design demands, although it is difficult to imagine a production of *Oh! What a Lovely War* stripped of its Pierrot costumes or *Playhouse Creatures* set in a period other than the Restoration.

One play that offers designers almost complete freedom to use their imaginations is *The Taming of the Shrew*. As with the vast majority of Shakespeare's work, it is open to an infinite number of interpretations and treatments.

The following section looks at the various issues and challenges that a designer working on a production of *The Taming of the Shrew* would have to address. He or she would need to consider:

- design fundamentals, such as scale, shape, colour, texture, applied to all visual elements
- use of lighting, such as its direction, colour, intensity, speed
- use of sound, such as its direction and amplification; music, sound effects, both live and recorded
- visual elements, such as costume, makeup, masks, props
- scenic devices, such as revolves, trucks, projections used to enable transitions or create special effects.

Preparing your designs

Stage one – initial notes

Before creating a design concept for a production, the design team in a professional theatre spends time in discussion with the director, as mentioned in Chapter 2. However, as *you* approach the task of designing for your set play you are the sole interpreter. You need to know *exactly* what you want *your* design interpretation of the play to communicate to your audience and exactly what effects you want your designs to have on them. You need to consider the style and genre of the play, its action and content, the nature of its characters and its underlying message or themes.

Whichever play you are studying, you need to be very familiar with the text. Re-read it from a design viewpoint and imagine the unfolding action on the stage. Make notes in your text, highlighting the fundamental requirements of the play, for example, the number of scene changes and the required number of entrances and exits. You should also note specific scenic design demands that are mentioned by the playwright, for example, the stove in *A Doll's House* or the fire in *Playhouse Creatures* or the newspanel in *Oh! What a Lovely War*.

When designing costumes you need to consider the characters and think about their relative ages, their status within the play and how their characters might be expressed in costume terms. You should note special events in the play when individual characters or groups might need additions to their costume or complete changes.

In *Antigone*, for example, **Antigone** will probably be wearing a different costume when she is led to her death from the one in which she initially appeared. She might even wear a 'distressed' version of her original costume when she is brought before **Creon**, after having buried her brother.

In *The Shadow of a Gunman*, **Minnie** appears smartly and 'charmingly' dressed in Act One, but her appearance in Act Two occurs late at night, as the house is raided, and when she rushes, desperately, into the tenement room she is 'only partly dressed' and her underclothes are covered with a shawl.

Nora requires the fancy dress costume of the fisher-girl from Capri in the final Act of *A Doll's House*.

Fig. 15.1 *Nora as the Capri fisher girl in* A Doll's House

In *Oh! What a Lovely War* the Pierrot costumes are adapted throughout the action with a vast array of different accessories and costume pieces.

In *Playhouse Creatures*, apart from the range of costumes needed for the characters when 'on stage', **Mrs Farley** needs to wear the distressed version of her once fine petticoat, as costume for her final appearance in the play.

In *The Taming of the Shrew* the wedding of **Petruchio** and **Katherina** requires not only 'best clothes' for the bride and her family but also **Petruchio's** ridiculous costume which he is wearing to test out his prospective bride.

Stage two – listing design fundamentals

Draw up a list of factors that will affect your design strategy.

Consider the following in relation to the setting design:

■ the play's original context
■ the period setting selected
■ the geographical setting of individual scenes
■ the style and genre of the play
■ the location(s) of the action of the play
■ the size of the cast
■ the required actor-audience relationship
■ thematic influences.

Consider the following in relation to the costume design:

■ the status of the characters
■ the age of the characters
■ the profession of the characters
■ the relationships between the characters
■ the personalities and characteristics of the characters
■ development of characters; changes in their fortune or situation
■ the actions or movements of the characters.

Consider the following in relation to the technical design:

■ locations to be suggested, for example, interior and exterior scenes
■ the style and genre of the play
■ the time of year or day when individual scenes are set
■ the mood and atmosphere of individual scenes.

Example plans for designs for The Taming of the Shrew

> ■ Activity
>
> Watch a live production, video, film or DVD version of the play to help you relate to some of the example points.
> ■ The BBC Shakespeare version stars John Cleese as Petruchio.
> ■ There is a film version starring Elizabeth Taylor and Richard Burton.
> ■ The BBC 2 'Animated Shakespeare' version gives a flavour of the story and its setting.

The setting design:

■ original context – Elizabethan England

■ period setting – open to interpretation; Elizabethan times? Contemporary times? The Victorian era?

■ geographical setting – the Induction is set in England; the play-within-a-play section, which includes all the main action, takes place in Padua and at **Petruchio's** country house in Verona

■ style and genre of the play – Elizabethan comedy, a fairly boisterous style, with no darker elements

■ location(s) of the action of the play – various, including the exterior of an English tavern, the bedchamber of an English Lord, a street in Padua, the interior of **Baptista's** house in Padua, a town square or churchyard, the interior of **Petruchio's** home in Verona, the interior of **Lucentio's** rented house in Padua

■ size of the cast – 20 named characters and several 'players'; in a number of scenes there are eight or more actors to be accommodated on stage at the same time

■ required actor–audience relationship – conventionally this play would be largely performed without acknowledging the audience's presence

■ thematic influences – some allusion to themes of love, of youth and age, of taming, testing and training in the scenic design.

> **AQA Examiner's tip**
>
> Remember to justify your choice of period. For example, if you select the Victorian era as a suitable setting for *The Taming of the Shrew*, you might justify it on the basis that attitudes towards women, marriage and money were similar in the Elizabethan and Victorian periods.

The costume design:

■ the geographical setting – as above, with some contrast indicated between the fashions of the English Lord and his retinue and the Italian characters

■ the period setting selected

■ the style/genre of the play – the costume designer will make a large contribution to the style of the production

■ the status of the various characters – the main cast is made up of wealthy men and their servants, in addition to the two daughters of **Baptista** and the rich **Widow**, who **Hortensio** finally marries; in the Induction, **Sly** and the Lord are seen at opposite ends of the social spectrum and Shakespeare is clearly exploring the very different living conditions of these characters, albeit in a comical way; costumes should reflect the difference in status

■ the age of the characters – there is a contrast between the younger and older characters that Shakespeare has fore-grounded in his text; highlight this contrast within the designs

■ the profession of the characters – the main characters are all gentlefolk and as such have no professions; their servants might be wearing uniforms or liveries that match their employers' costumes in some way, or they might wear very distinctive uniforms to show that they are servants, depending upon the period setting selected; the disguised tutors might be signified by appropriate costume, as might the Haberdasher and Tailor

■ the relationships between the characters – the rivals for **Bianca** might be dressed distinctively from each other; **Petruchio's** retinue of servants may all be wearing variations on the costume of their master

■ the personalities and characteristics of the characters – could signal **Katherina's** development from 'wild-cat' to obedient wife through her changing costume

▓ development of characters; changes in their fortune or situation – a wonderful opportunity for invention in relation to the wedding scene, especially in **Petruchio's** strange attire

▓ the actions or movements of the characters throughout the play; make allowance in **Katherina's** costume for her violent outbursts, for example

▓ the themes of the play – pick up the theme of deceit, which is expressed in variety of costume changes and disguises.

Fig. 15.2 *Katherina in a physical tussle with Petruchio – modern dress production of* The Taming of the Shrew, *2006*

The technical design:

▓ the geographical setting – the sounds of the English countryside, for example, birdsong or the huntsmen's horns; the sounds of Italy, for example, the hum of cicadas or the ringing of bells in the exterior scenes; the lighting states will be different for England and Italy

▓ locations to be suggested, for example, interior and exterior scenes – contrast is needed in relation to lighting states for interior and exterior settings; the use of directional light through windows or doorways, for example, and/or use of **gobos**

▓ the style and genre of the play – the light-hearted nature of the play will influence the lighting and sound design to highlight comic moments, for example, the noise of the lute breaking over **Hortensio's** head which could be heard off-stage

▓ the time of year or day when individual scenes are set – there are both daytime and nighttime scenes

▓ the mood and atmosphere of individual scenes – **Katherina's** moods and tantrums might be highlighted through technical means in the early part of the play; the festivities of the wedding(s) provide an opportunity for creating an atmosphere of celebration in the later stages.

Stage three – preparing designs based on your plans

When your fundamental design plans are complete, you can start making artistic decisions that will add detail to your plans. Think about colours, shapes, scale, fabric and texture for setting and costume; consider the structure of your set, its height, extent and method of construction. Remember to keep your design intentions at the forefront of your thinking. Keep asking yourself 'what effects do I want to create for my audience through my designs?'

In the case of *The Taming of the Shrew*, you'll need to decide whether to create a traditional style production set in Elizabethan England or Renaissance Italy or whether to **transpose** the play to a more contemporary setting. Recent productions have seen the play set in a wide variety of locations and periods.

In the 1995 production of the play, in which Josie Lawrence played Katherina, the set designer, Craig Russell, introduced a motorbike and a 'bubble car' on stage, giving the play a modern twist. Lucentio and Tranio arrived in Padua on the motorbike and then, in a sequence of action inserted between the wedding scene and the arrival of the 'happy' bride and groom at Petruchio's house, a truly bedraggled Katherina was seen pushing the clapped-out 'bubble car' across the stage during a torrential downpour of rain!

This production featured a range of costumes from different periods which resulted in a 'universal' style of design overall.

Fig. 15.3 *Josie Lawrence in the 1995 production of* The Taming of the Shrew

■ The 'universal' approach to design

Designers who choose to adopt a naturalistic approach to a production must do extensive research into the relevant period and location in order to recreate authentic settings, furnishings and costumes.

Some designers opt to take a more 'universal' approach to design. This involves setting the action of the play in a neutral or an abstract environment that cannot readily be identified as a specific place or period. Universal settings sometimes contain little or no furniture, although the set might be divided into separate areas and there may be places for the actors to sit. Some designers create a neutral stage, but use furniture from a range of different periods. Alternatively they might create imaginative furniture, for example, a settee shaped like a pair of lips for a love scene.

Another way of creating a 'universal' context for the action of a play is to make a non-naturalistic landscape, defined by colours and shapes, different levels and steps. This creates the impression of buildings or architectural design without actually representing a specific building on stage.

Sometimes designers use a neutral setting but design costumes for the characters that include designs from recognisable periods of history. For example, in the 1995 production of *The Taming of the Shrew* already mentioned, the dresses of the ladies included Elizabethan touches; they were full skirted and tightly bodiced; the women wore ruffs. The men, however, wore costumes from different periods, blending several decades from the 20th century along with those from previous centuries.

Fig. 15.4 *Impressionistic-style setting for* The Taming of the Shrew

The purpose behind the universal approach is usually to suggest that the themes from the play are relevant to all periods and to all audiences through the ages. The themes of love, rivalry, jealousy and marriage in *The Taming of the Shrew* are certainly as relevant today as they were in Shakespeare's time.

Where designers choose a contemporary setting for the play's action and include modern fashions for their characters, they are often able to draw parallels between the characters in the play and some recognisable stereotypes from our daily life in the 21st Century. This is often done for comic effect but it can also offer a serious comment on the type of character being depicted.

Form of staging

Before you can begin to draw up any set designs, you need to decide on your form of staging.

The problems created by the induction scene and the need for fluid scene changes from location to location might suggest that you could use the traditional features offered by a **proscenium arch** theatre or large open stage with **flying space** and possibly a **revolve stage** feature.

A **traverse staging** arrangement might be used with the induction scene played at one end of the space, **Petruchio's** house placed at the other end, and the sequences in Padua played in the larger acting space in the middle.

Whichever form of staging you choose will affect the design opportunities available to you. Think carefully about the technical resources needed to change locations and settings. Will you be flying scenery in or out? Will you use trucks or a revolve facility? Or will all your changes be achieved through lighting and sound?

Remember that *The Taming of the Shrew* in particular has a large cast to accommodate on stage and, even allowing for multi-role playing, you will need plenty of space. A number of scenes that are set in the main square involve action that is observed by others, which requires a lot of space. With the additional 'audience' of **Sly** and his party it's clear that clever use of space is crucial when designing this play.

Choosing the location for the action

A set designer of *The Taming of the Shrew* must consider each separate location in which the action takes place. The opening induction scene alone needs two distinct settings: the exterior of a tavern, where **Sly** is found in a drunken stupor by the passing Lord; and the interior of the Lord's manor house, in a bedchamber.

These two scenes are brief and, although the play suggests that **Sly** and his friends will be visible throughout the performance, you will have to decide how much stage space you want to commit to this relatively minor part of the production.

You might choose to set the induction on a different level on the stage, above the main action, or on a **forestage**, removing **Sly** and the rest of the extra audience from the real audience's main line of vision, once the main action begins. Alternatively, you might choose to highlight the play-within-a-play format of *The Taming of the Shrew*, giving the actors in the main play the status of travelling players, using a portable set and costumes to help them present their drama in front of the 'double audience'.

▪ **Activity**

Choose two characters from the play you are studying. Imagine how they might be dressed if you were to stage a contemporary version of the play. For example, how would you dress **Lucentio** and **Tranio** when they first arrive in Padua? Or **Nora** and **Mrs Linde** at their first meeting?

▪ **Key terms**

Flying space: the space above the stage where sets can be 'flown' (that is, lowered and taken up), to effect set changes.

Revolve stage: a revolving turntable for carrying two (occasionally more) scenes for a relatively quick change of location.

AQA Examiner's tip

In modern productions, directors often cut the induction, thus removing the dilemma for the designer. However, the Induction is a part of this set play and you should think about how you would present it, if you were either the director or the designer.

Once you have solved the Induction issue, turn your attention to the action of the main play. Using your original design plan, you will see that five distinct locations are required.

1   The exterior scene in Padua is often presented taking place in a town square, near to or just outside the home of **Baptista** and his daughters. Several designers have created a street scene for Act One of the play, featuring the facades of several houses referred to in the text, including the exterior of **Baptista's** house, the exterior of **Hortensio's** house and the exterior of the house that **Lucentio** rents for his stay in Padua. Sometimes a church and churchyard are also included in the 'square' to be used for the wedding scenes later in the play.

2   Act Two moves to the interior of **Baptista's** house, for the presentation of the tutors and the discussions of the suitors with **Baptista**.

3   A complete change of scene is required for **Petruchio's** country house in Verona.

4   The action then moves briefly to an indeterminate exterior, for the journey of **Petruchio** and **Katherina** back to Padua where they meet **Lucentio's** father, also on his way to Padua.

5   Finally, they all turn up back in the street outside **Lucentio's** rented house before the final scene, another interior, this time inside **Lucentio's** house for the wedding supper.

Fig. 15.5 *The wedding feast in Act Five of* The Taming of the Shrew

Fig. 15.6 *Katherina and Bianca in Act Two of* The Taming of the Shrew

The setting

Whichever century you have chosen as a period setting for your play, the references throughout the text to Padua, to Verona and to Mantua, are too numerous to ignore. The characters' names (with the strange exception of Curtis, one of Petruchio's servants) are uniformly Italian sounding. It seems logical, therefore, to choose an Italian setting for the main action of the play or at least to give some hint of Italy in the setting or costume designs.

As part of your research look at Italian architecture and art in order to convey some Italianate flavour through your designs. Your school or college art department may have some-resources that you can look at. There are also web-sites devoted to Italian architecture from the Renaissance period through to the Baroque that will give you plenty of ideas about what buildings looked like in 15th, 16th and 17th century Italy.

Fig. 15.7 *Italian renaissance facades*

You may decide to *suggest* rather than attempt to *reproduce* a typical Italian square for the opening of Act One. This could be achieved simply with the hint of the Mediterranean given in choice of colours and textures. Rather than a full-blown reproduction of an Italian piazza, a few terracotta pots and pantiles, whitewashed walls, a fountain, orange trees in tubs sprinkled around the set would be enough to suggest your chosen location. A plain background with some shuttered windows and perhaps an archway leading off the main stage, lit with bright 'sunlight' would help your audience to understand your intentions.

Alternatively, you may not want to foreground the Italian nature of the setting at all. You might read the play with its repeated patterns of play-acting, taming, teaching and testing in a more abstract way and choose a neutral setting against which to show your main interpretative ideas.

Costume ideas

The Taming of the Shrew offers wonderful opportunities for creative costume design. You will have to decide whether the costumes will complement or contrast with your choice of period and setting.

Not only is there the challenge of depicting different groups and types of character through their costumes; there are precise requirements for individual costumes at specific moments in the play.

You would expect to create costumes to differentiate between the masters and their servants in a play like this, but Shakespeare actually creates a situation which demands this distinction in the opening of Act One. Here, **Lucentio** and **Tranio** swap clothes so that **Lucentio** (now dressed in humble garments) can pass himself off as the schoolmaster to **Bianca**, and **Tranio** (now posing in the stylish clothes of his young master) can present himself as **Lucentio** and keep house in Padua.

> ### Activity
>
> ▪ If you are studying *The Taming of the Shrew* how might you differentiate between **Lucentio** and **Tranio** in their initial appearance?
>
> ▪ If you are studying one of the other plays, plan how you would costume two characters to distinguish between them in terms of status or class.

Comic style – its effect on design

There is opportunity to add to the comedy of the play through your designs for **Petruchio's** wedding outfit. Biondello describes **Petruchio's** outfit before he arrives, belatedly, at his own wedding. The trick for the costume designer, here, is to create a costume that matches the description and yet somehow still succeeds in surprising the audience and making them laugh. **Biondello's** description is worth quoting in full:

> *Why, Petruchio is coming, in a new hat and an old jerkin; a pair of old breeches thrice turn'd; a pair of boots that have been candle-cases, one buckled, another laced; an old rusty sword ta'en out of the town armoury, with a broken hilt, and chapeless; with two broken points …*

Biondello then describes **Petruchio's** servant **Grumio**, who is also dressed outrageously:

> *… with a linen stock on one leg and a kersey boot-hose on the other gartered with a red and blue list; an old hat, and The humour of forty fancies pricked in't for a feather: a monster, a very monster in apparel; and not like a Christian footboy or a gentleman's lackey.*

Give some thought to **Katherina's** wedding dresses. Unlike most brides, **Katherina** needs two dresses! One should be a picture of bridal perfection as she waits at the church for **Petruchio's** arrival. The second should be a **distressed** version of the same dress, tattered, torn and muddied, bearing all the signs of the terrible journey that she has made

Fig. 15.8 *Petruchio's wedding outfit from* The Taming of the Shrew

from Padua to Verona. Remember that she must also have two pairs of shoes, two veils, two headdresses, two trains, two posies – everything that she is wearing for the wedding scene must be reproduced, and appear utterly spoilt and bedraggled, for her arrival at **Petruchio's** country house.

Fig. 15.9 *Katherina's bridal outfit in perfect condition*

Fig. 15.10 *Katherina's bridal outfit spoilt and distressed*

▥ Lighting and sound design

Lighting and sound design plays an important part in *The Taming of the Shrew*.

Referring to your plans, you will see many opportunities for using lighting to establish the different locations in the play and sound effects to create both location and comic effects.

The contrast between England and Italy can be shown with the introduction of warm sunlight effects for the exterior Italian scenes. However, in the 1995 RSC production the lighting designer, Hugh Vanstone, set the wedding scene under umbrellas and leaden skies, as if the coming storm between **Petruchio** and **Katherina** were being anticipated by the weather! This led into the thunderstorm and torrential rain that hampered the journey of the 'happy couple' to their new home, which was lit as if by crackling firelight.

Sound effects can also be used to create location and atmosphere and a designer might introduce the sound of birdsong and hunting horns for the opening scene of the induction. When the scene moves to Italy, lazy sounds of cicadas and church bells might punctuate the naturalistic moments, while exaggerated comic effects might be created through the sound of **Katherina's** violent attack on **Bianca** at the beginning of Act Two, before we actually see the pair tussling with one another.

Applying design principles to your set text

Look back at the suggested steps for creating a design realisation of a play and apply them carefully to your set play. Try different approaches to your play, both naturalistic and abstract, historically authentic and 'universal'. Remember that you need to justify all your ideas, in terms of the effects that you want to create for your audience and in terms of your play's characters, action and themes. You do not need to stick slavishly to a traditional view of your play, but you do need to be able to explain and justify alternative designs.

16 The performer's interpretation

In this chapter you will learn about:

▦ how to respond to your set play imaginatively from the point of view of an actor, with reference to:
  – approaching a role
  – developing a role
  – presenting a role.

In the six plays available to you in this part of the specification, there are scores of different characters. This chapter focuses on a small number of characters from the set plays in order to explore the actor's approach to a role and prepare you for writing from an actor's perspective throughout your course and in your examination.

When studying your set text you need to understand all the *significant* characters from your set play and to be prepared to answer on any one of them. You should also understand the function performed by the lesser characters.

If you are studying *A Doll's House* or *Playhouse Creatures*, your task is relatively straightforward, as there are only five significant characters in each of these plays. *Antigone* has eight named characters, plus the **Chorus** of Theban Elders and various extras, and in **The Shadow of a Gunman** there are 10 main characters, plus an Auxiliary soldier. In *The Taming of the Shrew* there are at least 12 significant characters.

Oh! What a Lovely War is an ensemble-style play in which a cast of 15–20 actors **multi-role** to take over 70 separate roles between them. Only a handful, who represent historical figures, could be considered main characters, as they are named, for example, **Sir John French**, **General Haig** and **Mrs Pankhurst**.

▦ Approaching a role

To guide you on how best to approach the main characters in your set play, we will focus on one character from each, as an example. Ensure that you are familiar with the character listed in your set play below, re-reading the relevant parts in the play if necessary.

Antigone – **The Sentry**

The Taming of the Shrew – **Gremio**

A Doll's House – **Cristine Linde**

The Shadow of a Gunman – **Mr Gallogher**

Oh! What a Lovely War – **Sir John French**

Playhouse Creatures – **Mrs Farley**

Getting to know your role

First, make a list of points about your chosen character, under the following headings:

Who am I?

▦ Male or female?

▦ Young or old?

▦ Single, engaged or attached, married, separated, abandoned, divorced, widowed?

▦ In love or out of love, or unloved?

▦ In work or out of work?

- Rich or poor?
- Educated or uneducated?
- High-ranking (or superior), or low-ranking (or inferior)?
- A mother, a father, a daughter, a son, a brother, a sister, a grandmother, a grandfather, an aunt, an uncle, a nephew, a niece, a cousin, a distant relative?
- A friend or a foe?
- A lover or a rival?
- In sickness or in health?
- Visitor or visited?
- Giver or taker?

Where am I?

- Which country am I in?
- Which century and decade am I in?
- In my own home, or familiar territory, or somebody else's home or their territory?
- Indoors or outside?
- At work or at leisure?
- In or out of my depth?
- With friends, family, employers, employees, a lover or spouse, strangers, enemies?

Why am I here?

- A social occasion?
- To work or to play?
- A personal matter, a business matter?
- Invited, enforced, compelled or summoned?
- To escape someone or to find someone?
- To conceal something or reveal something?

How do I feel?

- Relaxed or nervous?
- Comfortable or uncomfortable in my surroundings?
- Curious or indifferent?
- Pleased or displeased?
- Surprised, shocked or satisfied?
- Disappointed, deflated?
- Outraged, horrified?
- Affectionate or dispassionate?
- Afraid or fearless?
- Anxious or relieved?
- Complacent or patronised?
- Proud or humiliated?
- Weak or strong?
- Optimistic or pessimistic?
- Well or ill?

Think

Some characters' feelings change over the course of the play or vary during individual scenes. You should include these changes in your planning.

Here are some example notes made about **Mrs Linde** from *A Doll's House*. They show how you might apply the information about your role to shape your performance.

Who am I? Mrs Christine Linde

- I am a woman – which will be shown in my appearance.
- I am in my late 20s or early 30s, but look older – casting or makeup will help here.
- I am single and widowed, although as the play progresses I rekindle my attachment to Krogstad; this change should be shown through facial expression and body language.
- I am unloved at the start of the play but in love by the end; I will use eye contact and touching hands to show this change.
- I am actively seeking work; this will be shown in my tone of voice with Nora and Torvald.
- I am relatively poor, as shown by my plain costume.
- I have had a hard life; humility has taught me to accept a fairly lowly position; this will be shown in my posture and initial sense of self-defeat.
- I have been a dutiful daughter and sister; this will be shown by my earnest tone when discussing my family.
- I am a friend to Nora, shown by my eye contact with her, my spatial relationship to her and my physical closeness and contact with her.
- I become a lover to Krogstad, shown by my vocal sincerity in addressing him.
- I am initially very weary, shown through slightly depressed posture and tired voice, but in health and improving in the short course of the play; I will wear blusher in the second half of the play to make myself look healthier.
- I am visiting Nora; this will be shown by my not looking entirely comfortable in my first appearance and looking quite intently around me, at my surroundings, when I arrive; later I am more at home in the Helmers' apartment and move more freely.
- I have come to ask a favour of Nora and gain a job – a taker – and so my voice will entreat; however I rapidly become a good friend to Nora and give her my support; this will be shown through encouraging looks and touches.

Where am I?

- I am in Norway, the country of my birth.
- I am in the mid-19th century – my costume, posture and demeanour will reflect this.
- I am in the home of a friend that I haven't seen for nine years; I will not be too demonstrative of my friendship immediately, but may appear reserved, quiet and slightly hesitant.
- I have come indoors from a cold outside and will have to remove my outdoor things.
- I am paying a social call and will be unfailingly polite, but I am seeking a favour, so I am not entirely at ease.

Fig. 16.1 *Mrs Linde in conversation with Nora in* A Doll's House

I am within my depth, talking to an old friend, and this familiarity will be shown through increased warmth in my tone of voice, exchange of eye contact and touching of hands and arms.

Nora is an old friend, **Torvald** and **Dr Rank** are strangers to me; **Krogstad** is an 'old flame' – I will distinguish between these character adjusting my eyeline and eye contacts, and the formality of my way of speaking to each.

Why am I here?

This is apparently a social call, but as my motive of seeking work becomes more evident and I will become quite serious in asking for **Nora's** help.

Later, I visit to help **Nora** and offer her support; my final scene is motivated by my desire to be reunited with **Krogstad**, which I will show by being distracted until he arrives and then both determined to persuade him and excited about the future – shown through voice, movement and facial expressions.

A personal matter, a business matter.

Through choice, so I am reasonably at ease after the initial hesitation.

First, to find a job, and then to find love.

My motivation in the final scene is to allow **Nora** to be enlightened about the state of her marriage; I will show this through the vehemence with which I insist on **Krogstad** not retrieving the fateful letter.

How do I feel?

At first, a little nervous, but then becoming more relaxed with **Nora**, shown through body, face and voice.

Comfortable or uncomfortable in my surroundings – as above.

Curious to hear about **Nora's** troubles; I will lean forward to listen to her.

Pleased or displeased – both at different times.

Shocked by **Nora's** marriage, and satisfied by the outcome for herself and **Krogstad**.

Affectionate with **Nora** and quite tender with **Krogstad** – shown through voice.

Anxious or relieved – both; see above.

Complacent – **Nora** accuses me of patronising her, so this must be evident in my voice.

Quite proud, but conscious of **Torvald's** lack of warmth towards me.

Strong, shown through increased energy and vigour.

Optimistic about both my own future and **Nora's**.

Looking better as the play progresses – makeup.

Activity

Choose a character from your set play and complete a plan like the one opposite.

💡 Developing your role

When reading or watching some plays it is easy to think about the characters as if they are real people with individual lives of their own. However, when studying a play in depth, although we might be absorbed by individual characters we should also be conscious of the playwright's intentions in writing the play, its central theme and meaning.

So when you are working on an individual character, as well as looking at the detail of your character, you should also consider why the playwright has included him or her in the play. Exploring your character's function will also help you understand how the playwright may have intended the role to be performed.

To explore a character's function in the play consider the questions below.

What is my function?

▥ Am I one of the central characters in the play; is the play's story *my* story?

▥ Is my function in the main plot or a subplot?

▥ Do I give the audience background details or useful information about other characters?

▥ Do my actions determine or influence the events of the play?

▥ Am I a **catalyst** in the play?

▥ Do I contribute to the audience's perception of the play's central themes and messages, by representing or discussing one of the main issues of the play?

▥ Do I act as a parallel or a **foil** to another character in the play?

▥ Do I help to bring out the nature of another character or other characters?

▥ Do I act as a mouthpiece for the playwright?

▥ Do I affect the audience, for example, creating comedy, pathos or shock?

Here are some example notes for characters from different plays.

> What is my function? The **Sentry** in **Antigone**
>
> ▥ I am a significant but not a main character.
>
> ▥ There is only one plot in **Antigone**.
>
> ▥ I give the audience information about **Antigone** having buried her brother.
>
> ▥ By bringing **Antigone** before **Creon**, I facilitate the unfolding plot, but I do not directly affect it.
>
> ▥ I do act as a catalyst; by 'arresting' **Antigone** and bringing her before **Creon** I contribute to the chain of action that results in the deaths of **Antigone**, **Haemon** and **Eurydice** and in **Creon's** ultimate tragic fall.
>
> ▥ I contribute to the theme of law and judgement through my exchanges with **Creon**, especially when I express my opinion that 'It's terrible when the one who does the judging judges things all wrong'.
>
> ▥ Although a very different character from Tiresias, like him, I attract **Creon's** suspicion that I have been bribed to act and speak as I do.
>
> ▥ I help to disclose **Creon's** tyrannical nature and cruelty (when he threatens me with torture) and his paranoia (when he accuses me of taking bribes).
>
> ▥ Sophocles uses me to accuse **Creon** of faulty judgement.
>
> ▥ I am certainly not a comic character, but my complete honesty with **Creon** and my blunt talking, even with one so powerful does surprise the audience and offers a contrast to the more respectful **Chorus** characters.

▥ **Think**

Think about the style of your chosen play. Do you think the playwright wanted the audience to believe in the characters, or are the characters more like storytellers, standing between their characters and the audience?

What is my function? Gremio **from** *The Taming of the Shrew*

- I am a significant but not a main character.
- I function mainly in the subplot, as a suitor to Bianca but I also appear in the main plot, as a commentator.
- I give the audience background details about Katherina, especially in relation to her 'diabolical' nature; I add to the chorus of voices describing Katherina as a shrew and I describe Petruchio's antics during the wedding ceremony that remains unseen by the audience.
- I am a rival for Bianca's hand and take a significant part in encouraging Petruchio to marry Katherina and in attempting to gain Bianca for myself; I do take part in the main action of the play, therefore.
- Simply as a wealthy rival (to Lucentio) for Bianca's love, I am partly responsible for Tranio's plot to pass off a stranger as Lucentio's father, Vincentio.
- I contribute to the theme of the contrast between youth and age, and to the theme of the relationship between love and money; in the wider theme of deception, that runs through the play, I am also one of those deceived through the stratagems of Lucentio and Tranio.
- I act as a parallel and foil to Hortensio and Lucentio in my role as suitor to Bianca; I oblige Baptista by providing a tutor for Bianca, where Hortensio actually attempts to deceive Baptista by disguising himself as a music teacher.
- My role as wealthy suitor to Bianca does bring out the extravagant roguery of Tranio, as each barters with Baptista for Bianca.
- I make some wry observations about marriage but am not strictly a 'mouthpiece' for the author.
- In my role as 'Pantaloon' figure and as a pedantic and elderly suitor for the love of a young girl, I create comedy for the audience; Grumio comments ironically about me 'A proper stripling and an amorous' comparing me to a young tree!

Fig. 16.2 *Pantaloon*

What is my function? **Sir John French** in *Oh! What a Lovely War*

▪ I am a significant historical character, but not a main character in terms of the action of this play.

▪ There is no 'plot', as such, in this play.

▪ I give the audience information about **Haig's** background in trade.

▪ I am one example of the incompetence of the strategists controlling the management of the war.

▪ Although a significant player in WW1, I have no such function within the storyline of this play.

▪ I contribute to the theme of incompetence in high office and to the class issue within the play.

▪ I play a parallel role to **Haig** and expose the backbiting and political jockeying for position that lay behind many military decisions during WW1.

▪ I help to reveal something of the nature of **Haig**.

▪ No, I am not a mouthpiece for the writers of this play.

▪ I am not a comic character but my stupidity and inability to speak French, coupled with my blatant xenophobia, revealed in my first scene, contributes to the black humour of the play.

▪ **Activity**

If you have a character who is an historical figure, find out more about him or her by doing some background research, using books and the internet. Remember that a playwright does not always present historical facts or characters accurately. Choose how authentic to be in your characterisation.

Fig. 16.3 *Sir John French*

Presenting your role

💡 How should the audience respond to my performance?

Having completed notes on the character from your set play, you now need to decide how you want your audience to respond to your character. You might want the audience to feel differently about you at different times in the play. If your character only appears on stage once or twice, there is less opportunity for the audience to vary their responses to you.

You might suggest the following responses for the characters that we have already looked at. A performer of the **Sentry** might aim to achieve the sympathy of the audience, as might the actor playing **Mrs Linde**, although they would almost certainly use quite different performance methods to achieve that sympathy.

The actor playing **Gremio** and the actor playing **Mr Gallogher** might be more concerned with achieving comedy for their audiences, while a successful performance of **Sir John French**, although potentially comic, will probably also provoke the dislike of the audience.

If you are thinking about how an audience might respond to **Mrs Farley** you need to consider how she changes during the play as she loses her position within the theatre company and ends ruined. Initial dislike or mistrust might change dramatically to pity by the end of the play.

Examination questions

In the examination, questions about performing a role tend to ask about a character in one or two specific scenes. If you have already considered each character's role throughout the play, it should be easier for you to focus on the specified section in detail. You will have your text with you to refer to in the examination.

Exam questions about performing a role will always give you a *specific* focus and will *not* simply ask you, for example, how you would perform the role of **Mrs Linde**.

Look at the following examples of the types of question that you might be asked. There is an example from each of the set plays.

AQA Examiner's tip

You are allowed to underline and/or use highlighter in your text and make brief annotations. These should be single words or phrases, *not* extensive comments and notes.

⬛

Antigone

1 Explain how you would perform the role of the **Sentry**, in each of his two appearances, in order to reveal his change in attitude from his initial fear for his won life to his relief as he brings a guilty **Antigone** before **Creon**.

(In some editions, the **Sentry** appears as the **Soldier** or **Guard**.)

The Taming of the Shrew

2 How would you want your audience to respond to the character of **Gremio** at the beginning of the play? Explain how you would perform the role in Acts One and Two in order to achieve your aims.

A Doll's House

3 How would you perform the role of **Christine Linde** in Act One of the play in order to engage the sympathy of your audience?

The Shadow of a Gunman

4 How would you perform the role of **Mr Gallogher** in Act One of the play in order to create comedy for your audience?

Oh! What a Lovely War

5 How would you want your audience to respond to Sir John French? Explain how you would perform the role in his appearances in Acts One and Two in order to achieve your aims.

Playhouse Creatures

6 How would you want your audience to respond to **Mrs Farley's** disgrace? Explain how you would perform the role in Act Two, Scenes Two and Four in order to achieve your aims?

You will notice that five out of the six questions refer explicitly to the audience and their response to the named roles. The 'odd one out', *Antigone*, requires suggestions for revealing the change in the **Sentry**; the word 'revealing', here, implies that the actor is revealing the change to the audience. So, it's not the 'odd one out', after all!

All actors must consider the audience when preparing a role. Every actor has a purpose in mind when making initial decisions about his or her character. In the professional theatre, of course, the director will often guide the actor's decisions in terms of their aims for the audience, because each individual character has to fit in within the director's overall interpretation of the play.

In this course, you are being asked to make your own decisions about how you play a particular role. But remember, your decisions must be based on the three aspects identified above:

- *who* you are
- what your *purpose* is within the play
- your preferred *audience response* to your role.

💡 How to achieve a specific audience response

Once you've identified the ways in which you would like your audience to respond to your character, you need to write confidently about how you will achieve that response through your performance. You should consider the following aspects: your appearance, your voice, your physical expression and how you interact with other characters.

🔍 *Your appearance*

On stage, as in life, first impressions are formed very quickly and are based on appearance. The experience of watching an actor play a character lies somewhere half way between the real-life experience of watching a stranger across a crowded room and making an acquaintance: we draw immediate conclusions about them from their appearance; we usually get to hear the character speak; we learn some of their views and attitudes; we see them interact with other characters, but we can't question them and we can't get to know them as we would in real life.

> ### Paired activity
>
> Watch 10 minutes of a recorded TV show that you don't normally watch and turn the sound off. Separately, make notes about your impressions of the characters. Then compare notes, turn the sound up and watch it again. Were your first impressions correct? Did hearing the voices alter your perceptions of them?

For that reason, in naturalistic plays, in order to help the audience form the correct impression of a character at the outset, actors tend to be cast, and/or made-up and costumed, to match the type of character they are playing.

So, when answering a question about how to achieve a particular audience response, it's worth including a few sentences on what your character looks like and is wearing. His or her appearance should be tailored to suit his or her personality, status and purpose within the play.

You should include a brief reference to each of the following aspects of your appearance.

■ Your age. Think about what decade of your life you are in. This will affect your movement and the audience's response. Are you young and cute? Or old and frail?

■ Your height and build. Are you tall and angular, short and plump, tall and well-built, or small and thin? This may be important in showing your authority or weakness or strength or the degree of confidence you might display, all of which will affect the audience in different ways.

■ Your facial features. Are you soft featured or harsh? Smooth-skinned or wrinkled like a prune? Mournful eyes or twinkling bright? Smiley or dour? Have you a pronounced feature that dominates your face? How do you wear your hair? What colour is it? How might the audience respond to your face?

■ Your posture. Are you straight-backed and purposeful? Do you have a tendency to shrink into yourself? Head up or head down?

■ Your costume.

Let's take a look at **Mr Gallogher** from *The Shadow of a Gunman*. After this you should apply the same task to a character from your selected set play.

O'Casey's stage directions are quite detailed. **Mr Gallogher's** appearance is described as follows: '*a spare little man with a spare little grey beard … He is dressed as well as a faded suit of blue will allow him to be … he carries a hard hat …*'

These directions guide the director and actor about **Mr Gallogher's** appearance, but if you were preparing to write about playing this role you would need to give more detail to achieve your preferred audience response. You would need to work out the answers to 'Who am I?' 'Where am I?' 'Why am I here?' and 'What am I feeling?' before proceeding to 'What is my function?' to help you to understand the character fully.

Mr Gallogher is only on stage for about 10 minutes in total. However, he plays a very significant role. The 'interlude' with **Mr Gallogher** and **Mrs Henderson** serves to emphasise, to the audience, the widely believed rumour circulating about **Davoren**, that he is a gunman on the run, associated with the IRA.

It is **Donal's** failure to deny this rumour that leads to **Minnie's** death, since, had he refused to listen to and then to accept **Mr Gallogher's** ridiculous letter addressed to the IRA, Tommy Owens would not have been boasting in the Blue Lion about 'his friend that was a general in the IRA'. It was this empty boast of Tommy's that almost certainly brought the Auxiliary straight to **Davoren's** tenement room and then to the cache of Maguire's bombs.

So is **Mr Gallogher** a serious character, or is he merely a figure of fun? Should the audience sympathise with him, because of the harassment that he and his family are suffering at the hands of his troublesome neighbours, the Dwyer family, or laugh at his outrageous request that the IRA should come and sort out the Dwyers and 'bring their guns'?

The example question for this character requires a comic treatment of the role; however, if you were asked, 'How would you want your audience to respond to **Mr Gallogher**?' you would be free to select your own treatment.

We learn from the text that **Mr Gallogher** is a respectable family man. He has a wife and two children and works for a harness maker. The fact that he lives in a tenement building suggests that he is fairly poor; the fact that he wears a suit suggests that he attempts to appear smart.

A serious treatment of the role, aiming to achieve a *sympathetic* response to the character might treat **Mr Gallogher's** appearance as follows:

- Your age – early forties (wife and two children).
- Your height and build – quite thin and fairly small, under-nourished; attracting sympathy.
- Your facial features – soft features, with a kindly face, quite drawn and tired looking; however, to show the strain of living next door to the Dwyers, large but sad-looking eyes; hair (slightly greying) neatly combed into a side-parting; the audience will feel pity.
- Your posture – a little nervous of the people in the room, somewhat rounded posture, with head generally downcast; might create empathy.
- Your costume – a faded blue suit, pressed and tidy but a little worn, over a white shirt; evidence of making an effort; attracts sympathy for evident poverty but decency.

If you were intending to create comedy you might want to consider a different approach:

- Your age – early forties (wife and two children)
- Your height and build – exceedingly thin and angular in appearance, looking almost comical.
- Your facial features – a large, bony nose on which is perched a pair of oversized spectacles, which have continually to be pushed back up the nose; the magnification on the lenses makes the eyes appear unnaturally large; a mop of unruly hair sticking up at odd angles.
- Your posture – unnaturally stiff, exaggerating the angularity, head up, to match the owl-like features created by the glasses and nose.
- Your costume – faded blue suit, rumpled and with the jacket too small and the trousers too large; the trousers held up with silly braces or odd-coloured belt.

In both cases, a clear impression of the character is created before **Mr Gallogher** even speaks.

🔍 *Your voice*

Appearance and voice should work together to help define character. We know that **Mr Gallogher** is Irish, so a Dublin accent is required, but what kind of character is he? Is he nervous and insecure, halting and hesitant in his speech? Does his volume vary? Or does his attempt at

Fig. 16.4 *One interpretation of* ***Mr Gallogher*** *in* **The Shadow of a Gunman**

formal, legalistic language in his silly letter cause him to read it aloud in an exaggeratedly 'educated' voice? If you want a comic response to **Mr Gallogher** you might choose to contrast his normal conversational voice with a quite affected tone when reading the letter.

When we are discussing voice and speech in the theatre, we usually refer to some of the following qualities:

- **volume** – this is the most straightforward quality and refers to the relative loudness or quietness of the vocal delivery
- **pitch** – refers, as in music, to the exact height and depth of any sound
- **tone** – refers to the quality of the voice, its thinness or richness, as well as to the modifications that an actor can make in delivery, for example, speaking boastfully or humbly, light-heartedly or with menace
- **inflection** – refers to the way an actor shapes the delivery of lines; it describes the rising and falling of the voice as well, for example, the way the voice rises at the end of any sentence that is a question; speech that lacks inflection is described as 'monotone'
- **phrasing** – refers to the way the actor shapes a speech, to the way individual words are stressed and to the use of **pause** within the delivery of speech
- **pace** – refers to the speed of an actor's delivery of speech; a good actor will vary the pace of delivery to match the situation he or she is in
- **rhythm** – refers to the pattern of speech, especially speech that is written in verse, where an actor has to work with the poetic metre that the playwright has chosen
- **accent** – this term has two separate meanings when used to describe vocal qualities; it can refer to the place where an actor chooses to put a **stress** or **emphasis** within a speech, or it can refer to the distinctive vocal 'signature' of people who come from a specific country, for example, we refer to an American accent or an Irish accent

▥ **dialect** – this term refers to the distinctive vocal 'signature' of people who come from a specific region of a country, for example, Cockney, Geordie or Brummie to signify someone from East London, Tyneside or Birmingham

How to write about vocal qualities

When writing about vocal qualities, you will probably only need to refer to a few of the qualities that appear in these bullet points, depending on the character that you are referring to and the level of detail that you are going into as you discuss the delivery of specific lines. Remember that, as an actor, you will be using your voice to help you to communicate your character and to achieve your preferred audience response.

We are going to look at **Mrs Farley**, from *Playhouse Creatures*, in terms of her vocal qualities. If this is your set play you will already know that **Mrs Farley** is an important character who undergoes a profound change in fortune in the course of the play. This will need to be reflected both in her appearance and in her vocal qualities. If *Playhouse Creatures* is not your set play, it is still important to read through this example and then apply the same task to a character from your own play.

Mrs Farley appears in the majority of the scenes in Act One, but only in two scenes in Act Two. We will look at moments from three key scenes in which the actor playing **Mrs Farley** would wish to achieve very different responses from the audience; the intended responses appear underlined.

Act One, Scene Two

This is **Mrs Farley's** first appearance; we learn that her father, a local preacher, has just died of the plague and she is attempting to preach in his place.

The stage directions indicate, *'Mrs Farley speechifies in religious tones'*, her first lines are:

> *And Lo*
>
> *It is written in our Lord's book.*

The preaching will require a loud volume and the direction suggests a sermonising tone. The audience might be impressed by her apparent sincerity and eloquence; alternatively, an actor might use inflection to draw out the 'o' of 'Lo' and to exaggerate the biblical rhythm of the lines for an almost comical effect.

When discussing her situation with **Nell**, **Mrs Farley** is likely to speak in fairly Standard English, given her position as daughter of a preacher, and this will achieve a contrast with **Nell's** rougher, cockney dialect. The audience may respond by trusting her, and then be shocked by her trickery of **Nell** when she rushes off to secure the job of actress that **Nell** had inadvertently tipped her off about and had so dearly wanted for herself.

When **Nell** offers to go with **Mrs Farley**, at the end of the scene, **Mrs Farley** would probably rush the pace of her response, 'No. It's not far. You wait. I'll meet you back here' and her pitch might rise as she is anxious to prevent **Nell** from realising where she is going. This might arouse the audience's suspicion. If she left a pause between each of the phrases, but spoke each phrase quickly, her phrasing would reveal her panic at the possibility of being found out and the audience would disapprove of her deceitfulness.

▥ **Activity**

In pairs, read through the extracts and pick out the key terms (listed above) used when discussing vocal qualities. Take turns to explain their precise meaning to your partner.

Act One, Scene Seven

By Scene Seven, **Mrs Farley** has become a successful actress, has caught the eye of the **King** and has begun a secret liaison with him. **Nell** has managed to trick her way into the theatre company.

At the start of the scene **Mrs Farley** is telling **Mrs Marshall** about her *rendezvous* with the **King**. She is later appalled to discover that **Nell** has been given the opportunity to appear on stage. She humiliates Nell about the state of her petticoat and boasts about her secret affair with the **King**.

Annoyed that **Nell** has finally been given an opportunity to act, **Mrs Farley** summons **Nell** for a 'private word'. Her simple line, 'Come here' could be delivered in a number of ways. A superior tone and a loud volume will make the audience **dislike Mrs Farley**; a dislike that might turn to **disgust**, if the actor adopts a sneering tone for the rest of the exchange:

Demanding tone, low volume.	*Mrs Farley: Show me your petticoat.*
Innocent tone, questioning, rising pitch.	*Nell: What for?*
Louder volume, accent on 'Show'.	*Mrs Farley: Show me.*
	[*Nell lifts up her skirt to reveal it. It's of greyish cloth. Mrs Farley laughs*]
Pause before 'rag', scornful tone.	*Mrs Farley: What a rag.*

Using vocal qualities in this way will ensure that the audience has a **negative** response to Mrs Farley.

When Mrs Farley speaks of the king, the audience may be able to see through Mrs Farley's sense of her own importance and recognise her for what she is – a somewhat naïve and exploited young woman. They might fear for her. She tells Nell about the king's gift to her:

These three phrases might be delivered in a boastful or in quite a childish tone. The underlined words might be accented for emphasis: if Mrs Farley raises the pitch of her voice, in each successive phrase, she might sound more innocent and arouse some sympathy in the audience. If she maintains a haughty tone, the audience is likely to continue to dislike her.

Mrs Farley: He's come to see me. He thinks I look continental. He gave me this.

[*She signals her petticoat*]

Fig. 16.5 *Mrs Farley in* Playhouse Creatures

Act Two, Scene Four

Mrs Farley's last appearance in Act Two, Scene Four reveals a great decline in her fortunes. Forced to leave the theatre company when she became pregnant, she has been abandoned by the king in favour of her rival, Nell. Mrs Farley appears here, wandering the streets as a dirty and bedraggled prostitute, trying, unsuccessfully, to pick up a customer. She speaks directly to the audience about having abandoned her little baby.

How would you use your vocal qualities in the following lines, to gain audience **sympathy** for Mrs Farley at the end?

> *I left it. Had to. Little white body. Laid it in some steps. What a cry when I left it.*

🔍 *Your physical expression*

All of us have the ability to vary our physical expression; think how you respond to the instruction to 'stand up straight!' Yet we each also have a very personal and distinct way of standing, walking, sitting, running, that is unique to us. When preparing a character for the stage, or considering a role to interpret in the examination, you need to give as much attention to the physical expression of the role as to the appearance and voice.

The term 'physical expression' encompasses the following qualities:

▮ **posture** – this refers to the way an actor stands or sits; it relates principally to the control of the back and to whether it is held straight or relaxed, erect or slouched

▮ **stance** – refers to the way an actor stands; this is sometimes termed deportment; some people stand tall, others shrink into themselves, some stand with their feet firmly set apart, other have their feet together

▮ **gait** – this refers to the way an actor walks; some people stride purposefully along, others take short steps, some waddle, some saunter, some stroll, some lollop along with a bobbing motion, some walk at an even pace; runners sprint, jog, dash (though not very often on stage!)

▮ **gesture** – refers to the way actors move their hands or other parts of their body to express themselves; it can include pointing, crossing arms, tapping fingers to the temple, offensive signs with the hand or fingers; thumbs up or down, beckoning, reaching out hands to invite or to plead, waving, raising a fist, shrugging, shaking hands, covering the face with the hands, cupping the ear, shading the eyes, nodding, kneeling

▮ **facial expression – (physical)** refers to the many different attitudes that can be expressed by the face, including, for example, smiling, grinning, crying, frowning, winking, blinking, 'pulling a face', putting out the tongue, wrinkling the nose, eyes to heaven (devotionally or sarcastically) rolling of eyes

▮ **facial expression – (emotional)** the face is also capable of communicating a huge variety of emotions by very subtle variations of the facial muscles; in life these adjustments are made involuntarily, as they are caused by genuine emotions, but an actor can imitate them on stage; these recognisable expressions include, for example, exasperation, disdain, despair, happiness, affection, adoration, inquisitiveness

Think

As people grow older they tend to acquire more idiosyncrasies; disappointingly, we often begin to do the very things we used to laugh at our parents for doing!

- **idiosyncrasy** – refers to a person's habits or personal peculiarities. Idiosyncrasies are usually adopted by actors playing character or comic roles; they might include, for example, twitching, coughing, yawning, scratching, sneezing, blowing your nose or mopping your forehead, jiggling money in your pocket, pushing spectacles up the nose or repeatedly polishing the lenses, crossing and/or uncrossing of legs, dusting yourself down or obsessively moving objects into place, readjusting your tie or repeatedly hitching up your jeans, playing with your hair or moving your hair out of the way

- **movement** – refers to the way an actor moves on stage; it includes posture and gait, but also refers to how mobile a character is, whether fidgety or static, still or always pacing; sometimes this is referred to as 'tempo'; all of us have our own natural tempo in life and actors generally strive to achieve a convincing tempo for the role they are playing on stage

- **use of space/spatial relationships** – refers to how an actor inhabits stage space; some characters isolate themselves from the others on stage; other characters invade the personal space of fellow players, either affectionately or aggressively

- **entrances/exits** – although not a separate element of physical expression, it is often worth giving special attention to the way in which your character makes entrances and exits, using the physical expressions of posture, gait, gesture, movement, tempo, and use of space; the audience can learn a lot about the way a character arrives on the stage, and how he or she leaves it and this, in turn, can determine their response.

Activity

In *Playhouse Creatures*, Mrs Betterton advises Nell how an actor can convey a variety of emotions by adjusting the head to match positions on a clock: 'If you imagine the stage as a clock. I shall demonstrate. ... Submission is well expressed at six o'clock. Shame at twenty to seven. Despair at five past twelve; not to be confused with heavenly abandonment at midday exactly. Death by strangulation is one of the only occasions on which an actress may employ a quarter to three.'

In pairs, try this out. Does it work?

How to write about physical expression
Look at the sample question on *Antigone*.

Antigone

1 Explain how you would perform the role of the Sentry, in each of his two appearances, in order to reveal his change in attitude from his initial fear for his own life to his relief as he brings a guilty Antigone before Creon.

(In some editions, the Sentry appears as the Soldier or Guard.)

This question does not ask you to specify your preferred audience response, although it would be a sensible approach to think about how you would wish the audience to respond first, to the **Sentry's** fear (sympathy?) and, then, to his relief (empathy?), as this will help you select your **performance methods**.

The **Sentry** appears twice, briefly, in the play. In his first appearance he has the unenviable task of informing **Creon**, the new dictatorial leader of Thebes, that, against the strict instructions of **Creon's** decree, some unknown 'criminal' has buried the body of the traitor, **Polynices**. Naturally he is more than a little nervous; he is in fear for his own life.

In his second appearance he is relieved to have caught **Antigone** attempting to rebury the rotting corpse of her brother, **Polynices**. This lets him 'off the hook', and he is evidently highly relieved. So, how might you show these contrasting emotions through physical expression?

First appearance – fear

When the **Sentry** first appears he makes a hesitant entrance, look at some of his first lines to **Creon**:

> My lord,
>
> I can't say I'm winded from running, or set out
>
> with any spring in my legs either – no sir,
>
> I was lost in thought … muttering [to myself],
>
> 'Idiot, why? You're going straight to your death'

The **Sentry** seems to be respectful of **Creon**, as well as scared. Perhaps, in terms of his use of space, he would linger by the entrance before coming directly in front of **Creon**. He is nervous and, while his movement across the stage might be slow and his gait a dawdle, his inner tempo might be racing.

> And so,
>
> mulling it over, on I trudged, dragging my feet,
>
> you can make a short road take forever …
>
> but at last, look, common sense won out,
>
> I'm here, and I'm all yours

The lines suggest that the **Sentry** is moving towards **Creon**, and that he reaches him and stops on 'I'm here and I'm all yours'. Perhaps the **Sentry** would kneel on this line. He might gesture, pointing first to himself and then to **Creon**, on 'all yours'. He might bow his head, in a humble stance to show his submission to **Creon's** will.

When **Creon** shouts at the **Sentry** to 'Come to the point!' the **Sentry** replies:

> First, myself, I've got to tell you,
>
> I didn't do it, didn't see who did –
>
> Be fair, don't take it out on me.

The repetition of the references to himself – 'myself … I … I … me' – suggests the **Sentry** struggling to justify himself. He might be gesturing towards himself again; he might be shaking at this point to show the nervous tempo; on the phrase 'I didn't do it' he might shake his head in a gesture of denial; on the phrase 'Be fair' he might hold out his arms

■ **Key terms**

Performance methods: all the various approaches that an actor may take to a role, including the use of vocal and physical skills and the modification of an actor's appearance through costume and makeup.

AQA Examiner's tip

The professional actor's own appearance cannot be considered to be a performance 'method', although it will have affected the choice of casting. However, you should always refer to your chosen appearance, for a specific role, when you are answering questions about performance in the exam.

in a pleading gesture. Throughout this first section his facial expression (emotional) will show apprehension and fear. He might use a prop, a cloth with which to mop his brow to show his nerves.

Before he leaves the stage, the **Sentry**, dismissed by **Creon** but threatened with torture and death if he does not return with the criminal, speaks briefly to the audience:

> *I hope he's found. Best thing by far.*
>
> *But caught or not, that's in the lap of fortune:*
>
> *I'll never come back, you've seen the last of me.*
>
> *I'm saved, even now, and I never thought,*
>
> *I never hoped –*
>
> *dear gods, I owe you all my thanks!*

It seems likely that his movement will be quicker here, as he is intent on escaping from **Creon's** clutches. He may shake his head in an emphatic gesture when he says he won't come back; his posture might be straighter now he sees a way out of his troubles and his exit is quick. He strides off with a purposeful gait, perhaps looking up or down, as if to the gods, with his hands in a gesture of prayer as he leaves. He has a facial expression (physical) of smiling or grinning.

Second appearance – relief

When the **Sentry** returns, bringing **Antigone** as his prisoner, his relief is very clear in his words:

> *My king ,*
>
> *there's nothing you can swear you'll never do –*
>
> *second thoughts make liars of us all.*
>
> *I could have sworn I wouldn't hurry back ... but*
>
> *back I've come, breaking my oath, who cares!*
>
> *I'm bringing in our prisoner – this young girl –*
>
> *... Now my lord,*
>
> *here she is. Take her, question her,*
>
> *cross-examine her to your heart's content.*
>
> *But set me free, it's only right –*
>
> *I'm rid of this dreadful business once for all.*

How would you employ physical expression during this speech to show the **Sentry's** relief at escaping the death penalty?

💡 🔍 *Your interaction with other characters*

Whichever character you are considering, it is important to remember that he or she does not exist in isolation.

When you look at a character from your set play with a view to writing about how you might perform the role, you should think very carefully about how to act the *relationships* your character has with the other characters both *on* and *off* stage.

Interaction involves both verbal and non-verbal communication and it is the non-verbal communication that an audience has to 'read' when your character is not speaking at all.

Activity

In pairs, act out both sequences, inventing your own physical expression of fear and relief. One of you read the lines while the other acts the role of **Sentry** in physical expression only. Then swap.

AQA Examiner's tip

Avoid writing about your character without reference to the way he or she listens and responds to other characters. Remember that your character must still be acting, even when not speaking!

How to write about interaction

When discussing interaction between characters on stage, we usually refer to:

Verbal interaction

▥ **Dialogue** – this refers to what we say to other characters and, of course, to *how* we say it. To achieve a good level of interaction on stage, you need to consider the 'lines' as being a channel of communication, both with whoever you are speaking to on stage as well as with the audience. This communication is substantially supported by an actor's use of non-verbal interaction; in other words you need to be 'acting' your lines and not merely 'delivering' them!

▥ **Subtext** – the non-verbal communication that accompanies spoken dialogue is sometimes referred to as the 'subtext', when it is used to expose deeper or opposite feelings to those expressed by the lines themselves. For example, you might be playing a character who meets a previous acquaintance in a formal situation. Your greeting of 'How nice to see you again' may be entirely sincere, or it may simply be the polite thing to say in the circumstances. Your use of non-verbal signs that accompany your delivery of the line might suggest to the audience that this is the last person on earth you wanted to see again, or they might suggest that behind the polite phrase lies a burning passion. Many naturalistic plays rely on the subtext to communicate meaning to the audience.

▥ **Pause, or silence** – subtext is sometimes communicated by the insertion of pauses within the dialogue that suggest that the speaker is lost for words or is feeling too much to actually voice his or her thoughts.

Non-verbal interaction

▥ **Spatial relationships** – you might think that characters who have close relationships with one another appear physically close on stage and that the more distant the relationship the more likely the characters are to be set apart on stage. However, this is not always the case. When two people are arguing they may get closer and closer to one another until their noses are almost touching, as their argument escalates. Alternatively, two lovers may be separated from one another by a physical barrier or other actors, but they could be desperate to touch and be physically close. However, this is often some correlation between the use of stage space and the relationship that actors are attempting to communicate; a stranger might stand at a distance from a group of established friends; rivals in love will not be keen to be close to one another; reunited family members may rush into an embrace.

▥ **Groupings** – this is another kind of spatial relationship where a character attaches him- or herself to one or other group of characters who are placed together on stage; sometimes being a part of a particular group conditions the character's behaviour.

▥ **Eye contact** – this refers to the way in which the character holds the gaze of another to whom they are speaking or listening. A character who looks directly into the eyes of another usually communicates sincerity to the audience, whether of love, friendship or respect for the person they are talking to. A character who constantly avoids eye contact, or engages and then breaks eye contact frequently usually communicates uneasiness, dishonesty or a reluctance to continue with the conversation. Other uses of the eyes to communicate relationships include:

- – a fixed gaze at another character
- – a series of secret or stolen glances (reciprocated or unreciprocated)
- – maintaining eyes downwards in modesty
- – looking over spectacles, as a gesture of superiority
- – glaring with disapproval
- – closing eyes in exasperation.

▥ **Physical contact** – this refers to how and how much a character touches other characters. There is a large spectrum of possibilities, from no contact at all to a full embrace or violent attack!

▥ **Body language** – this refers to how we use our bodies to communicate feelings. In life we can use body language consciously or unconsciously; on stage the actor must choose from a range of body language signals, for example:

- – turning away from someone unpleasant or offensive
- – taking a step forward to show interest, or backwards to show shock or disgust
- – tapping of feet or of fingers on a surface to show impatience, frustration or boredom.

▥ **Listening or watching and response** – this refers to the character's facial expressions and/or physical reactions to what other characters say or do during the unfolding action of the play. Some characters are passive; others become more fully engrossed by the action and/or words of other characters. Actors might use a combination of body language and eye contact to support their listening, watching and response.

Gremio from *The Taming of the Shrew* is an excellent example of a character who is on stage a great deal, but who has relatively few lines in each scene. He needs to communicate a great deal non-verbally about his feelings and his relationships with the other characters both on and off stage.

If you are studying the play, look in your text at Act Two, Scene One. **Gremio** is present for approximately 265 lines but he speaks only 54 of these lines. He must interact verbally with **Baptista**, **Petruchio** and **Tranio** (disguised as **Lucentio**), and must watch, first with admiration (as **Petruchio** presents his offer of marriage to **Katherina** to her father, **Baptista**) and then in amazement (when **Petruchio** claims to have won **Katherina**'s consent to marry him). Each of these responses needs to be expressed non-verbally.

At the end of the scene he reacts with respect towards **Baptista** (on stage), revealing his love towards **Bianca** (off-stage character) but with disgust and hatred when **Tranio/Lucentio** (on stage) outbids him for the hand of **Bianca**.

Remember that **Gremio** is generally interpreted as a comic character, and so his reactions might be more exaggerated than if the role were to be treated naturalistically.

Another good example of how actors need to use non-verbal communication can be found in Act One of *A Doll's House*. Here, shortly after the audience has been introduced to **Mrs Linde**, Ibsen wishes to establish a link between her and another character in the play, **Nils Krogstad**. Because Ibsen is writing in a naturalistic style, he chooses to reveal this link through **Mrs Linde's** actions, reactions and tone of voice, rather than through any direct statement on the matter. Ibsen is a master of the use of subtext.

▥ **Activity**

If *The Taming of the Shrew* is your set play, act out this sequence. If it isn't your set play, choose a similar section from your own play or improvise a situation where you must show, in quick succession, a range of emotions through non-verbal communication.

In this sequence, **Mrs Linde** has arrived to visit **Nora Helmer** in her home. The two women were once close friends but have not seen one another for nine years. **Nora** and **Mrs Linde** are talking confidentially together when the doorbell rings.

[The bell rings in the hall.]

Mrs Linde: (*gets up*) You've a visitor. Perhaps I'd better go.

Nora: No, stay. It won't be for me. It's someone for Torvald –

Maid: (*in the doorway*) Excuse me, madam, a gentleman's called who says he wants to speak to the master. But I didn't know – seeing as the doctor's with him –

Nora: Who is this gentleman?

Krogstad: (*in the doorway*) It's me, Mrs Helmer.

[*Mrs Linde starts, composes herself and turns away to the window.*]

Nora: (*takes a step towards him and whispers tensely*) You? What is it? What do you want to talk to my husband about?

Krogstad: Business, you might call it. I hold a minor post in the bank and I hear your husband is to become our new chief –

Nora: Oh – then it isn't –?

Krogstad: Pure business, Mrs Helmer. Nothing more.

Nora: Well, you'll find him in his study.

[*Nods indifferently as she closes the hall door behind him.*]

Ibsen creates a bit of mystery here about Nils Krogstad, doesn't he? Both Nora and Mrs Linde are clearly affected by his appearance and each expresses their surprise at seeing him, using non-verbal signals for the audience to pick up on. See how the subtext develops as the scene progresses; acted well, the audience will soon realise that Mrs Linde was once romantically attached to Krogstad and that she has feelings for him still.

Mrs Linde: Nora, who was that man?

Nora: A lawyer called Krogstad.

Mrs Linde: It was him, then.

Nora: Do you know that man?

Mrs Linde: I used to know him – some years ago. He was a solicitor's clerk in our town, for a while.

Nora: Yes, of course, so he was.

Mrs Linde: How he's changed!

Nora: He was very unhappily married, I believe.

Mrs Linde: Is he a widower now?

Nora: Yes, with a lot of children …

Mrs Linde: He does – various things now, I hear?

Nora: Does he? It's quite possible – I really don't know. But don't let's talk about business. It's so boring.

Activity

Try acting out this short section, using non-verbal communication, body language and pause to support or contradict your meaning and bring out the subtext for your audience.

Notice how, even in this very brief exchange between the two women, Ibsen gives the actors the means, although not the direct lines, to reveal their very different attitudes towards **Nils Krogstad**. **Nora** is clearly uninterested in him personally, while **Mrs Linde** is attempting to find out as much as she can. **Nora** blocks her at the end of the dialogue by changing the subject.

One final extract from the same scene shows Ibsen developing the audience's interest in **Mrs Linde's** true feelings for **Krogstad**. After **Nora** has introduced **Mrs Linde** to the family friend, **Dr Rank**, he begins to discuss **Nils Krogstad** with them both, unaware that **Mrs Linde** knows anything about the man.

> **Rank**: There's a moral cripple in with Helmer at this very moment –
> **Mrs Linde**: (*softly*) Oh!
> **Nora**: Whom do you mean?
> **Rank**: Oh, a lawyer fellow called Krogstad – you wouldn't know him. He's crippled all right; morally twisted …
> **Nora**: Oh? What did he want to talk to Torvald about?
> **Rank**: I haven't the faintest idea. All I heard was something about the bank.
> **Nora**: I didn't know that Krog – that this man Krogstad had any connection with the bank.
> **Rank**: Yes, he's got some kind of job down there. (*To Mrs Linde*) I wonder if in your part of the world you too have a species of creature that spends its time fussing around trying to smell out moral corruption? And when they find a case they give him some nice, comfortable position so they can keep a good watch on him. The healthy ones just have to lump it.
> **Mrs Linde**: But surely it's the sick who need care most?
> **Rank**: (*shrugs his shoulders*) Well there we have it. It's that attitude that's turning human society into a hospital.

Activity

Take it in turns to play Mrs Linde in this short section and test out your non-verbal communication skills!

How do you think **Mrs Linde** feels, hearing someone she once loved, described as a 'moral cripple'? How does the actress listen and respond in this sequence? She has to signal to the audience that she is upset or angry about **Dr Rank's** callous references to **Krogstad**, yet, at the same time hide her true feelings from both **Rank** and **Nora**.

Once again, you can see how complex a task it can be, to act convincingly, using both verbal and non-verbal communication.

💡 How to write as a performer in a non-naturalistic play

The final example is taken from *Oh! What a Lovely War*. In previous examples we have looked at how actors create realistic characters on stage, using techniques that enable them to mimic real life. An actor in *Oh! What a Lovely War*, however, has a very different task.

Oh! What a Lovely War was created collaboratively, and its purpose was to put forward an anti-war message. As a company, the original cast combined research with improvisation to present a scenario that highlighted the horrors of war. The play explores, amongst other things, the incompetence of World War One commanders, whose self-interest and general bungling led to the wholesale slaughter of soldiers and officers in protracted and apparently futile combat.

Although there are some named characters in the play, many of the roles are representative rather than specific. At one point in the play an actor might be playing **Sir John French** and, at another, a **German Businessman** and, at another, a **Soldier** and, at another, the representation of the entire nation of **America**. Remember that all the cast also appear as Pierrots throughout the play.

Multi-roling calls for different skills from those required to create a believable role in a naturalistic play. The actors must be adaptable and flexible. They must have a good range of varied vocal and physical skills. Where the naturalistic actor attempts to convince the audience of the truth of his or her performance, the multi-roler merely wishes to suggest a role and then move on to suggest another.

This does not mean that multi-roling actors do not undertake preparation or research into their roles, but that they apply this research differently. They still have to use their appearance and their vocal and physical expression to suggest the role that they are playing. However, faced with the task of playing 'America', an actor is not likely to resort to finding the subtext of the role. There is still scope for non-verbal communication, of course, which might show itself in the actor adopting a particular stance or attitude to the other 'countries' on stage and, naturally, he would need to work on his accent.

Look at the sample question below.

Oh! What a Lovely War

1 How would you want your audience to respond to Sir John French? Explain how you would perform the role in his appearance in Acts One and Two in order to achieve your aims.

This question focuses on a single character, making no mention of the fact that the actor playing **Sir John** would also be contributing to the play in a variety of other roles. Your task here, then, is to approach this single role like any of the other more conventionally written roles, as discussed above. However, bear in mind that the purpose of this play is to **parody** or **lampoon** powerful individuals like **Sir John**.

The point about multi-roleing is that some of the roles require one kind of treatment that is semi-naturalistic, whilst others require the skills of mimicry or cartoon-style acting, where the actor attempts to suggest the gist of the character rather than to create a fully rounded 'personality'.

An actor playing **Sir John French** has two main scenes in *Oh! What a Lovely War*. These are, in Act One, 'The Allies Confer', and in Act Two, 'Roses of Picardy'. If you are studying this play, re-read these scenes now and think about what response you would like to achieve from your audience.

Most suggestions will probably include fairly negative responses to **Sir John**, who is arrogant, pompous and completely self-serving. In many ways he represents everything that Littlewood and the Theatre Workshop were attacking in this play.

17 Affecting the audience

In this chapter you will learn about:

■ how audiences are affected by the choices you make as director, designer or performer.

So far we have considered how the work of each member of a production team – the director, the designers and the actors – affects the audience through the choices they make. Let's now consider how those choices, taken together, add up to the total experience that an audience has when watching a play.

When the curtain goes up at the beginning of any production, whether it is *The Taming of the Shrew* or *A Doll's House*, an intense physical theatre piece (with few words spoken), or a fantasy extravaganza, the performance that the audience sees is the result of thousands of decisions taken by the production team. All of those decisions are made with the audience in mind.

One of the *first* decisions that a director makes is selecting the most appropriate theatre venue and staging form. The director of *A Doll's House*, for example, might choose an intimate studio space to allow the audience a really close view of the disintegration of the Helmer marriage and to encourage their empathy with **Nora**.

One of the *last* decisions taken by the director of *The Taming of the Shrew*, for example, might be to rearrange the grouping of the wedding guests in the final scene, so that their reactions to **Katherina's** final speech will be more visible to the audience, who may share the same responses.

One of the *first* design decisions taken by the designer of *A Doll's House* might be to create a naturalistic set and costumes to remind the audience of its period setting. A *later* decision might be to adapt **Nora's** naturalistic costume by adding fur or feather trimmings, reminding the audience of **Torvald's** descriptions of her as a 'squirrel' or 'skylark'. A *final* design decision might be to adjust the volume of the final door slam as **Nora** abandons her husband and family, so that its effect is more shocking to the audience.

The actor playing **Minnie** in *The Shadow of a Gunman* might initially decide to adopt a flirtatious attitude to **Davoren** when she asks for her 'drop o' milk'. Later she might decide to ask more coyly to engage the sympathies of the audience.

Activity

Take a key moment from your set play, for example, the delivery of Haemon's final lines to Creon, the Auxiliary's questioning of Davoren, the Christmas truce in the trenches or Nell's first performance on stage. Think about how many choices have to be made to bring those brief sections to life.

If you alter any of the choices suggested above, the audience will experience a different play. For example, if you decide to stage *A Doll's House* behind a large proscenium arch, to dress **Nora** as a porcelain doll, performing in a setting with miniature doll's house furnishings, enclosed by three sloping walls that collapse when **Nora** finally slams the door, how would that change the way the audience is affected by the play? **Nora's** unhappiness would probably feel less real to the audience whose sympathy for her would be reduced.

Every detail that the audience sees or hears is the result of a careful decision tailored to affect their experience.

18 Preparing a blueprint for a production

In this chapter you will learn about:

- how to prepare a blueprint for a theoretical production of your set text.

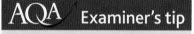

Examiner's tip

As you have been studying your set text you may have reached agreement on suitable staging strategies with the rest of your group. However, in the examination you are likely to gain more marks by offering your own individual response to the question.

Key terms

Traffic: in theatre terms, the comings and goings on stage, the stage business and action.

Examiner's tip

Beware of putting *too* much emphasis on the representative properties of colour within your costume designs in the exam. It is easy to get carried away with stereotypes, for example that black equates to evil and green to envy.

The earlier chapters of this section explored ways of interpreting your text from the point of view of the director, the designer and the actor; so by now you should have a clear idea about how you need to prepare yourself for the examination. You should return to these chapters throughout your course, to help you to answer examination-style questions that your teacher sets you as part of your practice for the AS exam.

In addition to trying out practice questions, you will find it helpful to prepare a **blueprint** for the virtual production of your set play. This should include details of staging ideas for every aspect of the production, covering every scene.

This blueprint needs to contain your personal ideas for interpretation and should give you a complete understanding of how the play will look and sound on stage, from the beginning to the end. Once you have this blueprint, you will be equipped to answer any question that might be asked about the play in the examination.

Your blueprint should contain detailed sketches for the setting design(s) for the play. Make sure that you consider any scene changes and that you have taken into account the general **traffic** of each scene. Check that you have made provision for entrances and exits and supplied any furniture or major props that are indicated in the stage directions or in the text itself.

Your design decisions should take account of the period setting of the play. (Remember to justify any decision you have made to deviate from the play's actual period setting.) Ensure that you match your designs to decisions that you have taken about your style of presentation, your chosen staging form and your intentions for the audience experience of the play.

Include sketches, or pictures, of your chosen costume designs for the principal characters. These should, of course, also reflect your chosen period and style. If you wish to achieve a realistic effect for your audience, do research carefully into the play's period when selecting authentic costume designs, fabrics and accessories, as well as appropriate colours for the characters to wear.

Supplement your design sketches with pictures or diagrams of authentic costumes and furnishings downloaded from the internet. These will support your understanding of the play and allow you to offer apt design ideas rooted in the play's original context. If you have transposed the setting of your production to an alternative period or location, you should undertake research into that alternative.

Your blueprint will include ideas that are the result of the decisions that you have taken as virtual designer for the piece, as director of the piece and as actor in the major roles.

An example for staging plans

The table below shows an example of how you might set out one strand of your overall blueprint. This table refers to staging decisions but you can adapt the formula to plan how to play a specific role in, or direct, any one scene or act.

STAGING DECISIONS: A Doll's House	ACT ONE	ACT TWO	ACT THREE
Staging form	Proscenium arch	As Act One	As Act One
Actor/audience relationship	Fourth wall in place	As Act One	As Act One
Set design	Realistic 19th-century, bourgeois living room – see Figure 18.1 Green and gold colours predominate; warm, cosy	Christmas tree standing stripped and dishevelled	Table and chairs moved centre stage
Costume design	Authentic period costume; Nora's coat is fur lined/hooded, her dress (green & gold) trimmed with fur	Nora's dress in peacock blue, trimmed with feathers	Capri fishergirl costume for Nora, replaced with solemn black dress
Lighting	Largely naturalistic	Largely naturalistic, some symbolic use of lamplight	
Sound effects	Doorbell; knock at the door	Letter falling into box	Party noises from above; knock at door The slamming of the door as Nora leaves
Necessary props	Christmas tree, macaroons, children's toys; bank notes	Stockings; costume	Letter, black-edged card from Rank
Mood and atmosphere	Initially joyous; flirtatious; more serious with Christiane	Rising tension, climbing to peak with tarantella dance	Optimistic for Krogstad; gloomy interlude with Rank Building anticipation to door slam

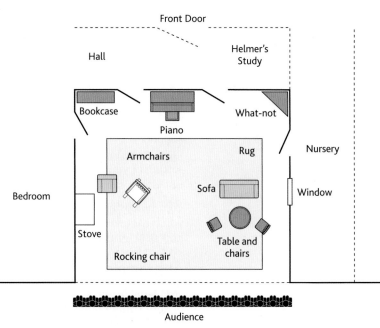

Fig. 18.1 *A sketch for staging plans of a production of* A Doll's House

Fig. 18.2 *Costume detail from* A Doll's House

How to be successful in the examination

How to write a successful answer

Whatever question is set, your answer should show that you understand how the play might work in performance. You demonstrate this through appropriate treatment of a small part of the play. Your answer should contain inventive staging ideas that will communicate meaning to a potential audience. You should also show your understanding of the period and genre of the play through the suitability of your ideas.

You gain marks for:

- creativity in your interpretation
- detail in your staging or performance ideas
- apt quotation from the text, with exact ideas for how the lines might be delivered
- consideration of how your ideas will affect the audience experience
- clear, labelled sketches to support design ideas
- equal treatment of each of the sections of the play referred to in the question
- accurate use of specialist theatre terminology
- fluency and good organisation and development of your ideas.

The following weaknesses will prevent you from gaining good marks:

- generalised statements of intention, without specific examples
- narrative answers without performance detail
- absence of clear quotation from the text to support your ideas
- ignoring or straying from the focus of the question, or only answering part of it
- ideas that are unsuited to the period setting or style of the play
- unevenness in your treatment of the sections referred to in the question
- absence of specialist terminology or inaccurate use of it
- poor expression, underdeveloped suggestions.

To gain good marks and eradicate your weaknesses get as much practice as you can at answering questions on your set text in 45 minutes.

Choosing the right question and focusing on its demands

There will be a choice of two questions on your set text. Choose the one that you feel most comfortable in answering, the one that refers to part of the play that you feel most confident about, or that asks for the perspective that you prefer writing about, whether that is a director's, a designer's or a performer's perspective.

When you have chosen a question, stick closely to its demands throughout your answer. Look at the questions below and make a note of the precise demands of each one. It doesn't matter which play features in the question. Questions like this are routinely set on all the plays.

Director's questions

Director's questions might be phrased in the following ways:

Antigone

1 What effects would you wish to create for your audience at the end of the play? Explain how you would direct the section from the entrance of Eurydice to the end of the play in order to achieve your aims.

A Doll's House

2 As a director, explain how you would stage the final section of *A Doll's House* in order to achieve your preferred effects for an audience.

(You should consider the section from Torvald's exit into his study to read his letters, in the second half of Act Three, to the end of the play.)

Playhouse Creatures

3 As a director, explain what effects you would want to create for your audience in Act One, Scene Six (Mrs Betterton's acting class) and how you would stage the scene in order to achieve your aims.

Each of these questions requires a response written in the first person and from a director's point of view.

Begin by stating the exact effects that you want to create for your audience. Then develop your answer, referring closely to the text, offering precise directions for the cast, as well as including suggestions for staging elements that will add to your intended effects.

Some questions do not allow you to select your preferred effects. These questions will demand a specific focus, for example:

Shadow of a Gunman

4 Briefly outline and justify your casting decisions for Mr Gallogher and Mrs Henderson and then explain how you would direct them in Act One of the play in order to create comedy for your audience.

Once again you need to write in the first person, from the perspective of a director, but you will need to make the creation of comedy your focus and keep that in mind, both in your casting ideas (which should be brief – no more than a paragraph for each character) and in your directions of **Mr Gallogher** and **Mrs Henderson**. You may refer to comical aspects of the characters' costume to support your ideas; however, you should not be dealing with wider staging issues, such as set or lighting.

Designer's questions

Designer's questions might be phrased in the following ways:

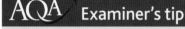

The Taming of the Shrew

5 As a designer, what effects would you want to create for your audience in Act Four, Scene One (Petruchio's homecoming with his new bride)? Explain how your set design for the scene and costume designs for **two or more** characters would achieve your aims.

Oh! What a Lovely War

6 As a designer, explain how your use of **at least two** of the following would help to create an appropriate mood and atmosphere for the opening sequence of *Oh! What a Lovely War*:
- setting design
- costume design
- lighting **and** sound design.

AQA Examiner's tip

The best answers usually begin with a concise introduction and end with a concise conclusion.

Each of these questions requires a response written in the first person and from a designer's point of view. Begin by stating the exact effects that you want to create (in the first question) and specify an appropriate mood and the atmosphere (in the second question). Then develop your answer, referring closely to the action of the given scenes, offering precise details of your designs in terms of **design fundamentals** that are directly related to achieving your stated aims.

Performer's questions

Performer's questions might be phrased in the following ways:

Antigone

1 Explain how you would perform the role of the Sentry, in each of his two appearances, in order to reveal his change of attitude from his initial fear for his own life to his relief as he brings a guilty Antigone before Creon.

A Doll's House

2 How would you perform the role of Christine Linde in Act One of the play in order to engage the sympathy of your audience?

Oh! What a Lovely War

3 How would you want your audience to respond to Sir John French? Explain how you would perform the role in his appearances in Acts One and Two in order to achieve your aims.

AQA Examiner's tip

Make sure that you use lines from the text (*not* page numbers or line numbers) to support all your practical ideas.

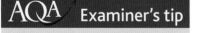

Each of these questions requires a response written in the first person and from a performer's point of view. In the first two examples, you need to keep focused on the precise demands of revealing a 'change of attitude' for the **Sentry** and engaging sympathy for **Mrs Linde**.

The third example requires you to state at the outset how you want your audience to respond to the character, then to match all your performance ideas to achieving that response.

Fig. 19.1 *Mrs Linde in* A Doll's House

■ Summary of this section

In these chapters you have learned about:

- how to interpret your set play
- the context, period and genre of your set play
- how directors interpret plays to create meaning
- how directors reach staging decisions
- how directors interpret stage directions
- how directors create mood and atmosphere on stage
- how designers contribute to the interpretation of a play
- how set designers create suitable locations or environments for the setting and action of a play
- how costume designers communicate various aspects of a character through design elements
- how technical designers contribute to the interpretation of the play
- how performers interpret their roles
- how actors prepare
- how performers condition the responses of the audience
- the vocal and physical skills of an actor
- how the choices made by the production team affect the audience
- how to prepare a blueprint for a production of the set play
- how to be successful in the examination
- where to find information about the set plays and how they have been interpreted in previous productions.

The e-resources and weblink associated with these chapters should be a continual source of inspiration as you work on your set plays.

Remember, too, that these chapters offer you practical ideas about how directors, designers and performers approach their work. This is valuable information to return to again and again, as you prepare for your written exam. You should also re-read the relevant sections when you are developing your chosen skill for the practical Unit 2, which is the subject of the next section.

2 Presentation of a play extract

20 Introduction to practical drama work

In Unit 1 you are judging live theatre and interpreting a set play, armed with the theoretical understanding of what directors, designers and actors do. In Unit 2 your work is assessed through your practical exploration of drama and theatre.

Unit 2 takes you from being a critical observer of theatre and turns you into a drama practitioner in your own right. Whatever skill you opt to be assessed in, be it directing, acting or designing, you are judged on your success in interpreting a play practically and in communicating your understanding of its meaning to an audience.

The building blocks for this unit are much the same as for Unit 1, but now you are putting into practice what you have learned about drama and theatre so far.

To help you to take this step, we ask you to find a model to follow by choosing an important practitioner, director, designer or theatre company, that has made a significant contribution to theatre, either in the past or in the present. Your teacher will guide you in your choice and provide you with the resources that you need to gain a full understanding of the work of your selected practitioner.

Although Unit 2 is not divided formally into two sections, there are, as in Unit 1, two parts to this unit. The first part relates to your study of relevant aspects of the work of your selected practitioner. This also involves your application of his, her or their ideas to the practical work that you are doing on your chosen play. The second part relates to your preparation and rehearsal of an extract from the play, leading up to its presentation for an audience.

Your teacher will help you to select an appropriate practitioner and ensure that you select a play that is compatible with the theories and/or practice of that practitioner.

Do refer back to the chapters that relate to your chosen skill as you prepare your presentation for the Unit 2 practical exam.

21 Influential practitioners

In this chapter you will learn about:

■ what is meant by 'influential practitioner'

■ how your chosen practitioner should influence your practical work.

What do we mean by an 'influential practitioner'?

This chapter looks at the examination requirement that, for Unit 2, the presentation of an extract from your chosen play should be evidently influenced by the ideas, theories and/or working practices of a recognised 'influential practitioner'.

Everyone involved in the creation of theatre is a practitioner. However, the word 'influential' defines people who have had a far-reaching effect on theatre in general. Their experimentation and/or theoretical writings have enriched and changed theatre; their efforts have inspired others and enlarged the scope of theatrical work, nationally or internationally. Perhaps, one day, you may become an influential practitioner yourself; but first, you need to understand the work and influences of others.

Theatre exists in an enormous number of forms. Both from your own experience and from the earlier chapters, you will be aware of the variety of styles and approaches that make up modern theatre.

Theatrical style does not simply emerge ready formed. Each recognisable historical or contemporary theatre style, however apparently radical, is the result of the experiment and vision of groups of like-minded people, sometimes led by one individual and sometimes working completely democratically. The practical exploration, descriptions and definitions of the theatrical work undertaken by innovators, throughout the ages, has profoundly affected the way theatre is presented.

In preparing for your practical exam you need to select one of these influential practitioners to help you shape your work. The research that you do and the way that you apply it will help you to achieve the following results:

■ You will extend your knowledge and understanding of drama and theatre and of your chosen practitioner's particular contribution to it.

■ You will give a unified style to your own performance piece.

■ You will appreciate the relationship between theory and practice in drama.

The following headings and categories, taken from the specification, outline what you need to know about your chosen practitioner. They are intended to guide you to focus on the features of your chosen practitioner that have been particularly influential.

They are arranged, for ease of reference, under six main headings, *all* of which you should consider when applying your chosen practitioner's ideas to your selected play. However, not all of the aspects in the *subheadings* will necessarily be relevant to your chosen practitioner or play.

1 Theories and approaches to creating productions

The theatrical and historical context

Every age produces individuals who challenge the theatrical conventions of the day and take theatre forward in some way.

These individuals include architects who have modified theatre spaces and playwrights who have experimented with dramatic style or content, as well as practitioners whose individual approach to communicating meaning to an audience has altered their experience of theatre.

Developing theatrical purpose

Practitioners rarely make changes to the theatre of their day without good reason. All practitioners have different theatrical aims and ambitions; you need to identify the motivating force of your selected practitioner.

Earlier practitioners of theatre, such as the Greeks and the performers in the Medieval Miracle plays, for example, had a religious purpose. Some drama of the late 19th century had a moral purpose. Contemporary theatre is multi-faceted and some practitioners intend to instruct, others to delight and inspire and others simply to entertain.

Once you have chosen your practitioner, you will need to adhere to his or her theatrical purpose, both in your choice of play and in its treatment.

Fig. 21.1 *Artaud as a young man. His key theories appear in his text,* The Theatre and its Double

Fig. 21.2 Complicité's *production* of A Minute Too Late, *2005*

Who's who

Konstantin Stanislavski (1863–1938) has had a colossal influence on the style of acting in modern theatre and his approach and ideas can be applied to many contemporary, **naturalistic** dramas as well as to the plays of Chekhov and Ibsen.

Antonin Artaud (1896–1948) reacted against bourgeois theatre, wanting to present the violent, repressed side of human nature on stage. His own productions were few, but the works of playwrights such as Sarah Kane as well as some dark, Jacobean tragedies, offer good opportunities to display his theories in practice.

Who's who

Bertolt Brecht (1898–1956) was a practitioner whose reputation rests on the socialist political impulse at the heart of his work. A significant playwright as well as a theatre director and theorist, he wrote extensively about his aims and developed theatrical theories for the creation of an 'epic theatre' style.

A major company such as **Complicité**, led by **Simon McBurney**, will be constantly evolving its working style. The company describe themselves as more than theatre, rather a 'state of mind', but their emphasis is on a collaborative approach both to devising and interpreting text. For further information online, see the e-resources.

The innovative nature of the approach

🗊 Theatre is constantly changing. Although the basic ingredients that make up a performance – the actors, the set, the costumes, even masks and puppets – do not change, the way in which these ingredients are mixed, does. Any one of the elements of a theatrical presentation can be treated in a significantly different way. Influential practitioners are influential because they are *innovators*.

You will need to identify what makes your chosen practitioner an innovator.

Theory and practice

Throughout this chapter there is brief reference to a variety of very different theatrical practitioners, but what unites them is that they have each written about his or her own work. If you choose a practitioner who has also written about their theatrical purpose and practice, you will have a ready resource to refer to.

Stanislavski's books, *An Actor Prepares* and *Building a Character*, changed the way that actors thought about their craft. **Augusto Boal** defined his work in community theatre and gave the lead to a number of disciples in his influential book, *Theatre of the Oppressed*.

Contemporary directors such as Peter Hall and practitioners such as Steven Berkoff have also written books about their craft; much of Berkoff's work is also available on DVD.

Find out how much information about your chosen practitioner's ideas you can easily access before you embark on your practical exploration.

2 Ideals, intentions for the audience and theatrical style

Artistic ideals

Above all, practitioners are working towards complex artistic ideals that need to be identified and defined in order for you to be able to understand them and to engage with them in your own work.

The text chosen, the style of acting advocated, the relative importance paid to design; all these aspects combine to create a piece of theatre that fulfils the practitioner's aims.

Almost all practitioners who spend a lifetime in the theatre experience shifts in their artistic ideals. Brecht's practice took him from producing *lehrstuck* or 'learning plays' that were **didactic** in intention to his famous, later, 'parable plays' that he labelled **dialectic** in approach.

Stanislavski's writings reveal a shift in his emphasis, within actor preparation, from a 'psycho-technique' to a 'method of physical action'.

Peter Brook's approach to theatre has changed so much over the decades that the elaborate theatricality of his productions of his early career and the extreme economy of those directed recently almost appear to be the work of two different practitioners (see the e-resources for more information).

Target audience

Some practitioners create theatre for a specific age group, others intend to appeal to (or scandalise) a particular social or even economic group.

▰ The names of theatre companies can give you a clue about the audience they are targeting. 'Shared Experience' is a name that suggests a particular relationship will be established with the audience. The name 'Forkbeard Fantasy' suggests the audience should be prepared to be surprised by the work they are about to see, while 'Kneehigh' promises informality as a hallmark of their work and audiences should be prepared for this.

Know your practitioner's target audience and shape your piece accordingly.

Intentions for the audience

One of the most important decisions for any company to make is to define what their intention is for an audience. Without such a definition the focus and clarity of the work is not achieved. Whether they want to tell a story in such a way that it will entrance an audience or challenge their thinking on a particular issue, the intention is all important. Once you have identified the intentions that your chosen practitioner had for the audience you will need to embrace them yourself.

Artaud assaulted his audience with loud noises and bright lights; through invading their space he intended to jolt them out of being merely passive observers.

Bertolt Brecht intended to distance his audience from the characters in his plays, thereby helping them to think objectively about the content and themes and to be ready to learn lessons from the past.

Political aims

The potential power of theatre often leads practitioners to use it a political tool. In response, political dictators through the ages have often taken control of, or censored, theatre, or even banned it altogether.

Agitprop is the name given to a form of theatre which makes no attempt to present a balanced view of the issues it presents: it is **propaganda**.

Contemporary practitioners, who wish to present a political viewpoint, generally recognise that a more balanced approach is most effective in influencing modern audiences.

In 1968 Peter Brook used an ensemble group to devise a piece of theatre, titled *US*, to expose the horrors of the Vietnam war.

▰ More recently, Max Stafford-Clark and the Out of Joint theatre company have collaborated with writers to produce **verbatim theatre**. David Hare wrote *The Permanent Way* for the company, a play dealing with the consequences of the privatisation of the railways and the subsequent major train crashes. *Talking to Terrorists* by Robin Soans was the product of hundreds of interviews with people who have been involved in some way with terrorist organisations.

If you have chosen a practitioner whose work includes a political impulse, make sure you choose a suitable play and do thorough research into the issues it deals with.

Theatrical Style

Some practitioners seem to create their own style of theatre, for example Artaud created the **'theatre of cruelty'** style. Others apply their unique approach to established styles of theatre in order to illuminate it, or occasionally, subvert it.

> ### ■ Think
>
> Other dictators have used literature and drama as their own form of propaganda, ensuring that their regime and personal ideals receive a favourable depiction in the Arts. Can you think of a powerful historical political leader who did this?

i Who's who

For a physical theatre group such as **DV8**, the style relies on the extremes of physicality. Their aim is to break the barrier between dance and theatre.

You will need to identify the style of theatre created by or favoured by your chosen practitioner and choose a play that is appropriate to that style.

Fig. 21.3 *DV8, The Cost of Living, UK staged performance, 2003*

▨ The director's role

Attitudes towards the role of the director

Practitioners often have contrasting attitudes towards the role of the director. For example, sharp contrast can be seen between the writings and practice of Edward Gordon Craig and the work of Joan Littlewood. Craig saw the director as the person who had total control of every aspect of the performance, insisting that actors performed exactly the moves he had devised. He also carried out much of the design work himself. Joan Littlewood, on the other hand, set up the Theatre Workshop for actors to work together as an ensemble, 'a place where people could act happily'.

Whichever practitioner you choose, however, you must ensure that you do not leave all the decisions up to an autocratic director!

Working methods

Most practitioners who write about their work will also define their working methods as well as their aims for affecting the audience. Working methods vary so much from practitioner to practitioner that it is isn't really helpful to give examples. Designers, directors and companies are bound to have little in common as they work on their projects.

Make sure that you research your chosen practitioner's working methods carefully as you will be adopting at least some of them as you prepare your extract for performance.

▨ Background information

Most influential practitioners have written about their working methods; Max Stafford-Clark's books, *Letters to George* and *Taking Stock* present fascinating accounts of his own work. Jerzy Grotowski's book *Towards a Poor Theatre* sets out his methods for creating a theatrical 'laboratory' for experiment.

4 The actor's role

Attitudes towards the role of the performer

A practitioner's approach to the performer's role is very much linked to 'attitudes towards the role of the director'. The position of an actor within an acting company is a very varied one and practitioners see the actor in many different ways.

Whatever practitioner you choose, you will need to identify the place of the performer within his or her theatrical vision. You will need to consider whether or not your practitioner requires the actors to appear to *become* their characters, as Stanislavski advocated, or merely to *demonstrate* them, as Brecht required.

If Berkoff is your chosen practitioner you will find that the actors need to develop a very physical, expressionist style. The physical skills of the performers will be tested further if you are influenced by Frantic Assembly or DV8. The influence of Peter Hall will demand an intelligent and clear delivery of text.

Here the specification requirement that you work as a collaborative group will also affect the role of the performer within your practical piece since, as mentioned above, student actors should never relinquish their rights to contribute to the interpretative process.

Fig. 21.4 *Berkoff's* Metamorphosis, *1988*

■ Theatre trivia

Groundlings were the audience members who paid a penny to stand on the bare ground in front of the stage in Elizabethan times; the cheapest place from which to watch the play. During the height of the summer the groundlings were also referred to as 'stinkards' for obvious reasons

Ideas about the actor-audience relationship

Whatever the performance, practitioners recognise that their work is incomplete until an audience is present. What they expect of the audience, whether it be quiet, disciplined attentiveness or audible, vociferous responses, is one of the hallmarks of individual practitioners.

Peter Brook spent three years with a company touring the world in order to learn about the nature of the actor-audience relationship. He took a group of actors into African villages and performed to people who had never seen theatre before.

The company simply arrived at a village and unrolled a carpet – the stage – and began to improvise a performance. The intuitive and natural response the actors received was more satisfying than the formal responses when work was presented to more 'sophisticated' audiences.

In a theatre such as the reconstructed Globe in London, the relationship between the actors with those who paid the least and who are standing around the stage is often the most exciting.

Remember you need to be aware of and plan for the type of response that your chosen practitioner intended.

Ideas about actor training

Learning about a practitioner's ideas on actor training can be helpful in suggesting ways you might prepare yourself for your practical exam, although you will not have the time to experience the type of intense, lengthy training that practitioners such as Stanislavski advocated.

5 Design issues

Attitudes towards the significance of design elements

Again, different practitioners have different attitudes towards the significance of design within their productions. While some, like Stanislavski, favour a **naturalistic** approach to setting and costume, others prefer their productions to be more **universal** in their design; some advocate **symbolism**, **functional representation** or suggestion.

Whether or not your group includes a design student, make sure that the overall look of your piece is in keeping with your practitioner's style of theatre.

The sketch in Fig. 21.5 is for a play called *The Dawn*, which is set in the trenches during the First World War. The central section, stretching towards the audience, is made up of trenchcoats, symbolising the men who have died.

The design above by Ralph Koltai for *The House of Bernarda Alba*, by Garcia Lorca, is deceptively simple but it manages to suggest the Spanish setting by its general design and to evoke an appropriate sense of entrapment by the use of the metal grilles.

Fig. 21.5 The Dawn

Fig. 21.6 The House of Bernarda Alba *by Garcia Lorca*

Ideas about theatre form and configuration

The change in theatre form through the centuries has had a profound effect on the nature of the theatrical experience and these changes are ongoing. Some practitioners envisage theatre taking place in one particular style of theatre and use the same configuration within that space. Others explore the influence of the theatre form on the nature of the theatre experience, and the development of promenade productions and site-specific theatre extend theatrical possibilities even further.

Artaud's idea was to have the audience in the middle of the space, with the actors surrounding them and invading their space. One of Brecht's ideas was to stage a production in a boxing ring, forcing the audience to be more interactive, like a crowd at a sporting event.

Make sure you choose a stage configuration in keeping with your chosen practitioner's ideas.

6 Projects, collaborators and influences

Productions and projects

Make sure that you are familiar with the productions and projects of your chosen practitioner. This is vital information that will guide you in your choice of a suitable play to perform.

Collaboration with others

Theatre is a group activity, however individual a particular practitioner's ideas may appear. Many directors work with a designer whose theories and style are compatible with their own, and the collaboration between certain directors and playwrights has resulted in exciting work.

Find out if your chosen practitioner has collaborated with another significant theatre artist to see how that might have affected their theatrical style.

Influence upon other practitioners

The whole artistic world of theatre is a source of constant cross-fertilisation of ideas.

Contemporary practitioners often pay homage to earlier practitioners in their own work. Sometimes they copy them, but more often they change or embellish what they admire.

Brecht was influenced by Erwin Piscator, a fellow exponent of political theatre, as well as by aspects of artists as strikingly different as Charlie Chaplin and a Chinese actor called Méi Lán-fang.

Peter Brook acknowledges how he has been influenced by a range of theatre styles and practitioners including Brecht, Artaud and Grotowski.

Katie Mitchell, one of the most innovative and individual directors of the present day, names Simon McBurney of Complicite as well as the dance choreography of **Pina Bausch** as two of her major influences.

Contemporary companies also have trademark styles, yet seem to owe their existence to any number of earlier companies. There are many practitioners who will nominate Peter Brook or Katie Mitchell as their own influence.

Get a sense of the place of your chosen practitioner within the intricate web of theatre practice.

Who's who

Pina Bausch (1940–) a German choreographer whose work is profoundly moving and yet sometimes also amusing.

Choosing a play

- how to make a purposeful choice of text.

AQA **Examiner's tip**

Your practical unit is worth 40 per cent of your AS grade. Make sure you make the right choice: one that gives all group members the opportunity to do justice to their skills.

Making a choice

For this unit you need to choose a play which offers you the right kind of opportunities in rehearsal and in performance. The play needs to be one that you can present in a style consistent with the ideas and practice of your chosen practitioner.

You will need to bear in mind the composition of your group; whether or not you have a director; how many designers you have; how many actors you have to find parts for and the gender mix of the group. These practical issues should be considered alongside your selection of practitioner and play.

Specification requirements

Before you make a choice of play, make sure you understand the specification requirements about period and genre.

One of the requirements of the specification is that your practical piece extends your theatrical knowledge, so you may not choose a play similar in genre or period to the set play you are studying for Unit 1.

Look at the grid below. Find the play you are studying and take careful note of the types of plays that are not available to you.

Play studied for Unit 1	Candidates must <u>not</u> choose
Antigone c. 441 BC	Genre: Greek tragedy Period: 5th century BC
The Taming of the Shrew early 1590s	Genre: Elizabethan comedy Period: 1558–1603
A Doll's House 1879	Genre: Late 19th-century naturalism Period: 1865–1905
The Shadow of a Gunman 1923	Genre: Irish tragi-comedy Period: Early 20th century 1900–1939
Oh! What a Lovely War 1963	Genre: Ensemble play with songs Period: Mid-20th century 1940–1970
Playhouse Creatures 1993	Genre: Historicised play Period: 1970–2000

This means that, if you are studying *A Doll's House*, for example, you may not choose to perform a naturalistic play from the late 19th century.

If you particularly enjoyed your set play, this may be a disappointment, but remember:

- there are thousands of plays that *are* still available to you
- you may find another category you enjoy even more.

▓ Choosing a play and a practitioner

It is likely that your teacher will either make the selection of practitioner for you, or will help you to select a suitable practitioner and suggest a range of appropriate plays for you to choose from.

Alternatively, your teacher might ask you to find a play that you and your group are interested in and then recommend a practitioner whose ideas might be applied to your exploration and presentation of it.

If your teacher gives your group a free choice of both practitioner and play, you will need to do a lot of careful research before committing yourself to either. You will need to look back over the earlier chapters in this book; if possible, follow up web-quests in the e-resources and read what you can in your school or college drama library to make sure that you choose the right combination for your group.

In the previous chapter there are explanations of how different practitioners' work varies. Make a list of the aspects of their work which you find most appealing. You will find this helpful as a starting point when searching for an appropriate text.

The more plays you know the better placed you will be to make a good choice. Although there is much flexibility in the way that some texts can be presented, not *all* plays lend themselves to *all* styles. You must seek advice from your teacher about the appropriateness of your selection.

The presentational style of a play is determined largely by its original style, by the intentions of the playwright, and by the linguistic features of the dialogue. You should also consider the themes and content of the play, as well as the design demands that you will have to accommodate before making your final choice.

Outlined below is some practical advice about ways in which you might find a suitable play.

Where to find plays to read

▓ School and public libraries usually have a good range of play texts, and in some areas of the country there are dedicated specialist music and drama libraries. (One of the advantages of these libraries is that you may be able to borrow a complete set of plays to rehearse with.)

▓ Book shops usually stock a variety of plays, and there are also specialist bookshops, such as French's Theatre Bookshop in London.

▓ Shops in theatres themselves often have well stocked supplies of plays, and many sell cheap copies of the text of a play being performed in the form of a programme.

Note that many texts have a clear definition of their content and style on the back cover; a quick read-through of the blurb will help you to eliminate some plays immediately.

Seeing the play performed

When you go to see a performance you will be able to identify the style of the play and determine whether or not the play (or one by the same playwright) might suit your preferred practitioner's ideas.

▓ The company performing the play may define their aims and influences, either in the advertising material or in the programme for the show.

■ You may see a play, a playwright or a style of performance which is new to you and which appeals to you. Ask yourself if it is suitable as a vehicle for the ideas of your chosen practitioner.

■ Videos and DVDs of stage performances are becoming increasingly available. A growing number of companies are choosing to record their performances – although some, as a matter of principle, do not. Such recordings will show you a particular style very clearly and allow you to view the techniques employed in more precise detail.

Searching the internet

There is an enormous amount of relevant material to be found on the internet, and the briefest of searches will help you to locate examples of plays, clips of performances and discussions with the practitioners.

■ The websites of major theatre companies such as Kneehigh, Cheek by Jowl and Shared Experience will give you examples of the plays they have performed in the past, and of productions they are currently touring or rehearsing. For example, Kneehigh create their own texts, which are published, and Cheek by Jowl offers podcasts discussing their work and short video clips of performances.

■ There are websites that provide lists of plays (see e-resources). On some of these you can enter the number of male and female characters you are looking for and find lists of matches. Do remember that these sites are not there to make your choice for you, only to give you a starting point.

Do use the internet with care because although there are complete plays published on the net, you must choose a play published in text form. The specification expressly *prohibits* plays which are only published on the internet.

This search for a play may appear quite a daunting task, but try to see it as a positive exercise and a way in which to extend your knowledge of drama. Share the effort between the members of the group, so that you can initially view a wide range of plays and the group gets used to sharing responsibility.

When you have made a short list of plays that fit your agreed criteria, you are then ready to start to experiment and explore and, finally, to make a definite decision.

The selection of a suitable play and appropriate practitioner(s) is a long process, but time spent now cannot be skimped and the right choice will make the next stage of the preparation much easier and more satisfying.

AQA Examiner's tip

Ensure you concentrate on the stage and not the film version of a play. When filmed, plays sometimes lose the theatrical qualities of the original.

■ Activity

Each member of the group should read two plays during a set time. Then share your opinions. Each of you should give a presentation to the rest of the group, highlighting the opportunities and challenges that the plays offer. Remember to focus on the suitability of text to practitioner.

23 Case studies

This chapter looks at the distinct approaches to theatre adopted by Konstantin Stanislavski, Steven Berkoff and the Kneehigh theatre company. You may be inspired to adopt one of these practitioners to inform your own work but remember there are many other suitable individuals and companies to choose from. Your teacher will be able to advise you of other choices, including those listed in the specification.

In the analysis below, the headings listed in Chapter 21 are used to identify the key features of each practitioner.

■ Konstantin Stanislavski

Konstantin Stanislavski (1863–1938) was a Russian actor, director and theorist, whose life's work was dedicated to helping actors to create realistic characters on stage.

Theories and approaches to creating productions

Stanislavski said, 'To play a part means to transfer to the stage the life of the human spirit.' He worked hard to explain to actors how they might achieve this. He wrote a series of books which outlined a system for actors to adopt in order to create, what he termed, 'truth' on stage. His influence on acting styles of the 20th and 21st century has been immense.

If you choose Stanislavski as your practitioner you will need to familiarise yourself with his books, *An Actor Prepares*, *Building a Character* and *Creating a Role*. Stanislavski intended the ideas in these books to be used during an extensive rehearsal period. As a student, you will need to be selective, employing only the techniques that are of value to the rehearsal process, to your chosen play and to your character in particular. Nevertheless, you must ensure that you allow yourselves enough time to do justice to his rehearsal methods.

Ideals, intentions for the audience and theatrical style

Stanislavski's ideal was for the actors to present 'a slice of life' on stage. He believed this could be achieved by the actors' understanding of the play and of its **subtext** creating a meaning for the audience that they could not gain simply by reading the play for themselves.

Stanislavski asked his actors to imagine that the audience were viewing the action as if through an invisible 'fourth wall' and to act as if the audience were not there at all. He felt this would give the audience an illusion of reality unfolding before them. He believed that any **direct address** to the audience broke that illusion.

If you choose Stanislavski as your practitioner, choose a play that lends itself to a naturalistic style and aim for truth in your acting. Belief in your characters and the situation they are experiencing is essential for both you as performers and for the audience.

■ Further reading

There are a number of guides to Stanislavski's key ideas, including *The Complete Stanislavski Toolkit*, by Bella Merlin (Nick Hern, 2007).

The director's role

Stanislavski saw the director as having total control of the performance and he expected absolute discipline and concentration from the actors. He believed that individual actors were not as important as the artistic whole of the production. Above all, he believed that the writer's intentions must be honoured.

Fig. 23.1 *Stanislavski surrounded by the cast of* The Seagull *and Chekhov and Olga Knipper*

Stanislavski believed that the director should establish the **super-objective** of the play, which defined the overall purpose of the production. He advised dividing the text into small units, each with its own objective, and rehearsing each unit intensively on its own before playing them in sequence to achieve the super-objective. He believed that this approach helped the audience to follow the shape of the whole play, recognising its themes, **motifs** and intentions.

If you choose Stanislavski as your practitioner, remember the group ethic of the exam and adopt a more democratic approach to defining your objectives.

The actor's role

Stanislavski's system for actors was extensive and complex. If you are using Stanislavski as your practitioner you will need to be familiar with all his ideas in order to select and apply those most appropriate to your needs.

Some of his key ideas are listed below.

- The need for an actor to master relaxation and breathing techniques.
- The need for an actor to understand the 'given circumstances' of the play, including its period, setting and background to the events depicted.
- The need for an actor to creates emotions from 'emotion memory' (his or her own emotional experiences).

- The need for an actor to use his/her imagination and the 'magic if' – a term to describe a method for actors to perform *as if* their circumstances were true.
- The need for actors to establish variation in the pace of their playing, creating individual 'tempo rhythms'.
- The need for actors to attain complete concentration on stage through establishing 'circles of attention'.

Design issues

Stanislavski wanted total authenticity in all aspects of a production, including the set and the costumes. He insisted that the décor used in his sets and the designs and fabrics used in the costumes were historically accurate to the location and period setting of the play.

The use of detailed sound effects was also crucial in his productions in aiding the actors' belief in the scenes.

Think

When Stanislavski was directing *Othello*, a play that is partly set in Venice, he travelled to Venice to acquire authentic fabrics. How far are you prepared to go to provide authentic props and costumes for your production?

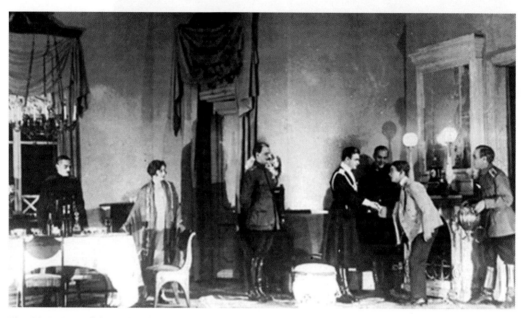

Fig. 23.2 Days of the Turbins *by Mikhail Bulgakov, staged 1926 by the Moscow Art Theatre*

Although you will be working with restricted budget, venue, and timescale, you should at least recognise Stanislavski's ideal. You might choose **end-on** staging and give some indication of the appropriate period and location in your choice and style of costume and props.

Projects, collaborators and influences

With Nemirovich-Danchenko, Stanislavski founded the Moscow Art Theatre, where he put his ideas into practice and continued his experimentation. His style of direction was particularly suited to the work of Chekhov. Stanislavski's production of *The Seagull* (1898) helped to establish the reputation of the Art Theatre and of Chekhov himself.

If you are choosing Stanislavski as your practitioner you will find a great deal of material about his projects in theatre history books as well as on the internet. You can apply Stanislavski's approach to a wide range of **naturalistic** drama.

Fig. 23.3 *The RSC production of* The Seagull *in 2007*

Steven Berkoff

Steven Berkoff was born in the East End of London in 1937. He is a director, writer and actor whose work is extremely individual and creative in style. His dramatised adaptations of novels and short stories as well as his original plays are readily available and several of his productions are available on DVD.

Theories and approaches to creating productions

Steven Berkoff trained in mime at **Lecoq** in Paris. He rejected the British theatre of his day as being outdated and obsessed with realistic plots and naturalistic acting styles. He saw himself as being part of a European theatre tradition rather than of an English one.

Berkoff names Artaud, Brecht and Grotowski as some of the people who had the greatest influence on his work, as well two English actors, Edmund Kean (1789–1833) and Lawrence Olivier (1907–1989), both of whom were known for a heightened style of acting. He was also inspired by the French **mime**, Jean-Louis Barrault (1910–1994) who promoted the importance of mime, movement, mask and ensemble work in the theatre.

Berkoff believes in the importance of the whole body and of ritualistic movement, which he combines with an emphasis on violent and challenging themes and material.

Who's who

Jacques Lecoq (1921–99): born in Paris in 1921, Lecoq was a leading exponent of mime and physical theatre in the twentieth century. His theatre school, based in Paris, was devoted to the teaching of mime and other physical theatre skills. Contemporary practitioners including Berkoff and Complicite have been profoundly influenced by Lecoq's teachings.

Reading Berkoff's comments on his own style of work and watching videos of his productions, such as *The Trial*, *Salome* and *East* will give you detailed knowledge and understanding of both the theory and practice of his ideas.

Ideals, intentions for the audience and theatrical style

Berkoff creates powerful effects by combining challenging and often controversial material with a very poetic style of language and a ritualistic style of performance. The term 'Total Theatre', which he applies to his work, defines both the style of presentation and the effect he wishes to have on the audience.

Both in his own writing and in the plays he chooses to direct, Berkoff achieves an almost musical and lyrical quality. In his production of *Salome*, for example, the piece is played in slow motion for most of the time, an idea he has adopted from its use in film to focus on a moment.

A play such as *Metamorphosis* offers opportunity to explore the most accessible aspects of his style. If you watch *Salome* you see just how demanding Berkoff's style can become; his own performance as Herod is brilliant and riveting, but it is not a technique to be easily mastered at AS level.

The director's role

Berkoff is a director with strong political and social ideals who believes in the supremacy of the role of the director. He wants to create an ensemble acting group yet within an autocratic vision.

Early in his career, Berkoff ran workshops teaching mime techniques. This was a way of finding actors with the skills and attitudes he required. He set up his own company, The London Theatre Group, in the late 1960s, ensuring that his actors accepted his individual style of direction and his demanding standards.

Uniformity of style is one of the outstanding qualities of Berkoff's work: in *The Trial* and *Salome* the majority of the actors form a kind of chorus, working together, peopling the play, even at times becoming physical embodiments of the props. The traditional role of the chorus within a play goes back to Greek times, but Berkoff has adapted and enlarged the technique.

The autocratic director is not acceptable for the AS examination; the ensemble nature of the work *is*. If you choose to follow Berkoff's techniques and approaches you will need to create a vision as strong as Berkoff's, without having one dominant authority in control.

The actor's role

When describing the style of his own work Berkoff says that everything is focused on the actor's body and voice. He says he wants to return the 'art of acting to the actor', ensuring that they remain the focus.

The sense of group identity is clear in most of Berkoff's work. In his play, *East*, the five actors create moments of physical ingenuity. The characters visit a fairground at one point and the actors mime their ride on the carousel, the dodgems, the big dipper and the ghost train with absolute clarity.

Versatility and creativity are acting skills required in all his plays; in *Salome* the beheading of John the Baptist makes a ghastly moment, while in *East* an actor 'becomes' a motorbike, complete with sound effects. In *Metamorphosis*, the actor playing Gregor must have the skills of a gymnast to perform the role, spent almost entirely climbing up, or hanging from, the bars of a large cage.

If you choose Berkoff as your practitioner you will face great challenges but also enormous opportunities. You will need to invest time in developing mime techniques. Clarity and precision are vital if you are to capture the essence of Berkoff's style.

Design issues

Berkoff refers to utter simplicity of design when describing his productions and yet his style is very distinctive. It is achieved with great economy but what *is* used is extremely effective.

Berkoff has said that too many lights and too many props destroy effective theatre, yet he does use lighting to suggest venue in his plays. In *East*, although the actors mime most of the props, they do assemble round a kitchen table and have to consume vast quantities of real food on stage.

White face makeup is another frequent feature of Berkoff's work, giving the face a mask-like quality. The costumes used in *The Trial* are individual in design but the uniformity and ensemble quality is created by using only black-and-white garments.

Music is used extensively in Berkoff's productions to give 'texture' to moments, to change the mood, to enhance the style of the language and to bring out the themes. It is also used to enliven the transitions from one scene to another.

If you choose Berkoff as your practitioner, you will need to ensure the design elements support the visual unity of your piece. If you offer a design skill to complement the performance you will have plenty of opportunities to be imaginative and creative, but bear in mind Berkoff's belief in economy of expression.

Fig. 23.4 *Galway Youth Theatre*, The Trial, *2004*

██ Further reading

Free Association: an Autobiography, by Steven Berkoff (Faber & Faber, 1996).

Collected plays

- ▨ *The Trial / Metamorphosis / In the Penal Colony: Three Theatre Adaptations from Franz Kafka*, by Franz Kafka and Steven Berkoff (Amber Lane Press, 1988).

- ▨ *Steven Berkoff Plays 1* (Faber and Faber, 1994)

- ▨ *Steven Berkoff and the Theatre of Self-Performance* by Robert Cross (Manchester University Press, 2004).

DVDs and videos

- ▨ *The Trial*, directed and adapted by Steven Berkoff

- ▨ *East*, written and directed by Steven Berkoff

- ▨ *Salome*, written by Oscar Wilde, directed by Steven Berkoff

- ▨ *East End through the Ages*, documentary presented by Steven Berkoff.

Projects, collaborators and influences

Berkoff is probably best known for his adaptations of Franz Kafka, in particular *Metamorphosis*. Robert Cross in his book, *Steven Berkoff and the Theatre of Self-Performance*, comments that Berkoff is often ignored in books about the theatre. One explanation he offers for this is Berkoff's originality, making his work hard to classify and categorise.

If you opt to use Berkoff as your practitioner, do give serious thought to the skills necessary for achieving success. You would be wise to choose one of Berkoff's own plays to present.

██ Kneehigh

Kneehigh are an innovative company, founded in Cornwall in 1980. They are a touring company, so there are frequent opportunities to see their work live with good media coverage about new projects and developments.

Theories and approaches to creating productions

Kneehigh's style of theatre has been described as 'joyful anarchy'. Their high reputation is based on the creative, innovative quality of their work. Emma Rice, their artistic director, explains her approach to theatre: 'For me, making theatre is an excavation of feelings long since buried, a journey of understanding.'

The company are a storytelling group who approach the fairy tale, not as a childish, improbable, or trivial story but as a surreal account of an aspect of life. For Kneehigh, folk tales reveal a dark core, uncovering universal truths and emotions; helping 'children' (of whatever age) to come to terms with the painful side of being human. Their work is collaborative and no production element is more important than another.

If you choose Kneehigh as your practitioner, you will find that their approach to storytelling can be applied to a wide range of plays. Remember, however that you must be using a playscript and not devising your own drama around a fairy story. The texts of Kneehigh's own productions are available.

Ideals, intentions for the audience and theatrical style

Audience response is at the heart of Kneehigh's productions. They don't just want a responsive audience, they want what they describe as a 'collaboration between actor and audience'.

They have achieved this in many different ways in their recent productions. For example, in *Tristan and Yseult* a chorus of 'lovespotters' observed the audience as they arrived, they then moved around the auditorium asking questions of individual members of the audience and writing down their replies in their notebooks.

The programme for the play contained 'Love Hearts' sweets for the audience, as well as balloons that the audience were invited to blow up and then release, to rocket around the theatre during the wedding celebration scene.

When it was time for the interval, a member of the cast told the audience to 'take a break!'

If Kneehigh is your chosen practitioner it is vital to plan your interaction with the audience carefully. Audiences vary in their responses, and the day of an examination can have an inhibiting effect. You need to rehearse how and when you are to use the audience and how you will cope if the response is unexpected.

The director's role

Kneehigh work as an ensemble and, although there is a designated director, the creation of the piece comes from the improvisation and creative exploration of the group as a whole. Bonding exercises and improvisation are at the heart of the creative process, encouraging a relaxed and productive working ethos. These exercises are not used solely as warm-up exercises but are designed to bring out the deep emotions of the cast as well as to enhance the humour.

The team as a whole undertake two different forms of research:

- the general research, relating to the topics within the piece
- personal research, finding material which directly relates to their own experiences of the theme.

Not all ideas explored in rehearsal are used in the final piece. A directorial judgement has to be made. In *Tristan and Yseult* a group of characters, known as the Unloved, appear dressed in anoraks, carrying binoculars and notepads, but until two weeks before the play opened they were represented as angels!

The idea of a group who can work together to produce a coherent style and who are not afraid to experiment, to take chances and eventually to change or reject ideas is a very useful model for you as a practical group.

Fig. 23.5 *Unloved characters in the Kneehigh production of* Tristan and Yseult, *2006*

The actor's role

For Kneehigh, the actor's role is a collaborative one. As part of the work on characterisation, for example, all the actors are invited to write on a large piece of paper any words that seem apt in relation to all or any of the characters. Each actor then selects the three most useful words to help develop his or her character role.

Actors are encouraged to respond through improvisations to create an individual approach to the story or interpretation of text. In a fairly constant ensemble of performers, some actors are more suited to creating the clown type, others to the physical portrayal, others to the more sinister or subversive characters. If you were adopting such an approach you would need to establish your own strengths as a group.

An aim throughout rehearsals is that the physical work that emerges must match the verbal imagination or poetry of the text. A good example from the production of *Brief Encounter* is when a love scene was performed as a flying sequence.

The technical demands of some aspects of Kneehigh's physical style of theatre may be beyond what you feel you can tackle, or beyond what health and safety allows. However, some simple devices can give an effective extra physical dimension, for example, the use of a trampette by one character in *Brief Encounter*, a toy scooter by another. The attitude to the role of the actor in general is easily adapted to your work.

Design issues

All aspects of design are integral to a Kneehigh performance. Music is chosen as part of the research process and used to provide a soundscape for the piece. The group experiment with different types of music to find those attuned to the needs of each piece. For example, in *Tristan and Yseult*, Wagner's stirring music was used, while a simple set of hand bells accompanied *A Matter of Life and Death*.

The group also integrate lighting during early rehearsals. Emma Rice describes the three elements of a Kneehigh production as music, text and design, and explains that the physical setting is as important as the play itself. She says, 'The design needs to create an environment in which the play can live.'

Fig. 23.6 *A Kneehigh production of* Tristan and Yseult, *2006*

Kneehigh gives opportunities for design candidates to create original environments, unusual costumes and imaginative sound and lighting. The energy and exuberance of the performance can be reflected in the design.

Projects, collaborators and influences

At first glance, the plays performed by Kneehigh may not seem to have much in common: *Tristan and Yseult* is a reworking of an ancient mythical love story; *A Matter of Life and Death* is a stage adaptation of a 1946 film about an RAF pilot who crash lands; *Cymbeline* is one of Shakespeare's less well-known plays dealing with very complex emotional relationships; *Nights at the Circus* is an adaptation of a story by Angela Carter about a circus performer who has wings.

What unites these distinct forms: a myth, a film, a classic play and a short story, is the fairy tale element.

Kneehigh is a very skilful company and their work requires enormous commitment, energy and ingenuity. If you choose Kneehigh as your influential practitioner it will give you the opportunity to explore a large range of theatrical ideas and techniques. Suitable texts should include a fairy tale quality that will exercise your storytelling skills.

AQA Examiner's tip

Remember that, in order for the actors to use the environment well, the design must be available for rehearsals from an early stage.

Further reading

Tristan and Yseult, The Bacchae, The Wooden Frock, The Red Shoes, by Carl Grose, Anna Maria Murphy (Oberon Modern Plays, 2005)

Nights at the Circus, by Angela Carter, edited by Emma Rice and Tom Morris (Oberon Modern Plays, 2006)

A Matter of Life and Death, by Tom Morris and Emma Rice (Oberon Modern Plays, 2007).

24   The skills of the group

The available skills and the makeup of the group

This chapter looks at the skills that are available for you to choose to be assessed in, for your practical exam, and also focuses on some of the guidelines that appear in the specification booklet.

In this part of the course you will be working in groups, and each member of the group needs to contribute to the interpretation and development of the selected play extract. Each member also has to work on developing their own skill, which must be chosen from the following list:

Directing (one candidate per group)

Acting (at least two candidates per group)

Costume design (one candidate per group)

Mask design (one candidate per group)

Design of stage setting(s) (one candidate per group)

Technical elements: lighting and/or sound (one candidate per element, or one candidate assuming responsibility for both elements)

The specification offers guidance about how each examination group must be structured, stating:

> Candidates are required to work in groups to present for an audience an extract from a published play of their choice. The group size is to be between two and eight acting candidates, plus, where appropriate, up to five candidates offering a design skill – set design, costume design, mask design or technical design (lighting and/or sound) – plus one directing candidate.

> Each group is to be self-contained and totally responsible for all aspects of the presented extract, which should realise clear dramatic intentions for an audience.

Although in theory you may choose any of the seven skills, in practice as a group, you need to follow the guidelines to make sure your group is the correct size and has the correct combination of skills.

This means that each examination group:

- *must* contain a minimum of *two* and a maximum of *eight* acting candidates
- *may* choose to work collaboratively as actors and *does not* have to include a directing candidate or any design candidates
- *may* choose to add to their group any or all of the following:
  - one director
  - one set designer
  - one costume designer
  - one mask designer
  - one lighting designer*
  - one sound designer*

* or one technical designer responsible for both lighting and sound.

If your group contains the *minimum* number of actors, and *no* additional non-acting candidates, then the group, as a whole, will contain *two* of you.

If your group contains the *minimum* number of actors, but the *maximum* number of candidates offering directing or design skills, the group, as a whole, will contain *eight* of you.

If your group contains the *maximum* number of actors and the *maximum* number of candidates offering the other skills, the group, as a whole, will contain *14* of you.

There are many different permutations possible but, whatever the make-up of the group, the specification stresses that:

> All candidates share corporate responsibility for the development and presentation of their finished piece.

▧ Choosing an extract

Once you have selected the play that you want to present for your practical exam, you will need to choose a suitable extract from it. By 'extract', we mean a portion of the play.

Depending upon the size of your group, your chosen extract might be a complete scene from the chosen play or only a part of a scene. If there are only two actors in your group, your extract will probably be a relatively short section from a scene.

If you have eight actors in your group, the chosen extract might be a complete Act, or two or more short scenes, taken from different parts of the play. You have complete freedom of choice about which parts of the play you wish to present. However, you are expected to choose sections of 'continuous action'. This means that you should not be cutting lines (or characters) out of your chosen extract to make it fit the timing guidelines.

Try to find an extract of appropriate length in terms of playing time and don't be tempted to work on more material than you need to satisfy the demands of the exam.

You will be guided in your selection by your teacher and by the suitability of particular parts of the play to demonstrate the influence of your chosen practitioner.

The specification offers the following guidelines:

> Candidates may choose to present a continuous extract taken from any part of their selected play or two or more sequences of continuous action taken from different parts of their chosen play. These sequences should be presented in chronological order and should take account of developments or changes in character and/or situation that occur in the play, as appropriate.

How long should the extract last?

The specification offers the following guidelines about the running time of your extract:

> Playing time for the presentation of the extract should be approximately 15–40 minutes, according to the number of acting candidates in the group; that is, a group with only two acting candidates should work to the lower limit, a group with eight acting candidates should work to the upper limit.

While all candidates share corporate responsibility for the development and presentation of their finished piece, each candidate must nominate for assessment a specific theatre skill, to be demonstrated within the performance of the piece.

The theatrical adage 'keep the audience hungry for more!' applies as much to an exam performance as it does in the theatre. It is better to be working on rehearsing and perfecting a presentation that lasts 20 minutes (if you are in a group of four) than to be struggling to learn and refine a piece that lasts 30 minutes.

Your teacher and the visiting moderator will expect to see carefully rehearsed, detailed and engaging work that fulfils the timings suggested by the specification.

Number of acting candidates	Recommended timings for the extract(s)
2 or 3	15 minutes
4	20 minutes
5	25 minutes
6	30 minutes
7 or 8	35–40 minutes

Although the recommended timings are related to the number of actors in each examination group, you should never think in terms of each actor having a specific number of minutes to perform in. Plays just don't work like that!

The style, genre and form of the chosen play will affect whether or not a group appears as an **ensemble** throughout or whether individual characters and actors come and go at different points in the extract. If there are five of you, for example, presenting a section from *Metamorphosis*, you might all be on stage throughout your chosen extract, lasting 25 minutes. However, another group of five might be presenting a 25-minute extract from Act One of *Hedda Gabler* where characters enter and leave the stage at different times.

All actors should make sure that the roles they are playing offer them plenty of opportunities to demonstrate their abilities within the chosen section. Note that this is *not* the same as trying to find an extract where all actors are on stage for exactly the same amount of time.

Building an ensemble

However many actors and/or non-acting candidates that you have in your group, it is important that, from the beginning of your work on your practical unit, you think of yourselves as a team or ensemble.

Whether you are working in a team of two actors or of eight actors, a director plus five designers, your individual success depends upon the whole group pulling together. You should all be prepared to contribute to artistic decisions, to make creative suggestions and to be willing to compromise and to accept (or at the very least try out) the suggestions of others in the group.

Your teacher will help you to decide how many students work together, guide you in your selection of an appropriate play and suggest ways in which you can explore the ideas of your chosen practitioner. Your teacher may also offer advice about your selection of extracts from your chosen

AQA Examiner's tip

There is no advantage in offering more than the recommended timings for your group size. In fact, a longer extract may mean that you reduce the quality of your performance.

play but the progress and success of your work depends on how much individual effort each member of the group puts in.

In this examination each student must be totally committed to the dramatic intentions of the group as a whole. In this way you will be able to share the responsibilities of creating your presentation and to enjoy the rewards of working together. Preparing a presentation is potentially a lot of fun and the harder each member of the group works the more fun it becomes.

Choosing skills to match your abilities as well as the needs of the group

Choosing your skill requires a lot of thought. You need to consider various aspects for each of the skills.

For the skill of acting, think about the following.

- Your particular strengths and weaknesses as a performer, vocally and physically.
- The demands of the play and the suitability of the available roles to your skills. For example:
  - Does the play demand a particular accent or regional dialect? If so, can you achieve and sustain it?
  - Does the play demand a high degree of physical fitness or agility? If so, do you have the ability to develop and/or attain the necessary stamina or physical flexibility to meet these demands?
  - Does the play contain older characters that need to be portrayed naturalistically? If so, do you have the skills to satisfy these demands?
  - Does the play contain characters that match the gender make-up of your group? If not, how will cross-gender casting affect the audience experience of the play?
  - Does the selected extract from the play offer you adequate opportunity to demonstrate your skill?

For the skill of directing, think about:

- your ability to make decisions, to take responsibility and your leadership qualities
- your inventiveness and creativity
- your understanding of the chosen play or extract and of the chosen practitioner
- your 'people skills' and relationships with the other group members, both performers and designers, if appropriate
- your ability to consider suggestions from your actors
- your ability to manage rehearsal time: your self-discipline.

For all design skills, think about:

- your design experience
- your design flair
- your knowledge of the demands of the skill
- your ability to cooperate with other designers in the group and with the director (if there is one)
- your ability to match your ideas to the needs of the piece and to the style of the chosen practitioner.

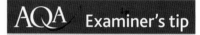

AQA Examiner's tip

For all skills, you need to think about the demands of working within the style of your chosen practitioner.

Link

Throughout the preparation for your exam presentation you should refer back to Chapters 3, 4 and 5 to refresh your memory about aspects of your chosen skill.

Go through this checklist before committing yourself to a particular role within the group. Remember that your choice of skill affects not only your own examination mark but also the marks of everyone else in the group.

The examination demands of each of the skills

To be successful in your practical exam you need to know precisely what is expected of you. Your teacher can give you the exact wording from the specification of what is required in each skill, although you may find the lists below provide helpful summaries. They can also act as checklists during your preparation, so you can ensure that you are approaching your chosen skill appropriately and that you are fulfilling all the requirements of the exam.

Remember, whatever skill you choose, the specification states that:

> … all skills are to be developed in relation to the group's chosen practitioner and to their dramatic intentions for an audience in relation to their interpretation of the selected play, as outlined in their supporting notes.

Directing

If you choose to be assessed as a director you must *do* the following:

- undertake research into the practitioner and the chosen play, its original context and period
- match your approach to directing to the needs of the chosen play and the style of the chosen practitioner
- guide your actors to achieve a clear interpretation of the extract
- bring out meaning for the audience through the following directorial methods:
  - choice and use of space
  - the actor-audience relationship
  - direction of the actors; groupings, movement, use of space and set; use of props
  - direction of actors' vocal delivery of lines
  - creation of pace, mood and atmosphere, climax.

In your *supporting notes* you should provide evidence of the above steps, plus:

- demonstrate your understanding of the director's role within the team and the necessary collaboration between the director and the actors
- outline your interpretation of the play and extract
- demonstrate your awareness of health and safety issues
- include a **prompt copy** of the extract as an appendix to your notes.

Acting

If you choose to be assessed as an actor you must *do* the following:

- develop and interpret a single role or a variety of roles, matching the theatrical style of the extract and the chosen practitioner
- experiment in your rehearsal of the role(s) with both vocal and physical techniques, for example:
  - use of vocal expression, pace, pitch, pause, projection, accent or dialect

– verse speaking

– movement, body language, ensemble playing, synchronisation

– facial expression, eye contact, listening and response

▥ perform in a way that fulfils the dramatic aims of the group and that suits the style and period setting of the chosen play.

In your *supporting notes* you should provide evidence of your understanding of the techniques that you have used and, in addition to that:

▥ give details of your approach to creating a role or building a character, including details of your experiment with the acting techniques appropriate to your chosen practitioner

▥ refer to your interpretation of the extract and your role(s) within it

▥ demonstrate your awareness of health-and-safety issues.

Design skills

The specification offers the following general advice to all students choosing to be assessed in one of the design skills:

> Candidates offering design skills are required to design and oversee the realisation/execution of their designs for the examination performance. Candidates may choose *either* to realise/construct/ execute their designs themselves *or* to deploy a third party, who must be a bona fide student, to construct/execute their designs, working precisely to the candidate's detailed instructions.

> Where candidates choose to deploy a third party to construct/execute their designs, they should include, as an appendix to their supporting notes, a copy of the instructions supplied to that third party. It is expected that these instructions will be supplemented by carefully labelled sketches, ground plans, plots, cue sheets, where appropriate.

> Where design skills are chosen, the supporting notes should include relevant sketches or diagrams.

So, if you choose to be assessed as a designer, in any capacity, you must do the following:

▥ design and oversee the realisation of your designs (by a third party, who must be a fellow student) or design and execute your designs (yourself) for the exam performance

▥ if you choose to delegate the execution of your designs to a third party you must include, as an appendix to your supporting notes, a copy of the instructions that you gave to that person, including sketches, ground plans or cue sheets, as appropriate to your chosen design skill.

In your *supporting notes* you should provide:

▥ relevant sketches and diagrams.

Costume design

If you choose to be assessed as a costume designer, you *must* do the following:

▥ design and oversee the realisation of your design or design and execute your design for at least one costume

▥ select appropriate fabrics, trimmings and ornamentation

▥ communicate a specific period, if appropriate

▥ supervise the construction, adaptation or selection of the remaining costumes worn in the performance of the extract

- consider the cut, fit and condition of the costume and the comfort or ease of movement and safety of the actor wearing it
- ensure that your design and costume is appropriate to the character wearing it (and that the other costumes also suit the cast as a whole). Check that it is in line with the dramatic intentions of the group, with your interpretation of the play and its characters and with the style of your chosen practitioner.

In your *supporting notes* you should provide:

- relevant sketches and details of construction and/or adaptation methods
- evidence of relevant research into the skill of costume design including, for example:
  - visual materials, sample fabrics
  - trial techniques such as dyeing and/or the simulation of textures
  - costings of materials and manufacture
  - durability and maintenance of costumes
- evidence of your understanding of the costume designer's role within the production team
- evidence of your awareness of health-and-safety issues.

Mask design

If you choose to be assessed as a mask designer, you must *do* the following:

- design and oversee the realisation of your design *or* design and execute your design for at least *two* masks
- design and supervise the construction of any remaining masks to be worn within the performance of the extract
- choose an appropriate style of mask; full or half face
- select an appropriate material for construction, consider style and scale, decoration and ornamentation
- ensure that your finished masks are appropriate to the characters wearing them and that their appearance is in line with the dramatic intentions of the group, with your interpretation of the play and its characters and with the style of your chosen practitioner
- ensure that the finished masks are fully practical in performance, facilitating audibility and unimpeded vision for the actors.

In your *supporting notes* you should provide:

- relevant sketches and details of construction methods, including photographs of the construction process
- evidence of relevant research into the skill of mask design including, for example:
  - visual materials
  - the purpose of masks in performance
  - consideration of the limitations that wearing a mask places upon an actor
- evidence of your understanding of the mask designer's role within the production team
- evidence of your awareness of health and safety issues.

Set design

If you choose to be assessed as a set designer, you must *do* the following:

▦ design and oversee the realisation of your design or design and execute your design

▦ ensure that your designs accommodate the action of the extract and offer creative opportunities to the rest of the group

▦ supervise the selection and assembly of the scenic materials and properties that you need to fulfil your design intentions

▦ consider the most appropriate staging form for the extract, in terms of the preferred actor-audience relationship; consider the scale of the design, the available space and the use of different levels, if appropriate

▦ consider entrances and exits as well as the ease of any necessary scene changes

▦ oversee the construction of the setting(s)

▦ ensure that your designs are in line with the dramatic intentions of the group, with your interpretation of the play, with its period, if appropriate, and with the style of your chosen practitioner.

In your *supporting notes* you should provide:

▦ detailed sketches, produced to scale, and/or a scale model of the set or settings for the presentation of the extract

▦ evidence of the development of the design ideas

▦ ground plans and working drawings with some photographic record of the assembly of the setting in progress and details of costings

▦ evidence of your understanding of the set designer's role within the production team

▦ evidence of your awareness of health-and-safety issues.

Technical elements – lighting and/or sound design

If you choose to be assessed as a lighting designer, you must *do* the following:

▦ design a lighting plot as appropriate to the requirements of the group presentation

▦ choose appropriate lanterns to meet the demands of the extract

▦ consider your use of lighting design to establish the style of the play, to create location and/or time of day, to enhance mood or atmosphere and/or communicate meaning

▦ consider the creation of special effects through the use of floor lights, **birdies**, strobes, and specials

▦ supervise the rigging and focusing of your design and the operation of the design during the performance

▦ create a lighting design that is in line with the group's interpretation of the play and extract, with the dramatic intentions of the group and with the style of your chosen practitioner.

In your *supporting notes* you should provide:

▦ a list of the equipment and accessories used

▦ final cue sheets and plot sheets

- evidence of your understanding of different types of lanterns and lamps and their various effects; use of **gels**, filters and special effects lanterns
- evidence of your understanding of the lighting designer's place within the production team
- details of the development of your design ideas
- evidence of your awareness of health-and-safety issues.

If you choose to be assessed as a sound designer, you must *do* the following:

- supervise the creation and/or recording of your intended effects
- supervise or execute the editing and mixing of your sound track
- supervise the setting up of equipment and the operation of the sound plot during the performance
- select your sound equipment, for example, microphones, amplifiers, loudspeakers, mini-disc players
- give consideration to your production of sound qualities, including, for example, levels, intensities and fade rhythms, reverb, echo, sampling recorded sound effects, **soundscapes** or music
- create a sound design that is in line with the group's interpretation of the play and extract, with the dramatic intentions of the group and with the style of your chosen practitioner.

In your *supporting notes* you should provide:

- a list of the equipment used
- evidence of your knowledge of sound equipment, including digital amplifiers, microphones, recorders, digital effects, speakers and audio software
- evidence of your understanding of methods of sound composition and compilation and of the potential of sound to create and change mood
- final cue sheets
- evidence of your understanding of the sound designer's place within the production team
- details of the development of your design ideas
- evidence of your awareness of health-and-safety issues.

25 Approaching the rehearsal process

Early rehearsals

Once your group has been decided in terms of:

- chosen practitioner(s)
- group members
- selected text
- selected skills

then you are ready to begin the rehearsal process.

Your rehearsal methods will vary according to the factors listed above. If you have a director in your group, for example, your initial sessions of discussing and analysing the chosen text are likely to be led by, although not dominated by, the student director.

If you are working as a group of actors without a director, you need to nominate someone to 'chair' initial discussions about your text. You may choose to take it in turns to oversee the rehearsals or you may choose someone to act in this capacity throughout the rehearsal process.

Whether or not you have a director, you should make sure that you voice your opinions about the development of the piece, your interpretation of the extract(s) and play, as a whole, as well as your ideas about your own role. This is important, as it ensures that everyone in the group has a sense of ownership of the finished presentation.

The same principles apply to those of you choosing design skills. You must ensure that your ideas are compatible with the interpretation of the actors (and director, if there is one) but you must also make sure that you have an input into that interpretation from the very beginning of the rehearsal process.

Designers, in the professional theatre, begin their work at the very start of the production process, and you too must never assume that you can wait and see how the actors are progressing before beginning to assemble your designs.

If there is no designer in your group you will need to make decisions corporately about how you are going to deploy design elements to enhance your production.

Whatever the makeup of the group, take turns in sitting out and observing the rehearsals from time to time so that you can take an objective view of what is working and what needs adjusting. Even if you have a director and a full complement of designers, everyone should be interested to hear the views of the rest of the group throughout the rehearsal process, and especially towards the end of the preparation period, so that adjustments can be made, if necessary.

Interpretation

Never underestimate the need to spend a portion of your rehearsal time working on the meaning of your chosen text. Whatever the length of your extract, you must understand the whole play in order to be able to interpret the extract, and you must take account of the meaning of the whole play in your interpretation of the extract.

You should devote a significant amount of time to carrying out relevant research into the text, including:

- its original social, cultural and historical context
- its theatrical context and production history
- its period setting and geographical location
- its main focus – what is it about?
- its characters and their relationships and concerns
- the themes of the play that need to be realised in a theatrical way.

You will already have carried out extensive research on the working methods of the selected director, designer, theatre company or other practitioner before you start to interpret your chosen text.

Your choice of practitioner is likely to determine your approach to rehearsal work but, whatever your influence, you must remember that rehearsal is about exploration, development and growth. Never assume that rehearsal is simply learning your lines and your moves. You must investigate the meaning of your chosen play and discover, through discussion and rehearsal, how to communicate that meaning most effectively to your audience, using the different skills of every member of your group.

Looking for meaning

Once you have shared your research findings as a group, a good way forward is to read the whole play, irrespective of which part of it you intend to perform. Read it through from beginning to end, taking several parts each if necessary and including members of the entire group, including designers.

In the professional theatre the director will have done a lot of preparation on the play, before beginning work in the rehearsal room. However, as AS students you may be working without a director and, even if your group does have a member who is offering direction as his or her skill, you must work as a group, initially, to arrive at shared objectives, shared intentions for the audience and of course a common understanding of the play's meaning.

On your second read-through of the play, you should feel free to stop and start during the read-through, asking questions about the text, jotting down points that you feel need clarifying and sharing opinions about the characters and their situation.

It is at this point, when you have got a feel for the text and its potential in performance, that you should select the extract(s) that you intend to perform and finalise the casting of the piece. Obviously, you will not embark on preliminary research into a play unless you know you have the right number and gender of actors to take specific parts, but the read-through might have thrown up some doubts about who might be best suited to which role.

Exploring possible extract(s)

The optimum playing time for your extract(s) in relation to the numbers of performers in your group has already been focused on in Chapter 24. However, do choose your extract with care and discuss the following questions with the group:

- Does the extract offer opportunities for demonstrating the strengths of the group?

AQA **Examiner's tip**

It is better to make adjustments early on in the process rather than after a lot of work has taken place. Ask your teacher for guidance. He or she is in a position to give you an objective opinion about what roles suit which members of your group.

- Does it include a key moment in the development of the plot: beginning, climax or **denouement**?

- Is there scope within a single extract or across more than one continuous section to allow each performer adequate (not necessarily equal) time to establish a character or demonstrate his or her skill?

- Does the extract allow for the revelation of emotion? Are there shifts of emotional temperature within the piece?

- Does it allow the actors to use all three means of expression: vocal, physical and facial? (This is not a requirement, but is an indicator of the opportunities and challenges within the extract.)

- Are there any particular performance demands in the extract that might present difficulties to the actors, for example, the need for one or more actors to present older or elderly characters convincingly, or to speak in a particular accent consistently?

- Are there any essential staging, setting or technical requirements beyond the reach of the group, for example, the need to fly a character in or to make a character disappear?

- Are there any practical demands in the extract that might present a problem, for example, the need to smoke, to stage a fight, or to serve and eat a meal during the scene while delivering dialogue?

Identifying opportunities and challenges within the extract before you begin to work on it will be useful in helping you to determine a rehearsal schedule.

Setting a rehearsal schedule

AQA recommends that you spend at least 40 hours in preparing your presentation for Unit 2. That's the equivalent of an eight-week rehearsal period, which you might arrange in two sessions of two-and-a-half hours per week, or five hourly sessions per week.

However, when you are discussing your timetable for progress, do build in additional hours for the final couple of weeks of your rehearsal period, to accommodate dress rehearsals and technical run-throughs.

Aim to have your work polished and ready for performance at least a week in advance of the exam. That way, you can perform your piece in front of a selected invited audience and benefit from their honest opinions that might help you to refine your work further. This also gives you time to put the finishing touches to your supporting notes and enables you to offer some meaningful assessment of the process and its likely outcome.

Some student groups actually sign a contract at the beginning of the process, in which they all agree to attend scheduled rehearsals, to arrive on time, to contribute productively to the process and not to disrupt rehearsals by being negative or uncooperative.

Activity

Draw up rules for your group to stick to during the preparation period. Work them out in a democratic way and take collective responsibility for their enforcement.

Uniting the individual skills of the group

Directing

If you have chosen directing as your skill, you will be seen as the lynchpin of the group. You will need to have a clear head and excellent organisation skills. The rest of the group will look to you for a lead during rehearsals and will expect you to have definite, but not unshakeable, ideas about the play.

Remember that very few professional directors know exactly how a play will turn out when they arrive at the first rehearsal. It is one of your jobs to help the cast come to a full understanding of the meaning of the extract and to direct them in such a way that the meaning, that you have agreed upon between you, is clearly communicated to the audience.

You will need to be thoughtful and tactful in the way you give direction, sensitive to the feelings of your actors, but firm in your intentions. Never begin a rehearsal without having some idea of your intended outcomes. These might be as simple as **blocking** a particular piece of text so that the most significant part of the action takes place downstage, or as tricky as rehearsing a fight sequence so that nobody gets hurt or coordinating a scene depicting a family supper, where the actors eat a meal.

You will not get the best out of your actors if you are bossy, stubborn or sarcastic. The best direction takes place in an atmosphere of mutual respect and, although you might find your task frustrating at times when nothing appears to be going right, there will also be rewarding rehearsals where you seem to reach a breakthrough in everyone's understanding of the scene.

A good director knows when to listen to the ideas of the actors, when to put an end to repeating a section of text and when to adopt a completely different approach to rehearsing a scene, perhaps through improvisation.

If you are working as a director in a group that has no designated designers, you may also be placed in a position where you need to help coordinate the ideas of all the group members about the most appropriate design elements to use to enhance the presentation of the extract. You might have very strong ideas about these yourself, but try to collaborate closely with the actors on this so that you are each happy with the final look and sound of the piece.

Acting: understanding your character(s)

Once you have a feel of the play, its style, its themes and concerns, its shape and structure and you have selected your extracts from it, you need to begin work on the characters.

Refer back to Chapter 17 to remind yourself of ways that might help you to understand and then interpret your chosen role. Your choice of practitioner will have a huge effect upon how you approach the role that you are playing, whether you are aiming for Stanislavskian 'truth', Kneehigh's energetic physicalisation of your role, or **Berkoffian expressionism**.

There is not enough space here to anticipate anything like a full range of possible approaches. The important thing is to research the appropriate approach thoroughly, to understand it and to apply it rigorously to your work on your character.

If your group includes a member offering directing as his or her skill, naturally you will also be influenced by that person's vision of the extract and your role(s) within it. This does not mean that you simply have to 'take direction'. You must undertake your own work on your role, in order to develop your skill and equip yourself to contribute to the making of meaning in the performance of the extract. If you don't agree with your director, you must find ways of resolving your differences, based on your full understanding of the play and the playwright's intentions.

Link

Remind yourself of what is expected of the director by looking back over Chapters 3, 13, 14 and 24. These should help you to construct your directorial strategy.

Further reading

- *Fifty Key Theatre Directors*, edited by Shomit Mitter and Maria Shevtstova (Routledge, 2005)
- *In Contact with the Gods? Directors Talk Theatre*, edited by Maria Delgado and Paul Heritage (Manchester University Press, 1996)
- *Taking Stage: Women Directors on Directing*, by Helen Manfull (Methuen, 1999).

Working without a director

If you are working in a group without a director you will have to be very disciplined about how you manage your own time.

In order to be effective corporate directors of your own work you will need to agree upon your schedule of rehearsals and apportion appropriate time to unpicking the meaning of the extract and exploring each character in depth.

You will need to set aside time to rehearse actors who may have monologues to deliver or pairs of actors who share sections of dialogue, as well as exploring the staging implications of scenes with larger numbers of actors, their use of space as well as their interaction.

It will be helpful to make up a group **prompt book** recording all the agreed moves, the delivery of key lines and other staging decisions that you make. Take it in turns to keep it up to date or designate one group member to take charge of it throughout the rehearsal process.

You should begin each rehearsal with a quick outline of what you intend to achieve. For example, you might want to work out some tricky moves for a sequence of synchronised action, or work on a particularly emotional moment between two of the characters, or do some off-text improvisation to help you get under the skin of a particular role.

Whatever your rehearsal aims, agree to them and stick with them and try not to leave the rehearsal without accomplishing at least some of them. You should also not leave the rehearsal without summing up what you have achieved and deciding upon the best approach to the next rehearsal. Write it down, so you don't forget!

You will need to be generous with one another and take time to watch and listen to all of the different actors within the extract, commenting and offering constructive suggestions for solving problems, as well as for improving everyone's acting techniques.

You may ask your teacher for his or her views throughout the rehearsal period, but remember that your teacher cannot direct you; he or she may only respond to your requests for feedback as you shape and refine your work.

Designing

If you are working within a group that has no director, your role as designer can be crucial in expressing the overall presentation or the performance, highlighting themes or establishing a very clear location and/or period for the extract.

The actors may turn to you for an 'objective eye'. However, you must never see yourself as an outsider. The designer's role, be it of set, costume, masks or technical elements, is to work alongside the actors and the director, if there is one, not merely responding to their demands but initiating suggestions and helping to drive the project forward, to stimulate their creativity as well as to accommodate their design needs.

If you have chosen any of the design options for this Unit, you must take an active part in the selection of the play and extract; not to do so would seriously restrict your opportunities. Don't be tempted into the attitude that whatever play is chosen has to have lighting, sound, set and costume and then just leave it to the other group members to pick a play for you to design.

▪ Further reading

- *Other Peoples' Shoes*, by Harriet Walter, (Nick Hern Books, London, 2003)
- *Year of the King: An Actor's Diary and Sketchbook*, by Anthony Sher (Limelight Editions, 1992)
- *The Actor and the Target*, by Declan Donnellan (Nick Hern Books, London, 2002).

▪ Link

Look at Chapters 4 and 15 to remind yourself of the factors that will affect your design strategy.

Hazer running from entry of audience (to create mist)

Front of House Clearance (cue that all audience are in place)
LX cue 1 (pre-set out/house lights out)
(LX = abbreviation for lighting effect, sometimes LFX)
(pre-set = dim lighting state on stage as audience arrive)

Macbeth Act 1

Scene 1
(An open place)
Thunder and lightning.

Enter three witches in black-out
LX cue 2 Lightning Flash
Sound Cue 1 Thunder and windscape
Smoke machine, cue 1, 3 seconds, during thunder

Enter Three Witches ●

● 1st Witch   When shall we three meet again?
               In thunder, lightening or in rain?

Pyrotechnic Cue 1 (fire in pile of stones)
Smoke Cue 2 (dry ice machine, off downstage left)
LX Cue 4 light in pile of stones on

3 witches in position
LX3 Lighting state builds

2nd Witch   When the hurlyburly's done,
               When the battle's lost and won. ●
3rd Witch   That will be ere the set of sun.
1st Witch   Where the place?
2nd Witch   Upon the heath.
3rd Witch   There to meet with Macbeth.
1st Witch   I come, Graymalkin.
2nd Witch   Paddock calls.
3rd Witch   Anon! ●
All   Fair is foul, and foul is fair:
               Hover through the fog and filthy air.
                         ● (Witches vanish.)

LX Cue 5 Lightning flash
Sound Cue 2 Thunder increase
Smoke Cue 3, 2 second

Exit witches downstage left
LX6 Cross fade to bright state behind door, fire light out
Sound Cue 3 Fanfare, 5 seconds
Bleeding captain on

Centre doors open , (cyclorama visible)
(Duncan revealed on throne, on shoulders of 4 attendants)
Enter two attendants, drape material from flies, fix with hooks to create tent
Enter Malcolm, Donalbain and Lennox, behind King
LX7 medium wash

Scene 2
(A camp near Forres)
● Alarum within.

● Enter King Duncan, Malcolm, Donalbain, Lennox, with Attendants, meeting a bleeding Sergeant.

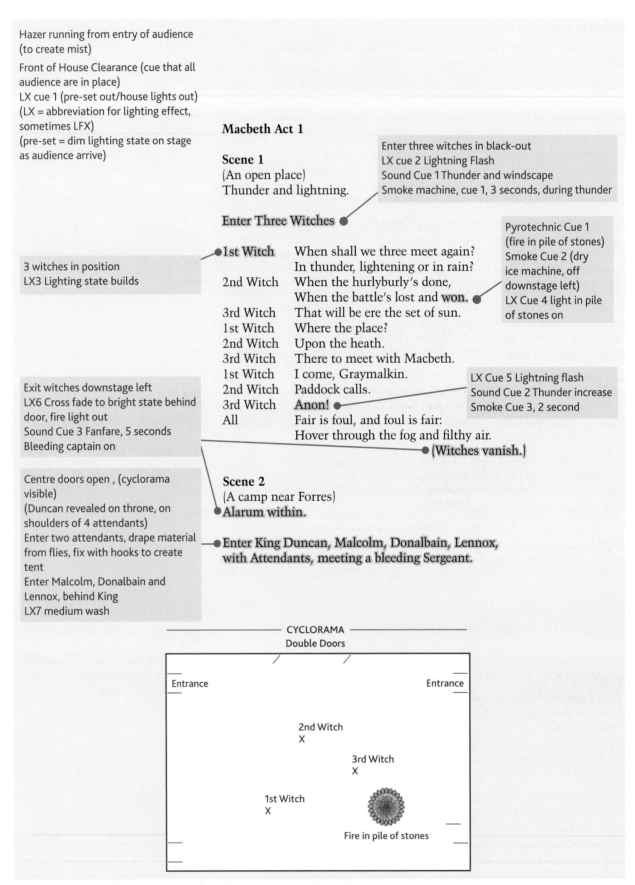

CYCLORAMA
Double Doors

Entrance   Entrance

2nd Witch
X

3rd Witch
X

1st Witch
X

Fire in pile of stones

Fig. 25.1 *An extract from a prompt book used for a production of* Macbeth.

While it may be true that all plays require these elements, not all plays offer equal opportunities or present the same kind of challenges to designers. You will be working with actors who have chosen a play to match their talents; make sure that it also matches yours.

If you are a set designer who longs to create a fantasy world, you will be frustrated to be designing a set for a naturalistic play or for a piece that depends largely upon the physical skills of the performers to create the set.

If your costume design skills will show most to advantage working on a historical period drama, your plans will be thwarted if the group picks a contemporary play. No student wishing to offer mask design should work within a group that is not prepared to find a suitable play or to perform in masks; no technical designers should be struggling to find technical opportunities in a play that demands very little by way of technical expression.

Fig. 25.2 *An imaginative costume from a production of* Toad of Toad Hall

Initial ideas

In the early stages of working on the chosen play, the designers' ideas can be really helpful in unlocking some of the play's meaning. The setting, costume and technical elements can help to define the group's understanding of the play and can be a major method for communicating meaning to the audience.

Be prepared to put your ideas down on paper and share your vision for the 'look' or sound of the play with the whole group. Don't be offended if your ideas don't always meet with unreserved delight. Working together is not so much about compromising your ideas as about adjusting your vision as the performance piece takes shape.

While the actors should be bringing their ideas about characters, movement and delivery to the rehearsal room, you should be armed with sketches, swatches of material or practical suggestions for creating mood and atmosphere in the scenes through technical means.

© Beckie Kravetz

Fig. 25.3 *Contemporary theatre mask*

Establishing a basic set layout from the outset will be immensely useful to actors during the rehearsal process, even if you have to modify your ideas along the way.

Spend some of your research time tracking down design details for previous productions of your chosen play and trawling books, galleries and websites for inspiration. (Several relevant websites are listed in the e-resources.) You should also ensure that your design ideas are entirely compatible with the influence of your chosen practitioner.

Working as a group without a designer

If you don't have a designer in your group you will need to make all necessary design decisions yourself.

To a large extent your design decisions will be influenced by the style of your chosen practitioner, but you must ensure that, as a group, you share the responsibility for the final look and sound of your piece and that you include discussions about potential designs from the very beginning of your preparation and rehearsals.

It's all too easy when you are involved in refining your own acting skills and rehearsing your extract to allow design issues to slip to the bottom of your priorities. If you're not careful, the exam date will be upon you before you have given proper attention to your set, costume and technical design. The earlier you make decisions about furnishings, costumes, accessories and props, the better.

Take some time to research and build up a bank of images from previous productions of your chosen play. You should not be slavishly copying previous productions but you may get ideas about the sort of design support that you need to communicate your interpretation effectively.

If you have a director, this could be an area where he or she takes the lead. If not, you need to add the design responsibilities to your general shared duties in translating your selected extract from page to stage.

Fig. 25.4 *Students rehearsing*

You might find it easier to divide non-acting tasks between you so that one actor takes responsibility for the overall direction, another for stage-management, another for set design, another for costumes and so on.

This approach can work well, but remember that you will not gain individual credit for the stagecraft that you undertake over and above your own acting. The success of the piece as a whole will be enhanced by judicious use of design elements but the credit for the staging elements that are used to support your performances will be shared equally between all members of the group.

26   Clear intentions for the audience

Dramatic intentions

Every theatre company has to think about its aims for its audience as it creates or rehearses a performance text. As we have said before, without an audience, there can be no theatre.

Your chosen extract will be also have to be crafted to meet clear intentions for an audience that may comprise fellow students, family and friends, and will certainly include someone whose job it is to assess your work in relation to the demands of the examination.

This is where your work differs from most professional companies. A professional company must sell tickets and fill the theatre to survive commercially. It must know the type of audience that it wants to appeal to and ensure that its work does just that.

You do not have the pressure of having to attract a ticket-buying clientele. However, you *do* face the pressure of having to conform closely to the examination demands of Unit 2 and to make sure that the hallmarks of your chosen practitioner are stamped clearly upon your work.

Your intentions for your audience might be to amaze them with feats of physical theatre, to make them laugh with skilful comic method or to move and disturb them with a piece of hard-hitting emotional realism. You need to ensure that your intentions are in harmony with the theatrical aims of your chosen practitioner.

For example, if your chosen practitioner is Stanislavski, you will want to lure your audience into believing in the reality of the situation that you present. You want them to empathise with the characters and, if you are a designer, to convince them of the reality of the setting and costumes used, allowing them to 'suspend their disbelief' and watch as if they are observing the unfolding of real life.

If your chosen practitioner is Brecht, you will want to teach your audience about social injustice, forcing them to confront a political issue and make them feel inclined to take action to right political wrongs. Your acting style will be detached and your design ideas appropriate to the social classes depicted, enhancing the action but not swamping it with unnecessary scenery or props.

Respect both your practitioner and your chosen playwright by choosing appropriate working and presentational methods, rather than causing your audience to be confused by a mismatch of content and form.

Do not ride roughshod over a text in order to make it fit into a style that it was not intended for. While plays by the Greeks and the Elizabethans lend themselves to a wide variety of approaches, it is difficult to justify giving an Artaudian twist to a piece of straight naturalism or introducing a physical theatre style to an 18th-century classic.

However, if you can justify your treatment and your teacher also agrees with your choice, you can be as experimental as the play allows you. Just remember that you need to include that justification, as well as a clear statement of your intentions for the audience, in your supporting notes.

27 Supporting notes

This chapter focuses on the supporting notes that you need to produce to supplement your practical work. At the end of the chapter there are some example supporting notes to demonstrate the sort of material that you might include.

Your supporting notes should show your understanding of the work and ideas of your chosen director, designer, theatre company or other practitioner. They should demonstrate how you have applied these ideas to your chosen play to achieve your dramatic intentions for the audience.

■ How should the supporting notes be presented?

The notes should be clearly presented, ideally word-processed and written as concise but *full* sentences. Use specialist theatre terminology wherever necessary. The notes should be divided into three sections as explained below and should be, *in total*, between 1,500 and 2,000 words in length.

You will need to provide evidence of the exploration that you have made into the work and ideas of your chosen practitioner, so you will have to include a bibliography and/or a 'webliography' and acknowledge the sources and resources you have used. This information does not count towards your word allowance.

You may include sketches and diagrams, whatever skill you are being assessed in, but make sure that, if you are offering a design skill, you know exactly what the examination requirements are.

■ Organising your supporting notes

You should divide your notes into three separate sections, each being between about 500 and 700 words long. You need to arrange your notes as follows:

■ Section one

In 500–700 words, outline the key features of your chosen practitioner's work and justify your choice of play and extract in relation to your exploration of the practitioner's work.

■ Section two

In 500–700 words, outline your dramatic intentions for the audience, explaining the main aspects of your interpretation of your play and extract and how your chosen practitioner has helped you both to shape your work and to achieve your aims.

■ Section three

In 500–700 words, offer a personal assessment of the rehearsal process and of the potential effectiveness of the piece for an audience. You should evaluate the development of your own skill in relation to both your chosen text and your chosen practitioner. You should also note the health-and-safety precautions that you have taken.

Further reading

Look back at Chapter 24 for the precise requirements of the notes for each of the available skills.

■ Preparing your supporting notes

You should begin to prepare your supporting notes at the very beginning of your rehearsal process.

Establishing the suitability of your selected play to your chosen practitioner

As soon as you have selected a suitable play to explore, using the ideas and methods of your chosen practitioner, make a checklist of the key features that have led you to make this choice. Remind yourself of the areas you should be looking at by referring to Chapter 21.

For clarity, arrange your thoughts under headings, such as the six listed below, as appropriate to your practitioner:

1 theories and approaches to creating productions
2 ideals, intentions for the audience and theatrical style
3 the director's role
4 the actor's role
5 design issues
6 projects, collaborators and influences.

Keeping a track of rehearsals and progress

Your preparation should include making notes about the research you do into the methods of your practitioner. Remember to note any books that you have read, relevant productions that you have seen and websites that you have visited. Make sure you keep a record of what these contained, how they helped you and how you used them. You will need to make a formal list of all your sources and resources to be inserted at the end of Section 1 of your supporting notes.

You should also keep notes about the progress of your rehearsals. Record any interpretative decisions that you make as well as any problems that crop up and solutions that you find as you work towards the final presentation.

Whatever your contribution to the final piece, whether as director, actor or designer, you need to keep a track of the whole process and of the artistic decisions that you take as a group and why. The more notes you make along the way, the easier it will be for you to construct your final set of supporting notes that will be seen by the moderator on the day of your practical exam.

■ Sample notes

Look carefully at the example supporting notes below. The student is performing in a presentation of extracts from *Haroun and the Sea of Stories*, a story written by Salman Rushdie and adapted for the theatre by Tim Supple and David Tushingham.

These example supporting notes should give you an idea of how much material you should include in each section of your notes, as well as the type of aspects to be covered. The student is offering acting as a skill. The notes include a photograph of the dress rehearsal of the piece but they do not include material that you will need if you are offering a skill other than acting.

■ Link

If you are choosing directing or any of the design skills, check the requirements for your supporting notes by looking back at Chapter 24.

Section one:

Key features of my chosen practitioner – the director, Tim Supple – and justification for our choice of *Haroun and the Sea of Stories* to illustrate his influence.

We decided to work in the style of contemporary 'storytelling' theatre companies.

We have seen a number of productions in this style, including the work of Kneehigh and Theatre Alibi; we also saw the amazing 'Indian' version of *A Midsummer Night's Dream*, directed by Tim Supple.

Tim Supple has been hugely influential in the storytelling genre, so we decided to select him as our practitioner.

Tim Supple began directing in the late 1980s. He took up the post of Artistic Director at the Young Vic in London in 1993 and has built up a reputation for the imaginative reworking and adaptation of classic works.

In the 1990s he directed a version of *Jungle Book* and of *Grimm's Fairytales*; coadapted and directed *Tales of Ovid* and coadapted and directed Salman Rushdie's *Midnight's Children*.

The key features of these productions were the spectacular effects created, incorporating physical theatre, dance, music and acting. We decided to choose a play adapted and directed by Supple to illustrate his influence and we chose *Haroun and the Sea of Stories* because the original production was a prime example of his work, as well as being a play about storytelling.

Fig. 27.1 *Student production of* Haroun and the Sea of Stories

Theories and approaches to creating theatre

Although Supple has not published theories about theatre, his adaptations tell us a lot about his approach to productions. He has given many interviews, especially about his recent work on *A Midsummer Night's Dream*. There are many reviews and references to his earlier work available, from which we were able to understand his aims and methods.

Ideals, intentions for the audience and theatrical style

The theatre company, Dash, of which Supple is Artistic Director, publishes a set of ideals and aims for producing new work and encouraging collaboration and experiment.

Supple aims to attract a diverse audience, drawn from all over the world, and is particularly interested in attracting young audiences who, he hopes, will be inspired and empowered to become artists in their own right. Many of his adaptations are intended to appeal to children as well as adults.

His style has been described as 'a feast of kinetic communal storytelling' (*Independent*).

The director's role

Supple's directorial style allows him to turn a group of actors, drawn from a variety of backgrounds, into a fluid and coherent ensemble of performers' encouraging them to achieve 'magical' results.

The actor's role

The actors are central to Supple's storytelling methods. He depends on his cast to be flexible, both physically and vocally, inventive and receptive to innovation in rehearsal as well as boundlessly energetic in performance.

Design issues

Supple's approach to design is eclectic. In *Haroun*, his codeviser and designer, Melly Still, drew inspiration from the East. The stage was fluid, made up predominantly of bare boards, surrounded by what appeared to be a whole library of books, to reflect the importance of storytelling at the heart of the play. The choice of fabrics was exotic, suggesting the mysteries of Arabia.

Projects, collaborators and influences

Tim Supple adopts a collaborative approach to his work. In *Haroun* he not only coadapted the piece with David Tushingham; he also codevised the play in rehearsal with Melly Still. His work, especially on *A Midsummer Night's Dream* has been compared to that of Peter Brook, a figure who Supple acknowledges as an important influence on him.

Bibiography/webliography: sources and resources

Haroun and the Sea of Stories by Salman Rushdie

Haroun and the Sea of Stories, the play adapted by Tim Supple and David Tushingham (Faber, 1998)

www.intermusica.co.uk

www.londontheatre.co.uk

www.stratfordians.org.uk

www.dasharts.org.uk

www.kneehigh.co.uk

Productions seen

Theatre Alibi – *Caught*

Kneehigh – *Nights at the Circus*

Tim Supple directs *A Midsummer Night's Dream*, Stratford, April 2007

(Approx. 550 words.)

Section two:

Dramatic intentions, interpretation of the piece and Tim Supple's influence on our ideas

Intentions

Like Supple, we wish to appeal to an audience of both children and adults; our aim is to tell the story of *Haroun* as clearly, but also as amusingly and inventively, as possible.

The hallmark of Supple's storytelling theatrical style is summed up in a review of his production of *Haroun*, that refers to 'spellbinding group tableaux, musical harmonies and sonorities ... explosions of colour and light and fabric ... gesture, and song, and great chunks of charm' (*Financial Times*). This is what we aim to achieve.

Interpretation

Interpretation of the play was not as straightforward as we had first thought, as *Haroun* works on more than one level. At its simplest, *Haroun* is about a boy whose quest to restore his father's storytelling abilities draws him into a fantastical world of water genies, monsters and a villain called Khattam Shud, whose aim is world domination; he is the enemy of free speech and imagination.

Khattam Shud's war on stories and his attempt to plunge the world into a metaphorical darkness reflects the position of the original author of *Haroun*, Salman Rushdie, who was issued with a fatwa or death sentence by the Ayatolla Khomeim in the 1980s for daring to write the *Satanic Verses*. *Haroun*, then, has a political message about the value of stories and the dangers of censorship.

We decided that the serious message of the play would be easily understood by the adults, but to appeal to a younger audience we decided to adopt an amusing, colourful staging strategy.

Tim Supple's influence

In *Haroun*, Supple shared the devising of sequences of action with the designer, Melly Still. We are working as a group of actors, without a single director, but we felt that by codevising sequences of action we are in fact following the precedent set down by Supple.

As actors, we have been completely open to experiment, and as in Supple's productions, we are using our bodies as well as our voices to make memorable images on stage. In *A Midsummer Night's Dream*, Supple uses a climbing frame made of rope for the fairies to climb and become entangled in; we use a ladder in a similar way creating interesting shapes that help us to tell the story. The play has a cast of 28 characters, excluding chorus; we have a cast of eight and we multi-roled as Supple did with his cast.

Like Supple, we have been inspired by the *Arabian Nights* in terms of our costume, using sheer, colourful fabrics, shawls, scarves and headgear allowing for multi-roling and fast changes from one character to another. We are determined to use the whole stage space so we create different levels using rostra and a ladder.

We intend to draw our audience into a magical and mystical world and use Arabian music to suggest the world of Kahani, where the action begins. When we move to the sequences set in the sea of stories, we use blue, turquoise and green fabric, which stretches the width of the stage, to suggest the sea, and we 'people' it with strange fish and other objects like miniature ships emerging from the waves, sometimes attached to the heads of the actors. This is the sort of inventive design that is a feature of Supple's work.

(Approx. 550 words.)

Fig. 27.2 Haroun *in* The Sea of Stories

■ Section three:

The rehearsal process; potential effectiveness for the audience. The development of my skill of acting. Health and safety.

Rehearsal

There are eight group members, aiming to produce a 40-minute piece; that's a lot to rehearse, refine and perfect! Rehearsals have been frenetic to match our fast-paced, energetic acting style.

Our reliance upon different props and pieces of costume means that exits and entrances must be perfectly timed and the various pieces (or substitutes) were ready well in advance of the performance. We have to know exactly who we are supposed to be showing to the audience and when! Storytelling theatre is not about 'becoming' a character but about telling a clear story.

Once we selected our extracts, we mapped them out on paper, like a military campaign. We noted the location of each scene: some scenes are set in Kahani, some on the ocean and some in Gup city. We made lists of which actors appear in which scenes, playing which character(s) and also which costumes and props are needed, when and where. This mapping process has been invaluable and highly complex since, although Jake only plays Haroun, the rest of us have up to six roles each!

First we mapped out the whole, then we devised action to support the text and cover costume changes, for example, when Rashid changes his coat. Our aim was to fill the stage with colour, movement and sound throughout.

Evaluation of skills and potential effectiveness

Multi-roling is a feature of Supple's productions that we have concentrated upon, achieving the distinctions between our characters using performance methods and costume.

I play two main parts, Haroun's mother, Soraya, and Iff the water genie. Initially, Soraya represents a loving wife and mother, which I show through my constant focus upon my husband and son and through my placid action of sewing. My gestures are gentle and soothing and as I sing, I sway rhythmically, suggesting domestic contentment. I wear a bright shawl, suggesting my Arabian origin but also to cover the costume I wear beneath it.

Iff, the water genie, is a fantastical, dream-like character – the opposite of Soraya. As Haroun's guide across Kahani, I wear a turquoise sequin-studded top and scarf, and transform myself from solid Soraya to ethereal sprite, moving nimbly and speaking with a lighter, higher timbre in my voice. Iff is played, simultaneously, by two performers; my other half, Hannah, and I use synchronised movements, necessary for the roles. Our movements and gestures are identical and we move, jump and creep, as one, to create the impression of creatures; not humans.

I have developed both my physical and vocal skills, achieving greater flexibility. Multi-roling techniques demand that the actor becomes acutely aware of the effect of pace or stillness upon characterisation.

In rehearsal, we would often demonstrate our role without words (or costume), to make sure that the rest of the group could instantly recognise which character we were showing. Delivering the text in a variety of vocal tones, pitches and accents has also helped. Charlie uses a rough accent with a staccato delivery style as Butt, the driver; however, as Hoopoe, his voice is gently modulated.

My only reservation about the success of the piece relates to the clarity of our diction. The pace is so fast that, occasionally, words are elided or lost; we need to remedy this.

Practitioner's influence and potential effectiveness

Taking our cue from Tim Supple's *A Midsummer Night's Dream*, we use jewel-coloured fabrics, atmospheric lighting and sound to suggest the mysterious East. We make inventive use of staging and props; for example, we have mounted book pages on sticks to represent the faces of an army; we bang the sticks on the ground to suggest their marching. We also create wild and wonderful sea-creatures bobbing above the waves of our 'ocean' and we use ladders to represent a castle, a generator and a monster, at various different moments.

We have not attempted to copy Supple's production of *Haroun*; rather, we took inspiration from it for our own interpretation, creating a kaleidoscope of characters to entrance our audience, young or old.

Health and safety issues

Physical theatre demands regular warm-ups, constant practice and accuracy to avoid injury.

We use many props, including swords, sticks and juggling balls, which might cause injury; in early rehearsals we practised with soft substitutes. To avoid hazards, these props are kept in a dedicated backstage space and only used in carefully choreographed sequences.

The use of fabric can be potentially dangerous, as actors could trip or become entangled. Again, its use has been meticulously planned. Rostra were checked for stability before every rehearsal and sequences involving the ladders were exhaustively rehearsed.

(Approx. 700 words.)

Further reading

You can find examples of prompt books, ground plans and theatre designs for set, costumes and technical elements by visiting the websites of individual theatres and theatre companies. Alternatively, type 'theatre ground plans', 'theatre set designs' into your search engine.

Assessing the finished piece

Assessing your own work

Self assessment is an important aspect of the final stages of any rehearsal period. You must look objectively at your piece of drama in order to improve and refine it.

You will have spent weeks in rehearsal exploring the ideas of a practitioner and applying them to the extract(s) from the play you have chosen. You will have experimented with the text along the way and invented sequences of action; you will have developed the delivery of the dialogue, trying out several different approaches before deciding on your final version. If you have worked hard, you will be feeling completely engrossed in your piece. Now you have to take a step back and review your work.

Assessment isn't simply asking yourself whether your piece is good or not. It's about finding ways to improve it and to enhance the audience experience of it. Here are some questions you should ask yourselves even before you show your work to an audience.

- Do all the cast know their lines and their moves for the whole extract?
- Can all the cast be heard and seen whenever they are on stage?
- Is the pace of the piece appropriate and is it varied where necessary?
- Are transitions between scenes handled smoothly?
- If the action or dialogue is meant to be fast and furious, is this maintained throughout?
- If there is physical theatre work involved, are all the cast demonstrating an equal level of physical flexibility and stamina?
- Is synchronised movement or choral speech properly coordinated?
- If the play is set in a particular region of England, Ireland, Scotland, Wales or America, are accents adopted and sustained equally well by all cast members? (For tips on accents, see the e-resources.)
- Have all necessary props been acquired and do all cast members handle props with equal dexterity?
- Have all necessary pieces of furniture and setting been acquired and is the setting appropriate to the style and action of the play?
- Do all cast members have appropriate costumes?
- Are all cast members wearing suitable shoes?
- Have the designers in your group completed their work? Is it appropriate to the needs of the group, to the style of the play and to the style of the chosen practitioner?
- Does the piece fulfil the exam requirements in terms of its playing time?

If the answer to any of these questions is 'no', you must take remedial action *before* you invite any kind of audience to see your work. This might mean putting in extra rehearsals to ensure all lines and moves are learned, pace and energy is injected into listless work and members of the group who are not 'up to speed' are given a wake-up call. If the piece is too long, you must either pick up the pace or make some judicious cuts.

If you are lacking essential props and furniture, you must also address this before you show your work. If your designers are delaying progress you need to get them refocused.

Inviting and responding to feedback

When you can answer 'yes' to all the questions above, it is time to show your piece to an invited critical audience. You should do this at least *a week* before your exam. The audience might comprise fellow drama students and it should certainly include your drama teacher(s) and any other individuals who are likely to give you some *honest* feedback.

You might ask your audience to respond to the questions below, although not all will be applicable to the style of your piece.

- Does the work appear to conform to the ideas of the practitioner as outlined in the programme notes?
- Is the action on stage intelligible? Can the audience follow what it is about?
- Is the play extract presented creatively?
- Are individual characters created clearly?
- Are relationships between characters revealed clearly?
- Do actors achieve the relevant age and or social class of their characters?
- Do the actors achieve, maintain and/or vary the pace of the piece appropriately?
- Is the dialogue delivered clearly and with appropriate emphasis and inflection? Are underlying meanings clear?
- Is physical theatre language clear?
- Does the piece create a specific mood or atmosphere? Is it appropriate to the nature of the material and to your treatment of it?
- Is emotion conveyed successfully?
- Is comedy achieved where necessary?
- Is the piece visually effective?
- Does the set serve the piece?
- Do the actors use the space well?
- Is there anything on stage distracting attention away from the action?
- Do wing areas need to be masked?
- Is lighting effective in illuminating the stage and in creating intended effects?
- Are costumes appropriate to the period, the location and the characters?
- Does the piece engage the audience's attention and maintain their engagement throughout?
- Are there any moments that are particularly effective and why?
- Are there any moments that are particularly ineffective and why?
- Does the piece achieve the stated intentions for the audience? How, or why not?
- Are there any obvious improvements that could be made:
  - to the actors' performances
  - to the visual appearance of the stage and its environs
  - to costume and/or make-up
  - to the technical design and support
  - to the actor-audience relationship?

> **AQA Examiner's tip**
>
> Give your critical audience a programme including some notes about your chosen practitioner and your dramatic intentions. You could take these from your supporting notes. This will help the audience to judge your work in context rather than just watching the drama unfold.

Assuming that your audience *is* a critical one and that they are keen to help you to improve your work, they are bound to make some constructive comments. It is vital that you listen carefully to your audience at this point.

Refining your work

You should have at least a few days before your exam to act upon the feedback you have received and refine your work. Do *not* feel despondent if the initial reactions were critical but take time to go through all the suggestions that have been made, evaluate the comments and see if you can make improvements.

Never be dismissive of criticism but, equally, don't accept any suggestions without testing them out and ensuring that they help you to achieve your original intentions.

This is your piece of drama and your examination. Good luck with it!

Summary of Unit 2

In this unit you have learned about:

- the term an 'influential practitioner'
- how your chosen practitioner should influence your practical work
- exploring the work and ideas of an influential theatre practitioner
- identifying key features of your chosen practitioner
- the work of three distinct influential practitioners
- choosing a suitable play for your practical presentation
- the skills available for assessment
- choosing your skill
- creating an ensemble
- working together to interpret your chosen extract
- setting a rehearsal schedule
- defining each group member's role in the rehearsal process
- working in a group with or without a director
- working in a group with or without a designer
- interpreting your chosen text; looking for meaning
- formulating clear intentions for your audience
- meeting your objectives
- preparing your practical work to illustrate the ideas of your chosen practitioner
- preparing your supporting notes
- presenting your supporting notes
- assessing your own work
- inviting and responding to feedback on your work
- refining your work for the examination.

The e-resources and weblinks associated with these chapters should be a continual source of inspiration and information as you work on your selected practitioner and play extract(s).

Glossary

A

Abbey Theatre: a theatre founded in Dublin in 1904 by W.B. Yeats and Lady Gregory and financed by Annie Horniman. It was the home of the Irish National Dramatic Society in the early part of the twentieth century.

Accent: a voice pattern particular to a region or nation.

Accessories: extra items added to a costume, such as shoes and jewelry to complete the effect.

Acoustics: the quality of the sound within an auditorium or area.

Act: 1) to perform the part of a character in a play 2) the name given to the major divisions of a play 3) the contribution of one performer or more in a show made up of different, unconnected items.

Action: the action of the play is the events that take place within it.

Actor: the performer who appears in front of the audience.

Actor manager: the actor who runs the company as well as acting in the play.

Actor-sharer: an actor in the Elizabethan theatre who had shares in the theatre company that he belonged to, owning part of the wardrobe and play-books.

Agitprop: theatre based on political propaganda.

Ambience: background atmosphere of a scene (adj. ambient).

Antagonist: the opposite of the **protagonist** in a drama.

Apron: the part of the stage in front of the proscenium arch.

Atmosphere: the emotional tone (mood) of a scene or section of a play. For example, a tense atmosphere.

Audience: the people who come to watch and listen to the performance.

Audition: the process by which a play is cast; the potential suitability of two or more actors is assessed by a variety of methods.

Auditorium: the area of the theatre from which the audience view the performance.

B

Back stage: the areas at the theatre used by the performers and stage crew which are not visible to the audience.

Backcloth: a canvas cloth that spreads the width of the back of the stage and onto which scenery is painted. (Also known as a backdrop, esp. in USA).

Bare stage: an acting area which does not have scenery on it.

Big name actor: a leading actor whose name is well-known, sometimes through film or TV as well as theatre.

Birdie: a very small spotlight, usually positioned on the floor of the stage angled upwards.

Black box: an acting area surrounded by nothing but black walls or curtains.

Black humour: a form of dark comedy that finds humour in serious issues and sometimes challenges good taste.

Blocking: 1) the plotting of the movements of the actors during rehearsals 2) one actor standing between another actor and the audience thereby blocking their view.

Blood capsule: a capsule containing fake blood that an actor can hide in the mouth and bite to create an impression of bleeding.

Blood sacks: packets of fake blood which can be easily broken to given the impression an actor is bleeding.

Blueprint: a highly detailed plan.

Bourgeois: a term that describes the conventional, respectable middle classes.

Boxes: the small seating areas containing usually four to eight seats at the side of older proscenium arch theatres.

C

Caricature: a cartoon-like exaggeration of peculiar personal characteristics.

Cast: all the actors taking part in the actual performance.

Casting director: the person responsible for submitting a shortlist of suitable actors from which the cast will be chosen, usually by the director.

Casting: the selection of actors for the parts required in the performance.

Catalyst: an agent of change in a play (the term originates in chemistry).

Catharsis: a concept defined by Aristotle as the purging of the audience's emotions through the release of pity and fear as they watch the tragic hero's descent from happiness to misery.

Chamber theatre: small-scale performance usually in a studio theatre.

Chase sequence: a piece of stage business in which a chase, usually prolonged and comic, takes place.

Choragus: individual patron paying for the tragic chorus for a performance in Ancient Greek theatre.

Choreography: the devising of movement sequences and dances; often created by a specialist choreographer.

Chorus: in Greek theatre, a group of actors who enhance the audience's understanding of the play by explaining the action, expressing opinions, or asking questions. In Elizabethan drama the role was frequently undertaken by a single actor.

Circle: the first tier of seats above the stalls in a theatre

City comedies: a series of comedies written around the turn of the 15th/16th century, depicting London life and times and portraying typical citizens of London in their plots.

City Dionysian: in Ancient Greek theatre these were annual spring festivals honouring Dionysius, the Greek god of fertility, wine and ecstasy.

Civic duty: referring to Greek theatre, the fact that citizens were expected to attend the plays.

Clergy: those people ordained to hold religious services in the Christian church.

Cold fog machine: a form of smoke machine in which the smoke is cooled so that it clings to the ground.

Colour palette: the choice of colours and shades used in the design of the costume and set.

Comedy of humours: a form of comedy based on the 'humours' or fixed personality traits that it was believed, in the 16th century, were created by the proportion of different fluids (humours) in the body. These fluids were blood, phlegm, choler (or yellow bile) and melancholy (or black bile). Characters in these plays were therefore portrayed as being. sanguine, phlegmatic, choleric or melancholic.

Comedy: a humorous play, usually with a happy ending.

Commedia dell' arte: a form of comic theatre that originated in Italy and which is based on improvisation.

Community theatre: performances aimed at and acted by a particular section of society.

Costume: the clothes, often specially designed, worn by actors on stage.

Courtyard theatre: the courtyard of an inn yard used as performance space during the Medieval period and later influencing the shape of Elizabethan theatres.

Curtain call: the moment when the actors come out onto the stage at the end of a performance to acknowledge the applause.

Curtain: a large curtain which hid the stage from the audience at the beginning of performances in conventional proscenium arch theatres; less commonly seen now; lead to expressions like "curtain up" which means the start of the performance and to "come down" meaning the end of the play.

Cycle: the term given to the group of plays in Medieval times covering the whole Bible story from the Creation to the Last Judgement.

D

Denouement: the unravelling of plot complications and resolution of the play after its climax.

Design concept: an over arching view of how a production will look and sound. It includes all aspects of theatrical design.

Design fundamentals: the basic principles behind design techniques in the theatre.

Designer (set/costume/technical): the person responsible for deciding what a particular aspect of the play will look like.

Dialect: refers to the distinctive vocal signature of people who come from different parts of the country.

Dialectic: designed to stimulate consideration of both sides of an argument.

Didactic: designed to instruct, especially morally or politically.

Direct address: when an actor, in or out of character, speaks directly to the audience.

Director: the person who has the overall vision of the production, the interpretation of the text and the performance of the actors.

Distressed: a technique for simulating the effects of age or wear and tear on settings, props and/or costumes.

Down stage: area of the stage nearest to the audience because a raked stage sloped towards the audience.

Drama: published texts, improvisation and workshop activity.

Drapes: curtains used to create a form of abstract scenery.

E

End-on: when all the audience view a play from one side, as in proscenium arch theatres.

Ensemble: a group of actors working together and taking equal responsibility for the performance.

Entrances and exits: 1) the various gaps in the scenery and the stage through which actors enter and leave during a performance 2) the act of entering and leaving the stage.

Epic theatre: political theatre appealing more to the intellect than the emotion; a Brechtian concept.

Establishment: a term applied collectively to authority figures, for example, in Government or other institutions such as the Church or the Military.

Expressionism: a form of theatre that originated in Germany in the early 20th century in which characters' inner feelings and/or thoughts are expressed outwardly in a form of physical expression.

F

Flats: a piece of 2D scenery consisting of a frame, usually covered with canvas, onto which scenery is painted; weights are used to keep a flat upright.

Flies: the area above the stage into which scenery and even actors can be flown.

Flying space: the space above the stage where sets can be 'flown' lowered or taken up- to effect set changes.

Flying: lifting scenery into the space above the stage or suspending an actor in a harness to give the illusion of flying.

Foil: a figure in a play whose characteristics contrast with one of the other characters completely, thus highlighting the other character's qualities.

Footlights: lights placed on the floor of the stage at the front to illuminate a performance; rarely used now.

Forestage: a part of the stage that projects in front of the proscenium arch and curtain.

Fourth wall: a term used by Stanislavski to describe how an audience in a proscenium arch theatre viewed the play as though through an invisible wall; the other three walls comprise the set.

Frosted gel: a form of gel which diffuses the light to give a more misty less harsh light.

G

Gait: refers to the way a person walks.

Gel: a coloured filter, placed into a lantern to cast either a strong or subtle light; short for gelatine, from which they were originally made hence the spelling.

Genre: a particular style of theatrical piece.

Gesture: movement of hand, body or face to express emotion or to convey plot.

Gobos: a cut-out stencil device used to create special lighting effects when placed within a profile spotlight – the beam is shaped to suggest, for example, prison bars, a dappled woodland or light pouring through a window.

Groundlings: in Elizabethan times, these were the spectators who stood in the open space around the stage, paying a penny for the privilege of standing throughout the performance (the Pit).

Guild plays: medieval plays performed by men from the same professional group.

H

Historicisation: a form of drama whereby the story is set in the past but the themes and issues are relevant to contemporary society.

House lights: the lights in the auditorium which are normally dimmed at the start of a performance.

Hydraulics: mechanisms which use pressure to raise or lower scenery and actors.

I

Icon: a symbol or emblem.

Idiosyncrasy: refers to a person's habits or personal peculiarities, usually adopted by actors playing character/comic roles.

Improvisation: a performance in which the actors work without a script, making up the words and action as they go.

Incest: a sexual relationship between two people who are considered, for moral or cultural reasons, to be too closely related to make such a relationship acceptable, for example, a relationship between brothers and sisters, mothers and sons.

Inflection: refers to the rising and falling of the voice during speech.

In-the-round: a stage with audience on all four sides.

J

Juxtaposition: the placing of two things side by side to create a specific effect.

L

Lampoon: a bitter, personal satire.

Lanterns: the correct term for lights used to illuminate the stage.

Leading actor: the person with the main role in a play.

Lift: when one or more actors lifts another during a performance.

Linguistic: concerned with the language of the text.

Live theatre: any performance in which the actors are present and performing in front of the audience.

M

Make up: cosmetics used on stage to enhance or alter the actor's appearance.

Mask: a covering for the face to create a stylised or drastically altered appearance.

Method of physical action: Stanislavski's theory on the need for an actor to be in total control of their physicality in order to reflect the truth of the character.

Microphone: a device to amplify or distort sound.

Mime: a wordless performance where movement and gesture are used to communicate meaning or simply to entertain the audience. A mime is also the name for the performer.

Miracle plays: originally French plays about the Christian saints and the Virgin Mary; used in England as an alternative to Mystery play

Mood: the emotional tone (atmosphere) of a scene or section of a play. For example, a sombre mood.

Motifs: a theme or idea in a play that recurs and which is elaborated upon.

Multi-role: when actors play more than one part in the same play they are said to be 'multi-roling'.

Musical director: the person in change of rehearsing the singing in a performance; often referred to as the MD.

Musical: a play in which much of the story and text is set to music.

Mystery plays: the medieval religious plays based on Biblical stories.

N

Naturalism: a type of drama that began in the late 19th century as an offshoot of realism and which presented human character as being formed by heredity and environment.

O

On-stage: the area that is visible to the audience, as opposed to off-stage which is not

Oracle: in Greek times, people believed that the 'oracle' was the fount of all knowledge; the word oracle can be used to describe both a prophet and a piece of prophecy.

Orchestra: 1) In Greek Theatres, the central performance area used by the Chorus. 2) Refers to the main seating area of the auditorium at floor level.

P

Pace: the speed at which lines are said and moves are made.

Pageant carts: the elaborate carts on which the Miracle plays were performed.

Pantomime: a traditional theatrical entertainment for children, usually performed at Christmas.

Parados: (Greek) Alleyway between the skene and the **orchestra** for the **chorus** to use as entrances.

Parody: in drama, a distorted/comical imitation of a character, a play or a style of play.

Paternalism: a style of government or management, or an approach to personal relationships, in which the desire to help, advise, and protect (like a father) may neglect individual choice and personal responsibility.

Patricide: the murder of a father by his child or children.

Performance: the interpretation of a play, ballet or opera by actors, dancers or singers. Some performances rely entirely for their effects upon the performers' words or actions, although most performers are also supported in a production by design elements.

Performance elements: all aspects of the performers' work; the acting/performing within a production.

Performance skills: the individual skills that an actor displays, including singing, dancing, etc. as well as acting.

Performance space: the area used by the actors, which is mainly the stage but can spread into the auditorium.

Phrasing: this refers to the way an actor shapes a speech and uses pause within the delivery of lines.

Physical theatre: a style of performance that places most emphasis on the movement of the actor rather than the delivery of lines.

Pit: the ground floor of a theatre auditorium, generally sunk slightly below ground level; these were the cheapest seats in the house in Elizabethan times and describes the sunken area occupied by the orchestra in modern theatres.

Pitch: refers to the exact height and depth of a sound.

Play: a written script consisting mainly of dialogue, which may be read and enjoyed by a reader, but which does not fulfil the playwright's intentions until it is performed by actors in front of an audience.

Playwright: the person who has written the play; it literally means the person who made the play.

Plot: the story line of the play.

Principal boy: the young male lead in a pantomime, usually played by a young woman.

Production: what the play (or ballet, opera or mime, etc.) is turned into once it has been interpreted by a director working with performers and with a production team consisting of designers, stage managers, technicians, scene builders and a wardrobe department.

Production elements: all aspects of a production reflecting the work of a production team which can be made up of some or all of the following personnel: a director, an assistant director, actors, stage manager(s), stage/set designer, lighting designer and technicians, sound designer and technicians, costume designer, make up artist, musical director, choreographer, fight director – even animal trainers, depending on the production.

Production team: the varied people who work together on a performance

programme: 1) the different parts which are put together to form performance of assorted acts 2) the booklet which gives and audience details of the performance they are about to see.

Projection: 1) an actor's ability to make his/her voice heard throughout the auditorium 2) a picture or design shone onto the stage as part of the set design.

Promenade: a production during which the audience stand rather than sit, and walk around with the actors as required.

Prompt copy: sometimes known as a prompt book, a master-copy of the director's decisions. It is a log of all the actors' moves, plus technical cues and props to be used in any one scene.

Propaganda: circulation of information which presents a one-sided view of events.

Props: movable objects used on stage by the actors. 'Props' is an abbreviation of 'properties'.

Proscenium arch: the framed opening that separates the stage from the audience in traditional theatres.

Protagonist: this term derives from the theatre of Ancient Greece when the Protagonist was the first actor to speak (aside from the **chorus**). It describes the leading character or 'hero' in a play who has to fight against / oppose the **antagonist**.

Psycho-technique: the process which Stanislavski described whereby an actor's performance is automatically appropriate if their understanding and exploration of their character is complete.

Puppetry: a figure worked by strings, rods or the hand; the puppets become the actors.

Puritan interregnum: the period of history between the execution of Charles I (1649) and the restoration of Charles II (1660) during which time the country was governed by Oliver Cromwell.

Pyrotechnics: this term refers to fireworks used on stage.

R

Rake: the slope of a stage, rising from front to back which helps and audience to see better.

Reactions: the responses of characters to the words or actions of other characters, to off-stage sound or to the unfolding events on stage.

Read-through: an initial read of a text by a cast before they start to work on the play.

Realism: the faithful representation of life in literature and theatre.

Rehearsals: the practice sessions in preparation for a performance.

Representational: a setting that represents a location on stage rather than attempting to create the impression of reality on stage.

Retribution: a punishment given to somebody for some offence that they have committed themselves.

Review: a written or verbal criticism of a play.

Revolve stage: a stage with a large circular area that can be rotated either as part of the action or to reveal new sets.

Rhythm: refers to the pattern of speech, especially when the lines are written in verse.

Ritualistic: a formal, stylised pattern of movement or ceremony.

S

Satyr play: in Ancient Greek Theatre an obscene farcical play, performed as an afterpiece to the tragedies in the Dionysia contest.

Scene: a shorter division of a play, which makes up the acts.

Scenery: what is placed on stage to suggest a location or a context for a play.

Script: the written words from which the actors rehearse.

Set dressing: items, usually quite small, which are placed on a set to make it look more realistic.

Setting: the sense of place created by the scenery.

Site-specific: the use of an area other than a theatre in which to perform and which adds a particular quality to the presentation.

Slapstick: originally two pieces of wood used by one character to hit another, making an exaggerated sound; general used now to refer to any boisterous physical comedy.

Smoke machine: a machine to create effects of mist, fog and smoke on stage.

Sound effects: the noises made to represent the sounds which would have been heard; sometimes

recorded sounds of the actual noise are used, sometimes the effect is suggested by other means.

Soundscape: a combination of sounds created live or pre-recorded that help to create an atmosphere on stage.

Special effects: a wide range of technical devices which create different theatrical illusions.

Spotlight: a narrow beam lantern focused onto a particular actor or area.

Stage blood: fake blood made in a variety of consistencies; sometimes called Kensington Gore, after an area of London.

Stage directions: the playwright's descriptions of characters, costumes and settings as well as indications of entrances and exits and suggestions for the delivery of lines or for reactions to the unfolding events on stage.

Stage left/right: the actor's left and right when facing the audience.

Stage machinery: mechanism installed to help move, raise or lower scenery.

Stage manager: the person in charge of the stage crew and responsible for the smooth running of the performance.

Stage: 1) the acting area of the theatre 2) a more general term to refer to anything theatrical.

Staging form: the arrangement of the acting and audience space in the **venue**.

Staging: 1) platforms on which plays are performed 2) the act of putting a play onto the stage.

Stalls: the ground floor area of seating in a theatre.

Standing Ovation: enthusiastic response from appreciative members of an audience who stand to applaud the cast.

Stock character: a character who represents a type of person rather than an individual.

Subtext: the meaning behind the lines; what a character is thinking rather than saying.

Super-objective: Stanislavski's term for the over-all ruling idea of the play.

Symbolism: an artistic/literary movement in which symbols represent aspects of characters' inner lives and ordinary objects are associated with deeper meanings.

Synchronisation: timing of action and/or speech so that one or more performers are doing/saying exactly the same thing at the same time.

T

Technical elements: the aspects of a production that require machinery and/or electricity to work.

Tenement building: a building divided into separate flats or rooms and rented to different tenants.

Tetralogy: in ancient Greek theatre a series of four related plays by the same dramatist consisting of three tragedies followed by a satyr play.

Text: the written script of the play.

Theatre of cruelty: a theory of drama proposed by Antonin Artaud in his book The Theatre and Its Double. The theory had many advocates in the 20th century, including Peter Brook. Productions in this style tend to present a violent and ritualistic form of theatre.

Themes: a unifying and repeated idea which form the basis for the play.

Thrust: a stage which juts out into the audience.

Tiered seating: rows of seats with each row slightly higher than the one in front.

Timing: the skill required when performing to know exactly when to move or speak.

Tone: Refers to the quality of the voice as well as to the intention behind a speech.

Total theatre: a relatively recent term to describe a theatrical performance, with strong physicality, which goes far beyond the delivery of a literary text.

Traffic: in theatre terms, the comings and goings on stage, the stage business and action.

Tragedy: a style of theatre that takes a serious approach to the topic and that usually ends unhappily.

Tragi-comedy: a genre that blends elements of tragedy and comedy; it can take one of two forms, either a potentially tragic series of events is resolved happily, or a comic situation is presented with dark or bitter overtones.

Transformation scene: the moment, usually in pantomimes, when a person or object is magically transformed into something different.

Transpose: to move the setting or period of a play, in production, from its original setting or context to a suitable alternative.

Trap-door: a cut out section of the stage floor through which actors or scenery can appear or disappear.

Travelling players: groups of performers, mainly in medieval times, who moved around the country, presenting various forms of entertainment wherever they could.

Traverse: a configuration of the audience where they sit in two sections facing each other across the acting area.

Troupe: a company of actors and performers.

Truck: a platform on castors which can be wheeled onto stage and locked into position as part of the scenery.

U

Universality: a term that suggests that the issues or situations presented in a play are relevant to all societies at all times.

Up stage: the area of the raked stage that is furthest from the audience.

Upper circle: (the gods) the second level of seating above the stalls and the circle; also known as the gallery and the gods, because that was where the gods were flown to above the Elizabethan stage.

V

Venue: a building or space selected for the performance of a production.

Verbatim theatre: a form of documentary theatre constructed from the actual words spoken by or written testimony of real people talking about real events.

Volume: the relative loudness or quietness of speech, sound or music.

W

West End musical: strictly speaking this refers to a musical performed in the West End of London but it refers more generally to an elaborate musical style.

West End: the Western district of inner London containing most of its principal theatres; the term is used as a collective term for the commercial theatre in London.

Wings: the area at the sides of the stage not visible to the audience where the actors wait for their entrance.

X

Xenophobia: a hatred of foreigners/strangers.

Index